Making Money in
Cyberspace

**Other Books by
Paul and Sarah Edwards**

Best Home Businesses for the 90s, Revised Edition

Finding Your Perfect Work

Getting Business to Come to You, 2nd Revised Edition
(with Laura Clampitt Douglas)

Home Businesses You Can Buy
(with Walter Zooi)

Secrets of Self-Employment

Teaming Up
(with Rick Benzel)

Working from Home

*Making Money with Your Computer
at Home, Expanded Second Edition*

**Other Books by
Linda Rohrbough**

Start Your Own Computer Repair Business

Upgrade Your Own PC, 2nd Edition

Making Money in
Cyberspace

Paul and Sarah Edwards
and Linda Rohrbough

JEREMY P. TARCHER/PUTNAM
a member of
Penguin Putnam Inc.
New York

Jeremy P. Tarcher/Putnam
a member of
Penguin Putnam Inc.
375 Hudson Street
New York, NY 10014
www.penguinputnam.com

Library of Congress Cataloging-in-Publication Data

Edwards, Paul, date.
Making money in cyberspace / Paul and Sarah Edwards and Linda Rohrbough.—1st trade pbk. ed.
p. cm.
Includes bibliographical references and index.
ISBN 0-87477-884-0
1. Business enterprises—Computer networks. 2. Web sites—Design.
3. Electronic commerce—Case studies. 4. Business enterprises—Computer network resources—Directories. 5. Internet (Computer network)
I. Edwards, Sarah (Sarah A.) II. Rohrbough, Linda.
III. Title
HD30.36.E36   1998   98-4004 CIP
658.8'00285'4678—dc21

DESIGN BY DEBORAH KERNER

Printed in the United States of America
1   3   5   7   9   10   8   6   4   2
This book is printed on acid-free paper. ∞

To Mark, Jessica, and Margaret

To Claude and Maxine

Acknowledgments

This timing for this book was suggested by Robert Welsch, who believed that we wait until the initial frenzied fever of the cyberspace "gold rush" had settled enough that we could do more than give best guesses about how to actually make money on the Internet. And for most of the several years it took to bring this book into being, we constantly heard, "The only people making money on the Internet are those telling others how they can make money." That's not true anymore. We are constantly and delightfully surprised by people—individuals—who from their spare bedrooms and living rooms are making excellent money from what they do online. In fact, recent surveys are showing that the smaller businesses are doing better than the larger ones. So Robert was right. Now is the time to let you know how to succeed in cyberspace while it's still young enough to offer lots of opportunity. At this writing, fewer than one in five small business have a Web presence.

Books are the result of a team effort, although the team members usually never meet face-to-face at the same time. But each has a role that deserves hearty acknowledgment. First is our co-author, Linda Rohrbough, who has earned the largest credit. Such is the utility of the ability to work collaboratively in cyberspace—we have been in the same room with Linda only twice. In New York is the team of people who guide and produce our books, including Joel Fotinos, our beloved publisher; Mitch Horowitz, our helpful and enthusiastic editor; Jocelyn Wright, the ever-dependable and competent super assistant editor who makes things happen. No book gets made without the people in production, including Coral Tysliava and Claire Vaccaro. Ken Siman and Kristin Georgio provide vital support for our efforts to spread the know-how we enjoy presenting to you.

The virtual team we relate to daily includes our assistant, Joyce Acosta, and, in her home office, Donna Gould, a source of wisdom and encouragement.

Finally, and perhaps most important, we acknowledge the hundreds of people Linda and we interviewed, many of whose stories provide examples in this book. Without their openness, honesty, and willingness to share their experiences, we could not have made this book as practical as we hope you will find it.

Contents

Introduction

Cyberspace: a term originally coined by science fiction writer William Gibson in the 1980s in his novel **Neuromancer**. *Cyberspace* has become a synonym for the interactive computing and communications base available in the worldwide electronic network known as the Internet. (Other sources say *cyberspace* is synonymous with the term *virtual reality*, or *virtual world.*) Cyberspace is ". . . 'where' the global community of computer-linked individuals and groups lives."[1]

 One of the biggest complaints about society today is its lack of interpersonal connectedness. Couple this lack with high technology and you get one of the biggest fears of our time—the Orwellian "Big Brother"—a merciless, domineering control of people with no thought for individuals and no personal joy or attainment. Noted psychologist B. F. Skinner expressed it this way:

Concentration of power in an agency is objectionable . . . because it destroys interpersonal contacts. If I work for a company manufacturing shoes and my neighbor for a company manufacturing shirts, and if we both earn enough so that I buy a shirt and he or she a pair of shoes, we have in a sense produced something

[1]*The On-Line Edition of the Hutchinson Encyclopedia* (Oxford, England: Helicon Publishing, Ltd., 1995), CompuServe's Reference Section.

of value for each other, but there has been no direct exchange. A
special opportunity to reinforce each other's behavior has been
lost. Companies are no doubt needed for the efficient production
of shoes and shirts, and we must have an economy rather than
simply a culture in the older sense, but something has been given
up.[2]

What if there was a place where that "something" that Skinner describes could be obtained without losing the economy of efficient production? What if this place allowed unprecedented personal freedom and successful businesses not only had to recognize individuals but also had to cater to them in order to survive? There is such a place, and it's called cyberspace.

As you'll see in the following chapters, cyberspace is a unique communications medium where individual freedom is paramount. It is a medium that resonates with the deepest components in our psychological makeup as humans.

A New Communications Medium

Each time a new communications medium has been introduced, opportunities abound, but there is always a learning process to find out how to use the new medium effectively. When the telephone was introduced, it took some time before people realized that they could speak differently than they did when sending a telegraph message. In the film industry, the advent of "talkies," or movies with sound, changed forever the way movies were made.

While a trial-and-error approach could work, it stands to reason the fastest and most effective way to take advantage of opportunities in a new communications medium would be to gain an understanding of the medium, learn the principles behind how it works, learn how to gain a response from people using it, and see how others have effectively used it.

[2]B. F. Skinner, *Reflections on Behaviorism and Society* (Englewood Cliffs, NJ: Prentice-Hall, 1978), p. 9.

For example, it seems obvious that an advertisement for an outdoor billboard would have to be redesigned before it could be placed in *USA Today* and redesigned again before it could appear in *Better Homes and Gardens* magazine. Each situation involves different audiences viewing the information at different speeds and from different points of view. It's obvious because we understand billboards, newspapers, and magazines—we've seen lots of examples, understand the principles behind how each is produced, and know how people tend to respond to each one.

Cyberspace as a medium has been widely misunderstood. Some characteristics of the medium have been defined, such as the emphasis on "netiquette" or proper ways to keep from offending people in cyberspace, but businesses have relied on trial and error to come up with ideas for using this new medium profitably. It is our contention that the trial-and-error approach is no longer necessary.

CASE STUDY

MARILYN BUTZ

BIZCARDPRO

HUNTINGTON BEACH, CALIFORNIA

HTTP://WWW.BIZCARDPRO.COM

SPECIALTY BUSINESS CARDS

Marilyn Butz was fifty-three and working for a print shop when the idea of doing business cards on the Internet came up. She'd worked for the previous ten years in the printing industry and was looking for something she could do herself starting part-time. Marilyn said the Internet was completely new and she'd never even sent e-mail. Her husband said she wouldn't get a single order her first year. But her grown son, who was working for an Internet Service Provider (ISP), said to her, "Mom, you can do this."

So in March of 1996 she decided to start her own Web site to sell specialty business cards on the Internet. She had a Macintosh Performa, so she bought a copy of *Adobe Pagemill* because she thought she wouldn't have to learn to code HTML (hyper text markup language) to develop her site. But after a short time, she found there were things the software wouldn't let her do and she had to learn HTML anyway. It took about three weeks. "I hated my son and I cried a lot, but now I can do everything by myself," Marilyn said.

While she put four hours a day in the evening and most weekends into her site, Marilyn said her biggest business challenge was the cost of accepting credit cards. She found it took $800 a month in gross credit card sales to make a difference in her bottom line, and it cost $30 a month just to rent the equipment, but she found it was a method people understood and accepted. Marilyn said her bank analyzed her Web site and decided they would allow her to take credit cards only if she accepted the information over the phone, not on her site or by e-mail. So she either arranges to call customers or encourages customers to call her twenty-four-hour message center to leave their credit card information.

One of Marilyn's biggest boons was discovering that Japanese businessmen have trouble getting business cards printed in raised print (thermography) in the larger Japanese card size of 3⅜ by 2⅛ inches. (American cards are 2½ by 2 inches.) She uses drop shipping and contracts with printers in other states like Texas to actually do the work once she has e-mailed the copy in the correct format. She also has a lot of clients in New York and New Jersey.

A big part of Marilyn's business is educating customers concerning file formats and fonts. She doesn't get involved in design work because she finds it too difficult to do printing and design, but she has designers she can make referrals to.

Promotion of her site is where she focuses much of her attention as well. She participates in discussion lists across the Internet and spends a lot of time in women's on-line sites. She met designers at the Field of Dreams site who helped her with her own site design and got business referrals there as well.

Marilyn's advice to businesses starting out is to "expect to spend some time on your site—dedicate yourself to doing this. Figure you need one additional employee to handle the Internet site to do it right. 'Right' means with the goal of making your on-line business grow."

Why Business in Cyberspace

Every community has businesses. Cyberspace is no different in that there's a place for businesses there as well, but it is a different medium with strengths of its own. These strengths include speed, low cost of entry, quickness of change, international distribution, personal touch, ease in searching, and the interconnectedness of cyberspace. Let's take a look at each one of these characteristics individually.

Speed

If there's one thing cyberspace has going for it, that one thing is speed. Although there are people who insist that the exchange of information on the Internet is instantaneous, it isn't. Messages sent across this vast network can arrive seconds, minutes, or even hours later. But even a slow Internet connection is faster than overnight delivery. Even more significant is the fact that information appearing on the Internet can be changed rapidly. So not only is it fast to put up the most recent information; it also is expected by people who use the Internet.

Low Cost of Entry

You can start doing business in cyberspace for $100, or even less. Lots of people—especially large companies who want to make an impressive showing—have spent more, but you don't have to.

Quickness of Change

It takes very little time to change your information in cyberspace. You can do so in less than an hour. Compare that to reprinting a brochure or redesigning even a photocopied handout.

International Distribution

Cyberspace knows no national boundaries. That means you can do business all over the world as easily as you can in your own backyard.

Personal Touch

The Internet tends to be a more personal environment. People expect to get a real person when they send mail, and there's a lot of personal information out there. This can work to your advantage, especially if you're a small, start-up company.

Ease in Searching

A big part of life in cyberspace revolves around the ability to find information. Computers are great at handling and dissecting information too big for any one person or even a group of people to deal with, and computers are at the heart of cyberspace. There are computers that go around cyberspace all day long just looking for information to index so that you can find it. As you'll see later in the book, that's one important way in which people will find your business.

Interconnectedness

Distance doesn't mean much in cyberspace. Because everyone is connected in cyberspace to a web of worldwide computers (that's why they call it the "World Wide Web"), information is transmitted at the speed of sound or the speed of light, depending on the type of connection. Either way, distance becomes meaningless, which makes you able to link to anyone on the globe and anyone on the globe can link to you. As you'll see, this ability to provide links makes doing business on the Internet attractive to customers.

If You Build It, They Won't Necessarily Come

Having said all that, we need to say this: If one thing is obvious by now, it is that you can't just put up a brochure in cyberspace and expect people to beat a path to your door. "If you build it, they will come" may work if you're opening a fast-food restaurant on a busy street corner, but it doesn't work in cyberspace. If it were that easy, you wouldn't need this book.

Much has been written about what works when trying to do business on the Internet. The problem is that the medium of cyberspace is too often defined in terms of other media that we already understand. For example, there have been predictions that at the current exponential rate of growth, by the year 2000 everyone on the planet will have Internet access. Now that's just silly. Everyone on the planet doesn't even have a telephone, much less Internet access (even if you consider the advent of wireless services). These theories are spouted by people who understand just enough to draw the wrong conclusions. Let us give you a couple of examples of this same type of thinking from recent history.

In the late 1800s, when the telephone was introduced, there were widely circulated cartoons that featured a single gentleman shouting into a telephone while auditoriums full of people in various locations listened to a single box connected at the other end. This made perfect sense in light of the ways in which people communicated then. It seemed natural that you'd go to an auditorium to hear an important speaker who didn't have to travel to your location to address your audience. Of course, people address audiences by telephone now, but that's not how we view the telephone. Who would have thought then that we'd be using something as revolutionary as a telephone to simply gossip about the neighbors or check the time? Yet it's convenience and utility that make the telephone valuable enough for millions of people to pay every month to have one.

Or take the more recent introduction of the video cassette recorder (VCR). It was widely thought that the VCR would hurt Hollywood, and the movie industry in particular, because people would rent movies rather than go to movie theaters. This was an argument based on convenience for the user. Why jostle in crowds in a theater when you can remain unjostled and pay less for snacks in your own home? But it hasn't worked that way. It's fun to see a movie on a huge screen in a theater, then buy the movie when it is released on cassette and watch it again and again at home. Or just rent it again. As a matter of fact, the VCR has helped the movie industry. Not only are the numbers of people attending movies in theaters increasing, but some movies— such as the Kevin Costner film *Waterworld*—that would have lost money have also been profitable because of the video cassette market.

So What Does Work?

Fortunately, the Internet has been around longer than is generally known, and there are people like Bruce Clay who have found what it takes to break into it and make a living there. The way to discover what works is to pinpoint what is actually working. Find a guide who knows something about the medium, then locate people who are successful and uncover what they're doing.

That is what we've attempted to do in this book. We have been living and working in cyberspace full-time since the 1980s. We understand the medium, its strengths, and its weaknesses. We've coupled our experience with that of people who are making it and boiled it down to its essential elements. In easy-to-understand terms, we present to you how cyberspace works using general principles, broken down into practical steps you can implement. You'll also read the stories of people who are actually making money in cyberspace and hear from them about how they got started as well as what they say about what works and what doesn't.

One of the things we are convinced of is that this isn't a zero-sum game. Someone else doesn't have to lose customers or business in order for you to gain in cyberspace. There are four basic human needs: food, shelter, clothing, and communication. In fact, it could be said in modern terms that communication outranks the other three, because if you can communicate, you can find ways to meet your other basic needs. Our need for communication is not even close to being met. Every device that brings us another way to communicate effectively will find a host of people eager to use it. Fundamentally, the Internet is a medium of communication. You can make it work for you—it's just a matter of knowing how.

CASE STUDY

BRUCE CLAY

@BRUCECLAY

NEWBURY PARK, CALIFORNIA

HTTP://WWW.BRUCECLAY.COM

CONSULTANT: WEB AND PRODUCT ARCHITECTURE,

DESIGN, MARKETING, AND PROMOTION

Bruce said he'd heard the hype about the Internet and decided to get in and use it to sell his consulting services to companies who want to launch new software products. He has a strong background in business and marketing and figured his background alone would be enough to get him in. He got serious about learning about the Internet; at one point he put in four hundred hours a month exploring cyberspace, and he taught himself the hyper text markup language (HTML) used to design Web pages. "I studied the Internet to figure out how to market myself as a service. Then I put up my site. I put up my background, I put up prices, and no one came. 'Call me,' I said, 'we'll discuss anything.'

"I started out with an 'I'm here,' but basically no one knew I was here. Building a Web site is like putting up a billboard in your basement—no one sees it," Bruce said.

"As I learned more about the Web, I tried to look objectively at my site, asking myself, 'Why would I visit this site?'" It was in asking himself what he would be looking for that Bruce realized he needed to give away as much information as possible about what he does.

So Bruce redesigned his site so that it gives away all the information you need to market a product and promote your Web site on the Internet. Bruce's tone is personal, informal, and friendly, and he talks to the reader using personal pronouns like *I* and *you*. The site provides a wealth of information and offers examples and checklists. He gives away so much useful information, you'd think he would put himself out of business.

In fact, Bruce says, "If you use my site and do it yourself, you don't need me." However, since having changed his site to provide so much free information, Bruce gets one or two unsolicited requests for consulting quotes and twenty e-mails a day—which he says is sufficient for him to operate a good consulting business. And he took off information about his per-hour rates, encouraging potential customers to contact him via phone or e-mail instead. "Everyone assumes I'm more expensive than I am," Bruce added.

Bruce claims that by giving away material, he develops trust. The free information has a twofold effect—it builds rapport without pressing and shows that he knows what he's doing.

Being a consultant is a lot like being a paramedic, according to Bruce. A consultant has to listen to the problems, examine the available material, and get the answer right the first time. Like a paramedic, the customer has no time or patience for trial and error. "If you do it right, they'll tell two friends. If you do it wrong, they won't tell anyone, or they may tell everyone else you did it wrong," Bruce added.

"Once I started giving away information, I started winning awards, links on other popular Web sites to my site, and mentions," Bruce added. He says he spends two hours a day on his site—one hour answering e-mail and the other keeping up the content on the site.

To those new to the Internet, Bruce says if you want to maintain a consistent customer base, give your customer something for nothing. Information is the most valuable commodity. In addition, he says, "You need to work smart, develop a proper marketing program, maintain a consistent visitor rate, and be content."

Bruce's goals are anything but modest: "I'm going to position myself over time as one of the top people in the industry who is recognized as an authority, rather than just thinking of myself as an authority."

Two Important Things to Remember

This book isn't aimed at big companies with a lot of money and resources, although it certainly would help them to read it. The first thing to remember is, despite what you may have heard about how much money big companies are spending, that cyberspace really is a level playing field. As a small-business person or self-employed individual, your business in cyberspace can be just as successful as a huge corporation's endeavor—maybe even more so. One highly successful company, Annie's Homemade, which sells all-natural macaroni-and-cheese dinners, started on the Internet with a $100 investment in their site and $60 a month to keep it up. Obviously, they did the work themselves, but you can too. If you want to pay someone, your expenses will be higher—closer to the $2,000 to $5,000 range to get started.

Second, making it on the Internet takes commitment, just like any other endeavor. You cannot build a site, then walk away from it and check back once in a while. The speed of the Internet makes people expect to hear back from you quickly, or they'll simply forget about you and your business.

Whom This Book Is For

This book is aimed at those looking for a new business to start, existing businesses who want to boost revenue, and businesses who hope to make their current Internet presence more profitable. As we said, if you're in a big company, this book can help you too, but the focus here is on the small operation that wants to make a good living serving customers in cyberspace.

How Much Money You Can Make in Cyberspace

We've talked with people who are earning a wide range of incomes in cyberspace, from $10,000 a year part-time to a gross of $250,000 or more a year. Their stories are all in here, along with their tips and tricks as to how they did it—information you can use to do the same. There's no magic formula. It's a matter of understanding the medium, working smart, and being persistent.

A Chapter-by-Chapter Summary

We've divided the book in two parts. Part I covers the business aspects of cyberspace at a higher level, while part II deals with the mechanics of what you need to know to get started.

The first two chapters of part I cover critical information about the medium with which everyone doing business should be familiar. The next four chapters offer information on the three main categories of businesses in cyberspace, with a fourth division for existing businesses venturing into the cyberworld. (Existing businesses will fall into one of those three main categories, but the challenges facing an existing business are different, which is why a separate section is devoted to these businesses.) Part II covers information everyone needs to know, no matter what type of business category they fall into. Next is a chapter-by-chapter summary.

Chapter 1 lists the characteristics that make the Internet different from any other communications medium ever employed. Entitled "Cyberspace Is Personal Space," this chapter explains how our physical and emotional makeup cause us to relate to cyberspace differently than we do to other popular communications media used in business, such as radio and television. This is information that is critical for an understanding of cyberspace from a business perspective.

In chapter 2, we cover opportunities in cyberspace, including the projected growth of business on the Internet, the income potential for businesses, and the basic three categories into which businesses in cyberspace fall.

Advertiser-supported sites are the focus of chapter 3. This is one of the basic precepts of doing business on the Internet, and we cover how successful cyberbusinesses are picking up those advertising dollars by drawing crowds to their sites.

Chapter 4 covers selling goods and services on the Internet, including what works well for sale in cyberspace and what you need to know to make selling on the Net work for you.

The amount of information on the Internet is mushrooming, and someone gets paid to develop that content and place it in cyberspace. In chapter 5, find out about writing content, developing Web pages, and helping others with their content and Web sites in this chapter.

Existing businesses face unique challenges in entering cyberspace. Chapter 6 is a guide to those challenges, and how to successfully meet them. You'll also find a list of the seven biggest mistakes businesses entering cyberspace make and how to avoid those mistakes.

Chapter 7 is focused on the do's and don'ts of building a successful Web site. This chapter covers a recommended procedure for making your Web site work, tools you'll need, design considerations, and practical tips to make your site a success.

Promoting your site is the focus of chapter 8. We'll talk about how you can make use of special characteristics of the Internet to promote your site as well as free and low-cost ways to get visitors.

In chapter 9 we discuss how to get paid electronically. The information in this chapter includes the most popular types of electronic payments, how you can get set up to take electronic payments, how to take advantage of commission sales from other sites, what to expect from Internet advertisers and advertising agencies, and quick and simple ways you can protect yourself from fraud.

And finally, chapter 10 winds things up with information on how to choose an Internet Service Provider (ISP) to host your site. In this chapter, you'll find out the important questions to ask and an explanation of what each question means so you'll understand the answers.

A helpful reference, the appendix contains the contact information for companies, tools, and resources mentioned throughout the book. In addition, we've included an alphabetized table of over 125 Internet businesses with descriptive information about each one. And we've provided a glossary of Internet terms and an index.

What You Need to Know to Use
This Book Effectively

You will get more out of this book if you spend time in cyberspace. You don't need a lot of money to make that happen. In fact, you can start spending time on the Internet even if you don't yet have your own computer and Internet connection. Your local public library, junior college library, or a university library may offer Internet access to residents of your community without charge. Or you can rent Internet access at one of the "cyber cafes" springing up around the country that offer a combination of coffee and Internet access billed by the hour. Perhaps you have a friend who will show you around the Internet. The important thing is to get access so you can become familiar with navigating the Internet. You may also want to go back to the Internet at various points in the book and look for examples of what we've presented.

To give you specific information to shoot for, we've included a short list of terms you should recognize to use this book effectively.

You can go through this short list and if you already know the terms and what they mean, then you're ready to jump in.

> ➤ *Internet browser.* Examples: Netscape, Internet Explorer
> ➤ *URL (Universal Resource Locator).* Examples: http://www.paulandsarah.com; http://www.putnam.com; http://www.netscape.com; http://www.PCbios.com
> ➤ *E-mail (electronic mail)*
> ➤ *Search engine.* Examples: Yahoo, Excite, Alta Vista, HotBot

Our Hope

We hope that the locations and descriptions of the businesses we've listed here remain accurate when you go to find them. However, cyberspace is a moving target and while we've done our best to present you with the most accurate information available, there's just no way we can make any guarantees. We do believe you'll find the information to be high-quality material that's practical and something you can implement even if the particulars about people and Internet locations may have changed.

It is also our hope in writing this book that you'll find a new road to personal empowerment and financial success. We're always interested in your stories and your experiences. Feel free to write us at the addresses below.

Paul and Sarah Edwards: www.paulandsarah.com
Linda Rohrbough: linda@PCbios.com

Part I
The Opportunity

Chapter 1

Cyberspace
Is Personal Space

Instant information creates involvement in depth.

—Marshall McLuhan,

*noted educator specializing in media,
technology, and communication*[1]

 **This chapter is the main building block for** what you'll read in the rest of the book. Information about what people are expecting from you in cyberspace and how to get them to respond to your presence there are critical building blocks to doing any type of business on the Internet. Here you'll find what makes cyberspace unique, why people behave the way they do in this medium, and basic principles for doing business on the Web.

In a nutshell, you'll see that *cyberspace is personal space* and, as you read on through the book, you'll see example after example of how this principle is played out in real situations. To understand what we mean by *cyberspace is personal space*, you'll need to understand something about our psychological makeup as it relates to our interaction with other people.

---

[1]Tony Schwartz, *The Responsive Chord* (Garden City, NY: Anchor Press/Doubleday, 1973), p. 104.

> **TIP**   *The terms* cyberspace, Internet, World Wide Web *(or* www*),* Web, information superhighway, *and* global information network *all refer to the Internet. While distinctions can be made between these terms (for example, the World Wide Web is the graphical portion of the Internet), you may safely consider them all to mean "Internet."*

What Makes Cyberspace Different?

Cyberspace uses multimedia, like sound and video, but it's different from television, videotapes, or movies. It offers information to read, but it's different from a book. It offers playback of music or other recorded sound, but it's different from radio. In fact, one of the problems of marketing in cyberspace has been defining what is different about this medium as opposed to other media of communication.

Our psychological makeup determines what techniques each communication medium must use to produce the desired response. For example, sound is vital to video or television viewing. Try this experiment. Turn off the sound on your television and see how long it holds your attention. Sound quality is so important that people who play video games report that the images they see are better when nothing is improved but the quality of the sound they hear while playing the video game.

Let's look at a medium based on sound alone, such as radio. Radio announcements have to be short and include lots of repetition. Why is that? Because people are usually listening to radio while they're doing other things, like driving or working. The radio is competing with a variety of other stimuli for the listener's attention. Therefore radio spots have to catch the listener's attention, and then get the message across quickly because the message is not going to have the listener's attention for long. Just as businesses who want to use radio and television effectively need to know how people relate to these media, so do those who wish to use cyberspace need to understand how people relate to it.

Cybercitizens Concentrate
and Have Their PC in Close Proximity

While there is evidence to suggest that many households have their computers in the same room with a television, surfing the Internet is an entirely different experience than watching television. One major indication of this difference is that the computer user is usually within two feet of the viewing area of the computer monitor and is often sitting upright, or even leaning forward. Television viewing is most often done in a passive position such as reclining or even lying down, and the distance between the viewer and the television set is five feet or more.

The level of concentration of an Internet surfer is much higher than that of the same person in a television viewing mode. Direct eye contact is made with the monitor, and the viewer is actively selecting, listening to, and reading material on the screen. The person viewing information on the Internet is more than likely to be viewing material he or she selected. Couple the power to select what is viewed with the "instant" access to that information, and you create intense involvement. The Internet surfer is often found leaning forward, looking directly at the computer monitor, obviously intensely interested in the material being presented. As advertising legend Marshall McLuhan put it, "Instant information creates involvement in depth."

Our Psychological Makeup and Personal Space

There have been a number of studies done concerning what is commonly known as "personal space." All creatures have boundaries created by their physical bodies, but there are psychological boundaries as well. This has been shown in the territorial habits of a number of animals, including dogs and cats. People have territorial boundaries as well, often referred to informally as personal space.

Personal space is an invisible territory around an individual. Objects and other people in that personal space zone receive more attention and tend to be under more scrutiny. All people have a personal-space zone, but it is handled differently in different cultures. In North America, intimate space is from zero to eighteen inches from the body, while personal space is the area from eighteen inches to four feet.[2] Edward and Mildred Hall, in their book *Hidden Differences: Doing Business with the Japanese*, say:

> *Sometimes when a foreigner appears aggressive or pushy, or re-mote and cold, it may mean only that his personal distances are different from yours.*

The Halls point out that the Japanese, who live in more crowded conditions, tend to compensate for the lack of personal-space real estate by avoiding accidental touching and any sign of spatial intimacy. They note:

> *It is important to remember that any violation of spatial patterns is experienced personally.*[3]

In situations where we are forced into physically crowded conditions, one of the ways we handle "forced intimacy" is to avoid eye contact. For example, we can be seated in chairs close together, but as long as the chairs are placed so that we don't have to face each other, we can still be relatively comfortable.[4] On the other hand, contact is even more intimate at close range if direct eye contact is involved.

Cyberspace Is in Your Face

So, what does this information about personal space mean for cyber-space? Here we have a communications medium where the person views instantaneous information at close physical proximity (usually under two feet) in an environment where there is usually no physical proximity to another user, but where there is direct eye contact (at least with the medium) and intense concentration. In addition, the

---

[2]Billie J. Wahlstrom, *Perspectives on Human Communication* (Dubuque, IA: William C. Brown Publishers, 1992), p. 94.

[3]Edward and Mildred Hall, *Hidden Differences: Doing Business with the Japanese* (Garden City, NY: Anchor Press/Doubleday, 1987), pp. 14–15, 48.

[4]Mark L. Knapp, *Interpersonal Communication and Human Relationships* (Newton, MA: Allyn and Bacon, 1984), p. 110.

cybercitizen's actual physical location is usually a place of complete familiarity within the person's own territorial bounds. Can we conclude, then, that the very act of surfing the Internet creates a situation of personal intimacy in the viewer unprecedented in communications media known previously?

If cyberspace is personal space or even intimate space, then you can assume that people you meet or who interact with information you place into the medium feel that you are in a position of personal intimacy with them. Does that sound preposterous? Let's examine the evidence. If indeed, our psychological makeup, our human nature, makes us feel a sudden intimacy in cyberspace, this would explain a number of behaviors exhibited in cyberspace that appear to be absent or not as intense in other communications media. Here's what we mean.

Even the Boss Answers His Own E-mail

One of the most notable features of cyberspace is that just about everyone still answers his or her own e-mail. So people you couldn't normally ever hope to reach by any other means of communication will personally read every electronic message sent to them. For example, a Microsoft employee living in Texas told us it is possible for any of the thousands of Microsoft employees to send e-mail directly to Bill Gates. Employees at other companies have similar privileges with their leadership. Sending mail of this sort is viewed as the equivalent of calling the boss at home on the weekend to ask about your retirement package and is commonly termed a CLM (career limiting move). So if you're going to do it, it had better be important. But before e-mail, who but a select few employees could even have hoped to have this type of access to management?

In one particular example we know of, a manager at a *Fortune* 500 company sent an e-mail regarding casual dress to a vice president in charge of operations of the region, bypassing several layers of management in the process. This produced a good deal of embarrassment for the people in supervisory roles above this manager and was viewed by many to be a CLM. However, several months later it was determined that casual dress would be adopted for the summer months, and now the regional office is considering casual dress on a permanent basis for employees who do not have to interface with customers. It appears that the manager who originally sent the e-mail was able to influence company policy in much the same manner as he might have if he had a personal friendship with the vice-president in charge.

Spamming

Spamming, the act of sending unsolicited e-mail, is another indication of the personal nature of cyberspace. It is met with hostility that seems out of proportion, unless you consider the intimacy factor of cyberspace. While technically, any unsolicited e-mail is considered a spam, what is usually meant by spamming is the practice of sending the same piece of unsolicited e-mail to hundreds or even thousands of users at once.

As an example, here is a question asked by a newcomer who joined a mailing list of entrepreneurs on the Internet in a discussion of spam and the answer from a member of that list:

> *I'm curious as to why people have a problem with spam . . . What's wrong with a little entrepreneurship when it could possibly MAKE money for someone . . . either the spammer himself or the person who receives the spam? . . . think about the people that only have e-mail access to the Net . . . how are they gonna find out about mailing lists and/or opportunities that they might be interested in. Just a few thoughts.*

Some of the comments made in reply were:

> *The First Amendment does not protect the spammer. You are free to speak your mind, but that doesn't give you the right to come in and set up your soapbox in my living room.*

> *. . . of course, the other approach is to increase the economic and social cost to spammers of their antisocial behavior, by subjecting them to lawsuits and even direct local pressure by informing landlords and people who live and work nearby of their misdeeds.*

One well-known spamming outfit, Cyberpromotions, is fighting numerous court battles over unsolicited e-mail. The company has been forced to get off every on-line service and ISP it has dealt with and instead has set up its own Internet server. *U.S. News and World Report* reported that Phillip Lawlor, CEO of spamming company Apex Global Internet Services, receives so many death threats on his home answering machine that ". . . sometimes—in a fit of morbid curiosity—he fast-forwards to get to the more frightening ones."[5] Now, however, people are doing more than just name calling. Both Apex and Cyberpromotions have been deliberately and maliciously hit by attacks designed to crash their computer systems.

The *U.S. News and World Report* article went on to say that anti-spamming sentiment has become fierce despite a survey from one Internet access provider who said 70 percent of its users said commercial e-mail is fine, so long as it's something the individual is interested in. All this sounds contradictory unless you realize that cybercitizens see spamming as the same as coming home to find an uninvited door-to-door salesman sitting in your living room. Being sold a product is not the issue. It's the fact that their personal space has been violated. If the salesman shows he has some interest in the cybercitizen by finding out beforehand about his or her interests, if there's evidence that a level of care for the individual has been taken, then the unsolicited mail is not an issue.

Flaming Enflames
Flaming is the act of sending insulting e-mail to someone else on the Internet. In an article entitled "Flamers: Cranks, Fetishists and Monomaniacs," the *New Republic* called flaming "a familiar sociological curiosity."[6] The article went on to describe the Internet as inhabited by "millions of electronic Walter Mittys nationwide" who take on a more "aggressive personality behind a computer and a modem."

A site dedicated to providing insults for flaming the homepage

---

[5]John Simons, "The Battle Over Spam Gets Ugly: Critics Take Aim at Junk E-Mail," *U.S. News and World Report* (May 12, 1997): 55 (1).
[6]Gary Chapman, "Flamers: Cranks, Fetishists and Monomaniacs," *New Republic* (April 10, 1995): 13 (3).

states, "Boiling anger sharpens your point of view . . . so what are you going to do about it?" One of the jokes on the Internet has it that the fastest way to get flamed is to enter a chat forum dedicated to a specific topic and then attempt to change the subject or introduce a new subject. However, we believe flaming is another symptom of the unprecedented levels of personal intimacy in cyberspace and we believe we can offer evidence to support that claim. So let's examine flaming in the context of what we know about cyberspace.

While the demographics of the people who have inhabited cyberspace is becoming more female and is starting to include wage earners at lower levels, the traditional demographics have been male, with an income over $60,000 a year, and usually well educated. A high proportion of the on-line services found the demographics included a large percentage of self-employed individuals. Prodigy did a survey that revealed a large number of people who own computers also have children, a result that came as a surprise as Prodigy previously believed the potential market was older men who were either single or had adult children. This demographic information hardly seems to fit the description of people who would regularly exhibit what appears to be uncontrolled, belligerent behavior.

One of the issues that has not been addressed is that the context of behavior makes a lot of difference as far as the acceptability of the behavior is concerned. The *New Republic* describes this e-mail from one cybercitizen to another as a "smart-alecky taunt":

> *Your reply was most impressive. You seem to have the ability to respond to mail with either profanity, inanity, or pointless threats of physical violence. Why don't you try those pills the doctor gave you, and take a nice long rest. It may do you no good, but I am sure the remainder of the viewers would be pleased by the absence of your moronic and asinine diatribes.*

If you view the places where people exchange information on the Internet as though they were a public hall, such as a PTA meeting or a party, then a reply such as this to anyone appears to be out of bounds when it comes to acceptable social behavior. But if this reply were made to someone who barged in on an intimate social setting, such as a private home or an office cubicle, the above quote almost shows remarkable taste and restraint.

Imagine a small conference room where the inhabitants are a group of executives having an intense discussion about a topic important to their future. The door leading to the room is clearly marked with a sign explaining that others may enter, but that all discussion must center on the topic at hand. Now someone enters the room, and in a break in the conversation, asks if anyone can make change for the parking meters down on the street or can give directions to a local restaurant. Such behavior on the part of the new person will be seen as a violation of the personal space and a lack of respect for the members of the group. Further, rather than leaving when rebuffed, the newcomer insists on asking the question again.

What complicates the picture even further is that the newcomer also sees the conference room as his or her own personal space. Thus the obviously angry response on the part of the participants to a polite question that the questioner is confident they know the answer to is seen as an unreasonable personal insult.

Add into the equation the lack of any body language to go with e-mail, so that an apologetic shrug or a handsome smile is missing, and the opportunities for insulting the other person multiply. Flaming is so commonplace that people have started putting in comments like "just my 2 cents" at the end of messages to avoid offense, or they joke about putting on "asbestos" long underwear.

A pattern forming among groups who share information on a certain topic, or "chat" groups, is to form a discussion on a certain topic and exchange worthwhile messages for a period of time, until some behavior insults a few members of the group. Then the majority of the messages become flames, other members of the group drop out, and eventually the discussion group is shut down due to lack of interest. Certain Web sites encourage chat but are run by moderators with experience who attempt to prevent flaming attacks that can result in the eventual destruction of the group.

Insulting someone is so easily accomplished in cyberspace that it's become a joke to go "trolling for newbies" by putting out "flame bait."

The bait is designed to stir up the novice or "newbie." Those with more experience in cyberspace learn how to keep their feelings, and responses, in check.

Other Evidences of Personal Intimacy

In discussing the intimate nature of cyberspace, a friend informed us she was often put off by responses she read on-line. She was surfing in an investing forum and the response from one member to another member who posted an investment idea was "that's stupid." We reminded her that people in intimate situations talk like that all the time. Close friends, lovers, family members all could get away with saying "that's stupid" to an idea presented by someone in their "intimacy zone"; and while it might not be welcomed, the comment would be acceptable. In fact, the comment might even make the receiver laugh.

One of the strongest evidences of the intimate nature of the medium are the marriages taking place between people who meet in cyberspace. What other communications medium can take credit for marriages? How many people who met over the telephone or the radio get married? Obviously, these people meet each other before they marry, but many have corresponded using e-mail for some time, and often have lived hundreds or even thousands of miles apart, but found each other because of common interests they could express in cyberspace.

From the beginning, personal pages have flourished on the Web. Personal Web pages have contained images of family members, the boat, and the family dog. Tools for putting these images on the Web, such as optical scanners and digital cameras, have experienced sharp price decreases and are selling as never before.

And material seems to be getting more, not less, intimate. We recently visited a homepage of a married couple where the husband spent pages explaining what they went through to have children—in great detail. The material read like a personal daily journal interspersed with editorial comments and included references to the husband's obesity and the dual six-inch incisions after a surgical procedure to increase his fertility.

Norwegian appliance manufacturer Electrolux had a popular Web site of a family refrigerator, but from the refrigerator's point of view.

Each time a family member opened the refrigerator door, a camera took a picture and displayed the image along with the date and time on the Internet. When we visited, the family had long since stopped posing for the camera or trying not to open the door too often. Thousands of people visited this site to see images of these family members staring blank-faced at their food.

Putting the Intimacy Factor to Work for You

The implications of the intimate nature of cyberspace can be summarized in four principles for building a successful business in cyberspace. They are: specialize, keep up with your e-mail, give people a reason to come back, and provide lots of information.

Specialize

With intimacy comes a heightened need for specialization. We, Paul and Sarah Edwards, co-authors of this book, have long emphasized the value of specialization for business start-ups. Being specific about what you do greatly increases your chances for success. However, as you'll see in the following chapters, the intimacy of the Internet forces even more specialization. It's not possible to be intimate about a general subject. Intimacy forces specifics, usually in great detail. From model horses to electronic greeting cards, you'll see that successful cyberbusinesses tend to specialize even more than standard business start-ups.

CASE STUDY

**JOHN MOEN
GRAPHIC MAPS
GALVESTON, TEXAS
HTTP://WWW.GRAPHICMAPS.COM**

John had been in broadcasting for a lot of years when his sister married a cartographer. He says he remembers asking the question that changed his life—"What's a cartographer?" As it turns out, his new brother-in-law traveled around the world for the purpose of producing two-dimensional cartoonlike drawings of cities. John joined his brother-in-law in the map business in 1981. After about eight years, the two "gently" parted.

On his own, John was drawing maps of cities like Houston. He'd travel to a city, draw a map of the buildings, landmarks, and points of interest, index the map, and develop a "pocket guide." He'd then sell the guide to someone in the city and would teach them how to sell the map to people like the chamber of commerce.

John met and married his wife when he had nine people working for him, including artists, designers, etc. His wife, whom John credits with being a very smart woman, looked over the business income and expenses and said, "Why do you have all these people?" John realized his business made a lot of money, but he spent a lot on employees. Looking back, he feels a lot of businesses make the mistake of having high operating costs "chasing a dream" when if they operated on a smaller scale, they could make more money. It was at that point John decided to be smaller and more focused. When John cut his business down to selling customized maps to corporations, he took in more money, with fewer people, made more of a profit, and had less to manage.

Up to this point, he'd been doing maps by hand, but he bought a new tool—a computer. His first computer, purchased in 1989, was a Tandy 1000 SX. It had two eight-inch floppy-disk drives. Later his son suggested he get a hard-disk drive.

After using the computer, John thought he might be able to draw maps on a computer rather than by hand. He did some research, purchased *Adobe Illustrator,* and spent time learning to draw using a computer. In six months of playing around with *Illustrator* and later *Adobe Photoshop,* he developed a way to draw maps on a computer. At that point, he went into a business partnership with a guy in Dallas and started a company called Illustrated Maps of Texas. The new partnership produced 11-by-8-inch maps of Texas.

But John was still looking for a better way. In about 1992, he was walking through a mall in Houston and saw a new Internet Service Provider (ISP), Phoenix Data Systems, doing a demonstration from a mall cart. This company offered direct access into the World Wide Web and John said while he was aware of the Web, he wasn't really "aware" of what he might be able to do there until then.

Phoenix helped John get onto the Internet, and the company hosts his

Web site today. Phoenix came to his home, instructed him in how to install the software, and showed him how to find file transfer protocol (FTP) sites where he could download interesting material. John said, in his opinion, browsing the Internet was a waste of time, but the Internet was quite useful when he wanted something specific. So, he went to the trouble of learning how to navigate the Internet himself. (He said he's learned running a small business that you have to be able to do almost everything yourself at least once. This way you don't get caught in the trap of not being able to deal with something that goes wrong and you avoid the trap of being too dependent on one person.)

John was bent on getting his own Web site up. He searched for software he could use to build his site and ended up going with a software package called *HotDog* from an Australian software company called Sausage Software. John said his biggest advantage was he already knew how to draw images and change them from one format to another in *Photoshop,* so he didn't have to spend time learning about data formats.

At first he designed his page on paper, but after a while, he started making changes without drawing them first—just using the software. At first, he changed his site, or Web page, over a dozen times in the first thirty days. At one point he got an e-mail from someone who said he should keep track of people coming to the site. So he put up a "counter" to count the number of visits, but that was depressing because he found out not as many people were coming to his page as he'd thought.

On the other hand, John said he found the low number of visits added substance to something he'd always believed: that to get business, you have to go out and get the business—if you wait for them to come to you, you'll be waiting a long time.

John's question was, "How can I get people to come to my site?" He tried posting his site with all the search engines he could find, and he joined newsgroups, but his "hits" weren't going up dramatically. And the people who did visit would leave him requests like "I'm working on a college paper and I need an image of every country in Africa by tomorrow morning."

So he decided to change his site. John had looked at other sites and made the observation that the successful ones offer a lot without charge. "They charge you for stuff, but they give you a lot," John said. So he spent a month designing almost a thousand pieces of clip art, then offered the images for downloading at no charge. "I said, 'Here's all the free stuff I offer and, by the way, I also do custom maps.' My hits went from thirty or forty a day to a thousand a day.'"

Once his hits went up John said, "My e-mail got almost uncontrollable." To answer, he found himself having to get up at 6 A.M. each day to work on e-mail for a couple of hours. The requests were wide-ranging, and some were unusual. For example, he had one from a rabbi in New York who was doing a book on the Persian empire and wanted a detailed map of a particular area. Another unusual request came from some government employees who were trying to win a contest and wanted a map of an area with the IRS site posted on the map. John said, " I was afraid not to answer because I was concerned I'd turn off these customers."

Once the site took off, John expanded it. He already had images and examples of maps he could draw, so he added examples of maps he'd drawn along with profiles of the people using them and how they're using them. This brought in even more business. For example, a company in Pittsburgh saw the exact kind of map on-line that they had in mind for their site, so they also placed an order.

As an additional incentive to draw people back, John has added a daily contest in which he describes a location on the planet and people have to guess the location. Prizes to winners have included things like $25 cash and an Indy 500 pin and pen. John said one of the surprising things he discovered by conducting the contests is that people are not geographically literate.

John said he's also been able to get big companies on the Internet who offer on-line maps to contract with him for those services. While contractual obligations prevent him from disclosing who all the companies are, he said his immense library of maps and travel guides has allowed him to get the work. He has work internationally as well. He is working with a company in Paris that is coming on-line with nautical and real estate sites, and he completed a project in Africa for a company who wanted to have maps of its African sites.

Lots of Web site bells and whistles and flashing lights are not relevant to a "now" buyer who wants to know what your price is, John says. Lots of people have told him they like the simplicity of his site and the way he makes it easy to use. He talks of a competitor whose site is so confusing he and his wife both had trouble navigating it.

John believes he's successful because he offers service at a fair price. He emphasizes the importance of the ability to be able to develop and maintain your site yourself. "If you rely on someone else to do it, you suffer because your site updates can get behind and you can't deal with people on a timely basis."

What's the secret? If you want to take in money, give stuff away, be educational, and provide a lot of information. Then you can attract customers who are willing to pay. "For serious users of the Web, information is the key," John added.

Keep Up with Your E-mail

If you suddenly found yourself eye-to-eye with someone less than a foot away from you, who is there because of something that interested her, and you wanted to get something from her, what would you have to do? You must gain trust, convey sincerity, and build a relationship. The intimacy factor of cyberspace operates in much the same way.

One of the most important ways to build trust is to respond promptly to e-mail. This tells the other person she's important to you. Successful Internet business owners spend one to two hours a day just answering e-mail. Cybercitizens are aware of how quickly the medium offers a response, and they have little patience for a lack of response or a slow response. The more successful your site, the more e-mail you can expect, so be prepared to spend time handling it.

Provide a Reason to Return

Return visits to your site are critical to your success whether or not you want to earn income by selling space to advertisers or sponsors. One of the reasons for the importance of return visits is building credibility and a relationship with the customer. If people only come once, they're not likely to trust you or to want to do business with you. In all likelihood, potential customers may visit several times before they offer you their business.

In order for people to come back to your site, there has to be something worth coming back for. This can be accomplished in a number of ways, including offering changing images people find compelling, handy reference information, software updates, etc. As an example, "I See You" is a service for working parents with children in participating day-care centers that allows them to view their child's classroom at thirty-second intervals on the Internet. Philip Margolis of PC Webopaedia offers an advertiser-supported site with constantly updated lists of commonly used computer and Internet terms along with related Web sites to visit for more information. Real Audio offers a software plug-in that allows users to play sound off the Internet, but sets a time limit on use so the user has to revisit the site every ninety days for an updated version or purchase the software.

Give Something Valuable Away

There are many ways to express caring for another person—e.g., a gift, a telephone call, a back rub.[7]

Notice that in this quote from Mark Knapp in his book *Interpersonal Communication and Human Relationships,* a gift is at the top of the list for building relationships because it expresses caring for the other person. Intimacy almost demands giving, and some of the most successful sites on the Internet have practiced this principle from their inception. Netscape was one of the most noted for giving away its Internet browser by the same name, and Microsoft has followed Netscape's example with Internet Explorer. Software developers have given away software packages for years in the form of shareware and freeware and some have made millions doing it.

Jim Button, a former IBM employee who developed the word processor Buttonware back in the '80s, made millions offering the software on the shareware "try-before-you-buy" premise. Today, John Moen of Graphic Maps offers free for downloading images of states and countries to promote his core business of selling custom maps. Bruce Clay gives away information on how to get your Web site more

---

[7]Mark L. Knapp, *Interpersonal Communication and Human Relationships* (Newton, MA.: Allyn and Bacon, 1984), p. 226.

attention from search engines to promote his consulting business. Aliza Sherman gives away information concerning issues particular to women in her advertiser-supported Cybergrrl site. These are just a few of literally hundreds of examples of people who started by giving something away.

What you give away depends on what is important to the audience you're after. Most Internet giveaway items are information, software, or images—things that can be downloaded to the user's computer immediately.

Conclusion

As we've seen, people on the Internet are responding to this communications medium in a highly personal and intimate way. In *The One to One Future,* by Don Peppers and Martha Rogers, the authors claim technology is changing everything for everyone from the corporation to your great-aunt. These changes will empower the individual and the small-business enterprise as never before. The authors say:

> *The old paradigm, a system of mass production, mass media, and mass marketing, is being replaced by a totally new paradigm, a one-to-one economic system.*[8]

Cyberspace is one of the first arenas for this shift, and we believe it is one of the forces causing the change to a one-to-one economic system. You'll see the four principles we've given you and the personal nature of this communications medium illustrated over and over as you read on. One of the indications of the changes ahead is the way people are flocking to this new medium. Growth in cyberspace has been unparalleled and opportunities abound, as you'll see in the next chapter.

---

[8]Don Peppers and Martha Rogers, *The One to One Future: Building Relationships One Customer at a Time* (New York, NY: Doubleday, 1993), pp. 4–5.

Recap:
principles that work in cyberspace:

1. *Specialize.*
2. *Keep up with your e-mail.*
3. *Provide a reason to return.*
4. *Give something valuable away.*
5. *Remember: Cyberspace is personal space. Treat people with care and concern.*

Chapter 2

Opportunities in Cyberspace

Today convenience is the success factor of
just about every type of product and service that
is showing steady growth.

—Charles G. Mortimer,

president, General Foods Corporation

 In the most basic terms, all we do in cyber-
space is exchange documents with one another over
the phone lines or other communications networks.
For the networks over which this communication
takes place we have to give thanks to the U.S. military.[1] If you remember, after World War II, our government realized it did not have
the means to effectively move men and resources from one end of the
country to the other. So it instigated the Interstate Highway system.
This interconnecting network of roads now crisscrosses the country
and allows all of us to use the Interstate Highway system.

Once the U.S. Department of Defense became dependent on computers, it didn't take long for them to figure out that computers fail

---

[1] If you're interested in the history of the Internet, you'll find no lack of it in cyberspace. Two good
places to start are the National Science Foundation and the Internet Society homepages. You can find
their homepage addresses (or URLs) in the appendix.

and that a computer failure could mean military disaster. The question was, What could be done? To prevent such disasters, over twenty-five years ago, in the 1960s, the military powers that be hired a group of thinkers from the Rand Corporation, and those bright minds came up with a network of interconnected computers to share information—the precursor to the Internet. Connected in this way, if one computer goes down, the network can still function. The interconnectedness was envisioned to be like a spider's web so that no one point held the entire structure and alternate routes could be found if one place was damaged or could not be used. This network had the added advantage of using the processing power of all the connected computers, making the whole more powerful than the sum of its parts.

Once the defense-related sites were joined in a new computer network called ARPANET, the next step was to hook up researchers in various universities. That's when the National Science Foundation became involved. In 1985 the NSFNET was formed to allow research and educational ideas to be exchanged electronically to free the flow of ideas unencumbered by the time and expense of travel and the restrictions of distance.

So, in the beginning just government-related sites could be connected, but the Internet was so exciting and so useful that after a while the growth of this government-funded network was growing way out of proportion. People from all over the world were finding ways to get on the "Information Superhighway" to access all the "free" information available there, and the U.S. government realized it could not afford to finance the entire world's access to the Internet. Nor did it need to. The decision was made to make the network public and turn over the cost of access to the private sector.

The Freedom Network

An important point to note here is that controlling access and content on the Internet was about as easy as controlling every person who uses the Interstate Highway system. It still is. Knowing that the Internet was born out of a government-funded operation has created apprehension that the worst parts of George Orwell's book *1984* and the notion that "Big Brother is watching you" could be coming true.

> **TIP** *On-line services, or non-Internet services, differ from Internet Service Providers (ISPs) in the type of access they provide users. On-line services, such as America Online, while allowing users access to the Internet, provide an added layer of complexity to the process that tends to slow Internet access. On-line services also tend to encourage users to stay within the service to shop or interact. However, these services tend to offer more control over the content that can be viewed, which is considered a plus when children are involved.*

But most of those fears are unfounded: if the U.S. government could have controlled access to the Internet, it would already have done so.

In fact, the Internet has been responsible for a lot of political change in the world. Totalitarian governments depend heavily on control of information and a lack of empowerment of the individual in order to maintain their power. The Internet takes control of information away from such governments, and their leaders hate it. For example, Iraqi government official Al-Jumhuiya of Baghdad said in an editorial in an Iraqi government newspaper that the Internet is "the end of civilizations, cultures, interests, and ethics." He called the Internet an "American means to enter every house in the world" and went on to accuse the U.S. of wanting to become "the only source for controlling human beings in the new electronic village."[2] But, in fact, the flow of information is the real threat to such regimes because the Internet shifts power to individuals, not goverment, and as such it could be called the "freedom network."

The Individual Choice Network

Having called the Internet the freedom network, let us emphasize a concept that is the underlying premise of this book and the means to your success in cyberspace. That concept is, the individual has total freedom in cyberspace. "Surfing" the Internet is a lot like television channel surfing, only without the obstacles. No one is held hostage by a commercial while waiting for a favorite show to come back on;

[2] Staff, "Technology Report," *Dallas Morning News* (February 18, 1997): 8D.

the user is totally free to stop the flow of information coming in or to simply move on if the information takes too long to arrive. No one is watching, so there's no social compulsion to politely stay.

In other words, people who visit anywhere on the Internet do so because they want to, and your job in doing business in cyberspace is to make them want to. That's what this book is all about. This empowerment of the individual is one of the things that makes cyberspace attractive to people. Where people are, businesses that meet their needs are likely to follow.

The Projected Growth of Business in Cyberspace

In 1997, the National Science Foundation said the Internet has grown from a handful of networks in the 1960s to over one hundred thousand networks. Each network can have one to hundreds or thousands of individual computers, so projecting the number of actual computers connected is an impossible task. However, as users register with on-line services and marketers conduct surveys, there are gauges for measuring the rate of growth of the Internet.

Exponential Growth Among On-line Service Providers and ISPs

Popular avenues of on-line entry reflect the exponential growth rates of cybercitizenry. In 1995, the three major on-line services—America Online (AOL), CompuServe, and Prodigy—reported a total of three million members. Three million was considered a staggering number of people at the time.

But in 1996, AOL said its membership doubled to 6 million and in the first half of 1997, AOL reported it had gained another 2 million subscribers for a total of 8 million. CompuServe reported in early 1997 that it was up to 5.4 million members, while Prodigy maintained its 1 million members. That's a total of 14.3 million members in early 1997 and a jump of more than 475 percent in just over a year's time.

The major on-line service providers admit a significant turnover in members, but even so the numbers are astonishing. In addition, there has been speculation that these services offer an introduction to members who, once they find themselves more familiar with on-line access, move to smaller Internet Service Providers (ISPs) where Internet access is faster and there is less competition for on-line resources.

While the number of ISPs is tough to estimate, *Boardwatch* magazine publishes a guide listing ISPs in 16,000 telephone area codes nationwide. Analysts at Forrester Research of Cambridge, Massachusetts, conservatively estimate 28 million cybercitizens from the United States alone will be going through ISPs to access the Internet by the year 2000.

> **TIP**   *In a nutshell, cyberspace is the world's largest word-processing application.*

People Accessing the Internet to Multiply

The rate at which people are entering the world of cyberspace is nothing less than astonishing. In 1995, the Internet Society said if the exponential growth rate continued, the number of Internet users could equal the entire human population by the year 2001. Predictably, the growth rate has slowed. Still analysts at Yankelovich Partners, Inc., of Norwalk, Connecticut, predict the cyberworld will gain cybercitizens at the breathtaking pace of 20 to 25 percent annually. Those are numbers any industry would envy.

However, the number of people accessing the Web is even more difficult to count than the number of companies providing access. Estimates in 1996 ranged from 28 million to over 50 million. While there is disagreement over the numbers, the one thing everyone agrees on is that the number of people accessing the Internet is climbing rapidly. International Data Corp., a consulting group based in Framingham, Massachusetts, said their research shows the number of people accessing the Internet should increase from their conservative figures of 28 million in 1996 to 175 million at year-end 2001.

Several cyberbusinesses reported a significant increase in the number of on-line orders back in 1995 when the major on-line services gave their members access to the Internet. As the numbers of people increase in cyberspace, the business opportunities are also sure to increase.

Sales Growth Takes Off

Healthy growth in the number of people on the Internet doesn't mean the businesses there have all been making money. Predictions of financial potential in the early days of the World Wide Web were, frankly, outrageous given the lack of experience of business on this new electronic frontier. The problem wasn't that there weren't businesses making money, but that businesses everyone expected to make money didn't.

"Despite these healthy growth rates, sales in the electronic marketplace have grown more slowly than expected for several reasons," cautioned Karen Burka, editorial director for the Stamford, Connecticut–based market analysis firm Cowles/Simba. "Existing electronic marketplaces—particularly those in the consumer market— have not demonstrated clear advantages over more traditional sales channels. Therefore, many potential buyers have not felt the need to change their shopping habits."

Saying that potential buyers have not seen clear advantages over traditional sales channels is an understatement. Businesses cannot just stick up a "virtual vending machine" and wait for the orders to come in.

Nonetheless, analysts at Yankelovich claim purchases on the Internet are increasing in number. "Cybercitizens are no longer just testing the waters," says Thomas F. Hill, vice chairman of Yankelovich. "They are coming of age as on-line buyers." AOL confirms the increase in buyers in cyberspace with its report that $2.6 million worth of flowers were sent via its 1-800 FLOWERS service to 55,000 moms for Mother's Day in 1997—a figure double the number sent in 1996.

Flowers are not the only item cybercitizens are buying. Nearly $7.5 million in goods were purchased on the Internet in 1996 (excluding non-Internet services such as AOL), according to analysts at Cowles/Simba. The group predicts that Internet-based sales of goods will climb to nearly $4.3 billion by the year 2000.

Analysts at Jupiter Communications are predicting a much faster climb to $15.6 billion in cybersales by the year 2000. *USA Today* reported that on-line sales more than tripled in a single year, mushrooming from $707 million in 1996 to $2.6 billion in 1997.[3] As the number of people entering cyberspace grows and Internet sales increase, advertisers are showing a growing interest in reaching customers on the Web.

Advertisers Investing in Cybercitizenry

Advertisers believe cybercitizens are worth investing in. In 1996, over $300 million was spent on advertising on the Internet, according to analysts at Jupiter Communications. While over $40 million was spent with the major on-line providers or "non-Web publishers," such as AOL and CompuServe, $260 million was spent in advertising on the Internet. "While on-line is still a spec on the media buyer's map, growth like this helps legitimize the medium and slowly but surely attract mainstream consumer advertisers to it," said Peter Storck, director of Jupiter's On-Line Advertising Group. The analyst said his company expects this steady growth in Web advertising to continue.

Analysts at Cowles/Simba are more conservative with their 1996 numbers, saying World Wide Web advertising revenue reached $171.5 million. These analysts say that's a 170 percent increase from the $63.5 million in 1995, but the group predicts Web advertising expenditures will reach $2.46 billion annually by the year 2000. The success of individual businesses on the Internet is what convinces advertisers to invest.

Income Potential for Cyberbusinesses

As we said in the Introduction, the income potential we've seen for those doing business in cyberspace ranges from $10,000 to six figures annually. However, we met few individuals doing over a quarter of a million a year and few making $10,000 a year part-time. Most businesses fell in a range between $40,000 to $120,000 annu-

---

[3]Elizabeth Weise, "Net Can't Fill All Your Stockings Yet," *USA Today* (December 10, 1997): 1D.

ally. Every business we talked with reported to us their revenues were climbing.

Existing businesses who branched out on the Internet varied. Some simply broke even, while others said a third or more of their current revenue was coming from on-line business. Some businesses expressed a need to have a presence on the Internet but were unable to track how much new business came in as a result of their Internet presence, though many were convinced a substantial amount of new business was due to the Internet. Some have gone as far as to offer stock via the Internet to raise funds for expansion.

Working part-time, it took most businesses we surveyed several months to show a profit. On a full-time basis, some businesses were profitable in as little as three months, while others found they took three years to become established. The average time it took most businesses to start making money on the Internet was a year. It's important to keep in mind that much trial and error went into the mix as these businesses started up.

Advertisers are bringing additional support to businesses serving Internet customers. However, not every business can be advertiser supported. We've divided the types of businesses in cyberspace into four categories.

Four Types of Businesses in Cyberspace

While there are lots of ways to categorize different types of businesses, we've determined that the most efficient way to break down cyberbusinesses into categories is by the way they generate their revenue. Businesses who generate revenue in the same way tend to do the same types of things to garner that revenue, and cyberbusinesses are no exception.

Successful cyberbusinesses fall into three main categories: those offering goods or services, advertiser-supported sites, and content development. In addition to these categories, we've added a fourth to include existing businesses entering cyberspace because these businesses face a special set of concerns. We'll take the next four chapters to examine each of these four categories in detail and explore how each category of cyberbusiness uses the four principles outlined in chapter 1 as well as how the personal nature of cyberspace affects the way businesses in these categories operate.

Recap:

four types of businesses in cyberspace:

1. *Selling goods and services*
2. *Advertiser supported*
3. *Content development*
4. *Existing businesses*

Chapter 3

Providers of
Goods and Services

Market research can establish beyond the shadow of a
doubt that the egg is a sad and sorry product and that
it obviously will not continue to sell. Because after
all, eggs won't stand up by themselves, they roll
too easily, are too easily broken, require special
packaging, look alike, are difficult to open,
[and] won't stack on the shelf.

—Robert Pliskin,

vice president, Benton & Bowles,
speaking to the National Packaging Forum in 1963

 Selling goods and services in cyberspace is
hardly new. One of the most popular goods to be
sold in cyberspace was software. Phil Katz with his
compression utility, Pkzip; Jim Button, a former IBM
employee who developed the word-processing application Buttonware; and John McAfee with his antivirus product, Scan, all made it
big selling software in cyberspace.

Once graphical services such as Prodigy and America Online
came into being, the ability to see products offered for sale changed
forever the way business would be done in cyberspace. In this chapter, you'll see what makes cyberspace a great place for marketing
goods and services, what type of products do well in cyberspace, and
how successful cyberselling is done.

The Strengths of Selling in Cyberspace

The most significant strength of selling in cyberspace is that it is inexpensive. Companies we talked with spent from $100 to $5,000 or more to get a Web site on-line to sell products. The average cost was $500 to $1,000. Compare this to the price of designing and distributing a full-color printed brochure to hundreds or even thousands of people, and the cost of placing material for sale on the Internet is a bargain indeed.

Not only is a Web site inexpensive to set up, but giving people the information they need to decide whether or not to buy can also be less expensive. For example, Mike Smith of Joshua Tree Wood Trim says he's found it much less expensive to sell wood trim kits for automobiles over the Internet because customers can get all their questions answered on-line. This saves him money, as he doesn't have to pay for toll-free calls to answer questions, and he doesn't have to send out a catalog to educate the customer as to what the wood trim kits look like, how they're installed, or the selection of woods available.

Not only is it relatively inexpensive to put up a Web site with items for sale, but changes can also be made to the Web site in a matter of hours. Even inexperienced computer users can set up a Web store in a day or two. The most time-consuming task is knowing what to sell and how to get Web visitors to buy. We'll address those issues next.

CASE STUDY

DENNIS FETT AND DEBRA JOAN BUCK
PEACOCK INFORMATION CENTER
MINDEN, IOWA
HTTP://WWW.PEAFOWL.COM

Dennis calls himself a city boy who graduated from East Side High School in Paterson, New Jersey, and went on to major in music at the Yankton Conservatory of Music in Yankton, South Dakota. While in college, Dennis also dabbled in photography. Upon graduation, he got a job teaching music in South Dakota, then he accepted a position near the small town of

Minden, Iowa, where he met Debra Joan Buck. The couple dated for four years, got married in 1980, and rented a farm near Minden.

Debra had a pet pig named Charly who grew to be over eight hundred pounds. One day an accident befell Charly, and Debra went in search of a new pet. She told Dennis she'd like to have a peacock, so after much searching Dennis got three peacock eggs, one of which hatched.

Dennis and Debra found that there wasn't much information out there on "peafowl," which is the term they discovered was all-inclusive for peacocks, peahens, eggs, and chicks. Their first bird, whom they named Junior, died unexpectedly and upon taking the bird to the vet to find out why, they discovered the bird had a deformed heart. They were also surprised to discover that Junior was female, not male.

By then, the couple was hooked on peafowl, so they bought two blue males and three blue hens. Then they heard about white peacocks and purchased five of those. By this time, they had a breeding operation started. They also started selling the birds, as well as eggs, feathers, and jewelry.

Dennis, who had struggled with English in college, decided to start keeping notes on what he learned about peafowl, since there was so little information available. By 1986, he felt he had enough information to write a book. Since no one seemed to be interested in publishing the book, Dennis and Debra borrowed money from a bank, Dennis took his own photographs, and the couple published a book on peafowl themselves titled *The Wacky World of Peafowl*.

Dennis said that when the fifteen boxes of books arrived from the printer, he realized he was going to have to start selling. He took out ads in poultry magazines and did his own public-relations work, which garnered him an article in the *Washington Post*. Public interest in the birds and the books seemed to accelerate and, inside six months, the couple was able to pay off the bank note.

By 1987, the couple had an opportunity to purchase a four-acre tract of land near Minden and moved the entire operation onto their own property for the first time. By the time Dennis was reprinting the first book, customers were starting to ask him if he was going to do a second book. With plenty of material on his hands, Dennis and Debra took advantage of interest in the new book to get prepaid orders in advance, which financed their second book, *The Wacky World of Peafowl, Volume II*.

Meanwhile the couple's peacock operation was getting plenty of attention from a variety of publications from *Organic Gardening* to *Vogue* magazine. Television crews visited the farm, and the couple made several national television appearances. When the *New York Times* said, "Dennis Fett has an encyclopedic knowledge of peafowl," Dennis realized he'd established himself as an authority on the birds.

In 1991, Dennis and Debra were getting pressure to write a third book, but they decided to publish a subscription-based color, bimonthly newsletter instead. The next year, Dennis was called in as a consultant to the city of Rolling Hills Estates in Southern California when a crisis situation erupted over a conflict between city residents and the local, wild peafowl population.

In 1995, although the peacock business was good, Dennis found himself having to take work as a substitute-teacher and Debra worked part-time as a secretary to make ends meet. A shortage of substitute science teachers caused the high school to offer Dennis a short-term assignment in a biology class. It was there he overheard students talking about the Internet, so Dennis asked questions and the students volunteered information. One thing led to another and one student, Matt, offered to design and support a Web site for the Peacock Information Center.

Dennis struck a business deal with Matt (and made sure Matt's parents were involved) to get the Web site going. A local ISP hosted the site, and Dennis paid the expenses as well as Matt. "At the time, we didn't even own a computer," Dennis said.

The site was an immediate success. Since Dennis didn't have Internet access, he provided self-addressed, stamped envelopes and Matt printed off the e-mail questions and mailed them each day. Dennis would then write answers for Matt to send back. Business was still conducted via mail order with the Web site acting as an on-line catalog.

After several months, it became obvious that Matt was becoming overwhelmed with the volume of e-mail and simply couldn't handle the load any longer. Plus, Matt was a junior in high school, and Dennis realized he wouldn't be around to help with the site forever. Dennis and Debra decided to once again go out on a limb and borrowed the money to purchase a Macintosh and a copy of *Claris Home Page*.

While the couple was grateful for the job Matt had done, with more control of the homepage, Dennis and Debra were able to make changes and see results much more quickly. Debra redesigned the homepage, and the couple noticed an immediate increase in the number of visitors and the amount of sales.

Dennis said he's had a lot of people comment on how much they like the simplicity of his homepage and the fact that it loads fast. Dennis also noted that a recent change in the page increased book sales dramatically. The couple thought it was a rule of Web page design that users shouldn't have to scroll through the first page to find information, and additional information should be available via menu options. However, Debra violated that rule by listing all the book information, including pricing, right on the first page. Dennis said orders for the books have gone up dramatically as a result and credits the increase in sales with making it easier for visitors to get to the book information.

Currently, the couple does almost 100 percent of their business on the Internet, the most lucrative of which is book sales. They also use the immediacy of the medium to let people know about the availability of hot items, such as eggs, which are often sold out months in advance. Some of their business is international, despite the fact that they don't take credit cards and they require checks drawn on a U.S. bank. "We do hardly any business in Iowa or in the states that border Iowa," he said.

Dennis is building for the day when his only job will be the peafowl business, and he feels the Internet has done a lot to move him in that direction. As another step toward independence, Dennis pursued and was awarded a fellowship from Creighton University in Omaha, Nebraska, to study peafowl mating habits. Their future plans also include expanding the newsletter and including other peafowl products for sale on the Web site.

What Sells in Cyberspace

The most important characteristic of selling in cyberspace is offering specific and unique products and services. As we've emphasized before, it pays to be specific: sites that are making money selling in cyberspace are on the razor's edge of specific and unique. For example, John Wells offers phasers that make real sounds for Star Trek fans. He also offers T-shirts, mugs, and other memorabilia for popular shows such as *The X-Files, Friends,* and *Rosie O'Donnell.* Dennis Fett concentrates on live peacocks, while Rick and Ralph Fazio sell plastic pink flamingo yard decorations. Raj Khera sells information about government contracts, and Paul Graham of ViaWeb sells custom Internet stores in his ViaMall site.

Cyberspace is also a nurturing place for talented individuals to bypass traditional marketing channels to gain an audience. Even well-established musical artists, like the performer formerly known as Prince,[1] are using the Web to reach fans directly. He decided to leave Warner Brothers to sell one hundred thousand limited-edition copies of his *Crystal Ball* music CD from his own Web page on the Internet.

But you don't have to be famous to find a market in cyberspace. Debra Joan Buck, wife of Dennis Fett of peacock fame, found the Internet to be a previously untapped market for her father's stories. Lowell Buck had written profusely about his World War II experiences and country life, but no one knew about it until Debra found the volumes of handwritten work in her father's attic after his death. Debra compiled the previously unpublished works into a book titled *Lowell's Limericks & Life Stories* and now sells the book via the couple's Web site.

Hard-to-Get Goods

Items that are difficult to get through regular retail channels are excellent candidates for sale in cyberspace. There may be a number of reasons why an item is difficult to obtain. The item may be perishable, new, available only in limited quantities, or it doesn't create enough demand with the general public to be sold in standard retail outlets. Items you might think of as being mail-order products often work well for Web site stores.

One of the major advantages of cyberspace for the consumer is that shopping becomes so much easier. What might take several days of asking around and searching to find can often be found in a few moments on the Internet. From buyers of antique washing machines to fine art worth millions, you can find it on the Internet.

Even mundane items can be sold in cyberspace if there's a com-

---

[1]The artist formerly known as Prince changed his name to a symbol, probably in anticipation of this graphical world.

pelling reason for the consumer to buy. Take macaroni-and-cheese dinners as an example. Annie's Homegrown, co-founded by Ann Withey of Hampton, Connecticut, sells all-natural, one-step pasta dinners aimed at people with young children. There's even a bunny named Bernie on the box.

Another example of mundane items sold in cyberspace is Peapod. An on-line grocery-ordering service, Peapod (http://www.peapod.com) allows subscribers to select items from their local grocery store using their PC and can deliver the groceries the same day. Started by the Parkinson brothers in the Chicago suburb of Evanston, Illinois, in 1989, the service boasts that 80 percent of its customers are women. The company went public in 1997 and is now one of the largest on-line interactive grocery shopping services in the U.S.

In the case of products or services like Annie's Homegrown and Peapod, the consumer may pay more than for competing products not offered on the Internet. However, each offers a compelling reason for consumers to buy and provides a convenient way to meet a specific need. Annie's Homegrown addresses the concern that parents have about food additives while providing quick meals for children, and Peapod offers time savings and convenience.

CASE STUDY

RICK AND RALPH FAZIO
FLAMINGO SURPRISE
CLEVELAND, OHIO
HTTP://WWW.FLAMINGOSURPRIS.COM

Identical twin brothers Rick and Ralph Fazio of Cleveland, Ohio, decided in 1991 that they had a unique idea for celebrating special occasions. The brothers came up with the idea for a service that places fifty plastic, three-foot-high, pink flamingos in the front yard of an unsuspecting person as a practical joke. The decorations are placed in the yard in the early morning, left there all day with a sign that identifies the occasion, then picked up at night, and used again the next day on another unsuspecting victim. So in the spring of 1992, the special-occasion service Flamingo Surprise was born.

The Fazio brothers say Flamingo Surprise was an immediate hit. "It's such a shocker to wake up to fifty hot-pink flamingos on your lawn," Rick added. Soon Flamingo Surprise had expanded to include four U.S. cities and a variety of lawn decorations including elephants, barn animals, dinosaurs, mutant frogs, giant musical notes, and even huge baby bottles.

In fact, the pink flamingos were so popular, the brothers started a mail-order business selling them in pairs. The company also started selling via mail order the "Birthday in a Box" containing twenty flamingos, a 16-by-22-inch sign that can be personalized, and two three-foot-long birthday banners. This product was aimed at people who had heard about Flamingo Surprise but didn't have the service in their area.

Rick Fazio says the plastic pink flamingo was invented in 1957 as a yard ornament, and the popularity of the bird caused a number of "knock-offs" that are a "Pepto-Bismol" pink and not as graceful-looking. Flamingo Surprise makes a point of only using birds made by the original creator. "Kmart carries flamingos for a couple of months in the spring, but when they're gone, they're gone. We're just about the only source for them outside those two months," Rick said.

Taking the business to the Internet hadn't occurred to the brothers until one of their employees who was attending college told them his class project was to create a Web site. The employee asked Rick and Ralph if he could use Flamingo Surprise and wanted to be reimbursed for expenses. Rick said he never thought the Web page would be a revenue producer. The idea was to make an inexpensive, on-line catalog by taking pictures of different surprise lawns once they were set up and then displaying the photos on the Internet. So then when someone wanted to see what a display of thirty mutant frogs looked like, it would simply be a matter of referring the person to the Web page.

The site was officially open to the public in June of 1996, but Rick said that somehow people managed to stumble upon the site before it was announced. With no more promotion than printing the Web site address on the company's own advertising materials and the word-of-mouth promotion on the Internet, the Flamingo Surprise homepage generates about 5 percent of the overall company revenue. The site is now managed by Cyberexpress Netvertising, a company based in Cleveland, Ohio, that also maintains a homepage of their own focused on flight simulation games.

Rick says he's been impressed with the innovative ideas Cyberexpress has come up with for his homepage. For example, the Chicago Flamingo Surprise office gets lots of calls from people who want to come by, so Cyberexpress has already added the capability for visitors to enter their address and then get a map from their location to the store.

Even without a secure server, business orders have poured into the Web site by e-mail, although some people prefer to call the 800 number to order. When the fortieth anniversary of the pink flamingo gained media attention, Rick said orders reached unprecedented levels. In fact, some people have ordered via e-mail, and Rick says they've even supplied their credit card numbers right in the e-mail. However, most people ask a couple of questions via e-mail before ordering.

Future plans for the site include an enhancement so that the company can accept secure credit card orders on the Internet. Rick also has plans to further promote the site through advertising campaigns for the company.

Items Particular to Cyberspace

Items for use in cyberspace can also be sold there. For example, Netscape sells its Web browser on the Internet, Real Audio sells add-on sound playback software for Internet browsers, Sausage Software sells a Web page creation tool called HotDog, and so on. It's important to note that these companies started as small one- or two-person businesses, giving away their software in much the way that the pioneers of marketing software in cyberspace have done. Only instead of the try-before-you-buy approach of shareware, the software was licensed on a trial-period basis and sometimes incorporated a "clock" that shut the software down when the trial period was over. This risk-free introduction served to introduce users to new computing concepts, create a market for power-user versions, and stimulate a corporate market for products aimed at serving cybercitizens using the freely distributed version.

In addition, items for use in electronic mail are popular. Electronic mail, or e-mail, has been the most popular application on the Internet since its inception. So it stands to reason that new products that make e-mail delivery and sending easier, items that can be sent via e-mail, and add-on products to enhance e-mail are popular in cyberspace.

The popular Eudora from San Diego–based Qualcomm is one example of an e-mail tool sold on the Internet. While Internet browsers have e-mail capability, Eudora makes e-mail easier with the ability to scan incoming messages and software for computer viruses, encrypt and decrypt messages for privacy, and compress messages for faster transmission.

Electronic greeting cards and stationery for use with e-mail are becoming popular on the Internet. A number of companies offer electronic greeting cards. These include traditional companies such as Hallmark and American Greetings, who got the idea from start-up companies such as Artec International, which was started by the wife-and-husband team of Laila Rubstein and Eugene Yushin.

CASE STUDY

LAILA RUBSTEIN AND EUGENE YUSHIN
ARTEC INTERNATIONAL
NEW YORK, NEW YORK
HTTP://WWW.GREETING-CARDS.COM
ELECTRONIC GREETING CARDS AND STATIONERY

Laila and Eugene are both Russian immigrants, but Laila said they had to travel to the United States to meet and marry. The couple met in Washington, D.C., through common friends and discovered that their mutual interest was multimedia. Laila has a computer science degree and was working for newspaper publisher Gannett doing a lot of graphical user interface design. Eugene is an artist.

Laila said that, almost immediately after they met, they decided they were a unique match professionally and wanted to do something together involving multimedia. After bouncing around a few ideas, the couple decided to try designing and marketing multimedia greeting cards on the Internet. Their plan was to develop animated, colorful, and customizable cards that included sounds and music. The cards had to be entertaining, yet small enough to be sent across the Internet. The cards also had to be self-executing, so they didn't require Quicktime or some other multimedia software engine to run.

Eugene started designing and Laila started programming. In November of 1995, the couple launched their own Web site on the Internet to distribute their new products. To finance the venture, they invested their own funds and borrowed money from relatives.

The hardest part, according to Laila, was being first. There were obstacles to overcome in developing the cards and, because they were the first, there were no models to follow and no one else to imitate. "We were the only ones with a full life-cycle product," Laila said, meaning that they were responsible for every aspect of their product from creation to promotion, marketing, and distribution. "When we came up with this idea, there weren't even secure servers for accepting credit card orders," Laila added.

On the Web site, their cards (called Multimedia Interactive Greetings or MIGs) are divided into categories. Visitors can see a picture of what the card looks like and a description of each card, and they are encouraged to download a free card to try out. The free demonstration card is just like the card available for purchase, but the customized message cannot be saved. Users can then choose to download, customize, and send the card themselves via diskette or e-mail, or visitors may have the card customized with their messages and sent for them by either diskette through "snail mail" or e-mail. This allows visitors in cybercafes or other locations where the computer equipment is "on loan" to still be able to send a MIG.

While the site was developing, Laila and Eugene discovered there was demand for multimedia work in the corporate market. So to supplement their income, the couple accepted animation projects for corporate clients.

To expand their Web site business, Laila and Eugene have sought and found other sites who will promote the greeting cards for a percentage of the profits. The couple also includes a link on the site to on-line florists who offer flower delivery at a discount.

The couple says their business, which now includes several employees, has been international from the start. While they hadn't intended it to be a service to the disabled, Laila says customers with disabilities are especially grateful for the availability of MIGs.

As for advice to people starting out, Laila says to be prepared to work a lot, especially at first. She says she and Eugene have worked many fourteen-hour days and some even longer. "But the best part of the business is that it's fun," Laila added.

Items Sold at a Discount

Commonplace items sold elsewhere can also be sold in cyberspace if the consumer will save some money by buying on-line. Flowers are a good example. We personally found that ordering flowers on the Internet presented a significant savings of as much as 50 percent over ordering them via a toll-free number. On-line ordering also offers the added advantage of allowing customers to view the floral arrangements they send, so when Grandma says she loves the heart-shaped vase, we know what she's talking about.

Traditional services, such as printing, are being done at discounted prices on the Internet. Marilyn Butz, of Huntington Beach, California, started Bizcardpro as a part-time business selling specialized business cards at a discount to clients in the U.S. and abroad. Marilyn takes advantage of the ability to transfer files electronically on the Internet to show proofs to clients, and she can do custom work, such as gold foil or making the cards the size used in Japan instead of the standard U.S. business card size.

Royal Farros of Moffett Field, California, offers the opposite of the specialized services Marilyn offers by printing generic business cards and stationery that users can design and order right on the Internet. Iprint (http://www.iPrint.com), Royal's "on-line printing company," offers discount prices and allows site visitors to select and input their own information into standard business-card, letterhead, and stationery configurations. Customers can then choose from a selection of fonts and colors as well as insert graphics of their own design or those available on the site. Orders are paid for with a credit card and then shipped in a few business days.

Since the Internet makes it easy for consumers to shop around, offering the lowest price can make a big difference in sales. Mike Smith of Joshua Tree Wood Trim said lowering his prices made his Internet orders jump significantly—enough to more than compensate for the lower profit margin. In addition, cyberspace is a growing place for discount items and clearance sales. Andy's Garage Sale, an Internet store fully owned by Fingerhut Corporation, is an example. Items for sale change from one day to the next, depending on availability. Internet auctions are also popular, and items for sale range from computer components to cargo containers for hauling freight. CityAuction, started by Andy Rebele of San Francisco, is an interactive, on-line combination of classified advertising and an auction. At CityAuction (http://www.cityauction.com) individuals from around the country place items for sale, and Internet visitors bid against one another.

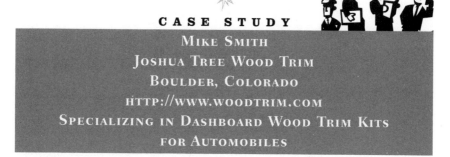

CASE STUDY

MIKE SMITH
JOSHUA TREE WOOD TRIM
BOULDER, COLORADO
HTTP://WWW.WOODTRIM.COM
SPECIALIZING IN DASHBOARD WOOD TRIM KITS
FOR AUTOMOBILES

When Mike was in college, he used to detail cars to make money. While working with his brother on cars in Boston, he met a guy who owned a car accessory plant and was hired to work at the plant. That's when Mike was first introduced to the wood trim kits that he now markets on the Internet.

He said that the first time he saw one of the kits, something just clicked for him. "I thought it was a truly elegant accessory. With one of these kits, you can make a Honda Civic look like a Mercedes," Mike said.

Mike knew he wanted to sell the wood trim kits as a business, but he needed to get positioned to do so. So he took a job working for a publisher and moved to Boulder, Colorado, because he didn't feel he fit in with the culture in Boston.

It was in Boulder that Mike met some people who were starting a home-page design business. They proposed to Mike the idea of doing a Web site for only $1,200 so that they could use the results to market their services.

Mike said it was important to him to have high-quality images on his Web site because his product has a strong visual orientation, so he agreed.

Although he sells the wood trim kits through retail channels, Mike says the Internet is the only part of his business that's been profitable. He's advertised in magazines such as *Road and Track* and *Car and Driver* and gotten 200 to 300 calls a day, but only three orders a week. "We spent a lot of time answering questions," Mike added.

On the Internet, people can view the kits, see step-by-step illustrated installation instructions, and look up their vehicle make and model to get a price before they order, so they don't have to call and ask questions. The Internet orders are pure profit, as there's no catalog to send and no toll-free telephone support is required, Mike added.

As an experiment, and due to increasing competition on the Internet, Mike decided to lower his prices. To his surprise, a dramatic increase in sales accompanied the price decrease, and the increased volume more than made up for the lower profit margin.

Mike did some banner advertising on Yahoo but didn't feel the ads worked for him. He spent $1,000 to get 40,000 page views targeted toward visitors who entered keywords having to do with autos or auto accessories. Unfortunately, he didn't get enough orders to pay for the ad, and of the orders he did get, he got several returns. So he advertises his Web site address, or URL, instead of his phone number, in an ad in *Autoweek* magazine, a publication geared toward readers who are more educated about autos and have a higher median income. Mike says he's found that his *Autoweek* ad is more effective than the Yahoo advertising.

Mike guarantees the product for the life of the vehicle as long as the same person owns the car. He says that he gets very few returns, and the few he does get are from people who think the kit is a replacement for the vehicle's dashboard, not an overlay. Mike's returns are only 3 percent, which is below the average of 5 to 12 percent standard in the mail-order business.

Not only has the Web site turned out to be a success for Mike; the deal also worked out well for the company that developed the site. Mike says the designers attracted the Boulder Museum of Art as a client, and now they won't touch a Web site design project for under $5,000. Mike's advice for products where eye appeal is important is to hire a professional to design your site.

Subscription Services

Services that charge the user for access to the information on the Web site or for information delivered are commonly run as subscription services. This is one of the oldest ways to market services in cyberspace; subscription-based access has been practiced by non-Internet services such as America Online and Prodigy for years. In addition, extensive databases of magazine and newspaper articles are available for electronic access either on a one-time or a subscription basis by companies such as Lexis/Nexis of Dayton, Ohio.

Subscription services can be a hard sell, since so much information is free on the Internet, but services that gather an unusual amount or type of information and then tailor that information to the subscriber appear to do the best. Take GovCon of Rockville, Maryland. GovCon offers a subscription service to those interested in government contracts with specific information on past contracts such as the nature of the bid, who got the contract, and the amount of the contract. The information is compiled from several source documents and is collected over a period of time, then provided to the customer in the format that suits the customer's needs.

CASE STUDY

RAJ KHERA
GOVCON, INC.
ROCKVILLE, MARYLAND
HTTP://WWW.GOVCON.COM
SUPPLIER OF INFORMATION TO THE GOVERNMENT
CONTRACTOR COMMUNITY

In 1995, Raj Khera and his brother, Vic, started to build what they thought was a Web site consulting company. Raj put in his own $10,000 to put up a "sample" Web site titled the Business Resource Center.

The Business Resource Center (BRC) site was never intended to be a moneymaking operation but instead was aimed at providing helpful information to small businesses that the company hoped would become clients.

The business information came from Raj, who had a personal love for the small-business community and constantly updated the site with articles and information. Soon the BRC site was generating a lot of traffic and the consulting business got their first client, the government contracting firm of Freidman Fuller. That was when Edward Rosenfeld joined the team.

The Freidman Fuller Web site had been built to the agreed specifications, but it did not generate the same amount of traffic that the BRC site did. Barry Freidman, one of the principals of Freidman Fuller, proposed to Raj that they combine Raj's knowledge of the Internet with Freidman Fuller's knowledge of government contracting to build a site that would provide information to businesses concerning government contracts. After all, the government is the single largest U.S. purchaser of goods and services, but the requirements for becoming a government contractor can be daunting, Edward Rosenfeld said.

A deal was struck, and Raj's trio began work on a new site called Gov-Con. Like the BRC site, the GovCon site would provide free information regarding government contracts to anyone who registered. The site was an immediate success. "We found an underserved market," said Edward.

The first information they published was entitled the *Commerce Business Daily* (CBD). The CBD takes advantage of a government requirement that any new contract information has to be made public. The government publishes lists of new contracts regularly, so the CBD organizes the contract information and presents it in a way that would be attractive to businesses trying to obtain government contracts. GovCon hoped the CBD would prove useful enough to businesses to draw people to the site on a daily basis.

The original business plan called for an advertiser-supported site. Gov-Con was expected to draw company principals who made purchase decisions and would therefore be a forum for advertisers who wanted to be noticed by these decision makers. GovCon's first advertising clients were service businesses such as lawyers and accounting firms, but the list quickly grew to include other vendors such as Sprint and Riggs Bank. Advertisers were attracted by the idea of being able to reach decision makers directly. "If you're Peat Marwick and you want to reach the guy who's in charge of purchasing for Lockheed, that guy visits GovCon," said Edward.

At first, GovCon was just information, and most of it was available elsewhere—but not as fast or as conveniently. Much of the information was available in a printed format, but it required the businessperson to hand-search an entire document just to find out if they could bid on anything in the document. To provide the printed information in an electronically searchable format, GovCon had to retype the government documents.

Edward said they were able to eliminate the typing by purchasing a feed to get information in electronic format directly from the Government Publications Office (GPO). The company wrote a search engine for this electronic information and then allowed visitors to GovCon to use keywords to search through this large pile of information to find what they wanted. Not only was the feed faster, but it also allowed GovCon an edge. Before the GPO shipped the print version of the contract bidding information, GovCon had it available on-line.

Then something unexpected happened to change the original business model. Edward said that GovCon started getting requests from businesses for more specific information. And these businesses indicated they were willing to pay extra to get the information in a way that suited their particular needs. Some users wanted information that fit certain keyword criteria e-mailed directly to them on a daily basis. The time-sensitive and competitive nature of government contracting made it worthwhile to some businesses to pay extra for this service.

So GovCon put together a subscription service for businesses. This service offers specific information on each government Request for Quote or RFQ. The subscription service allows businesses to learn about RFQs based on a number of criteria, such as dollar amount, products involved, and so on.

The dollar amount is important because one RFQ could be for a single copy of a software package while another could be for a seventy-five-seat license for the same package. Since bidding requires the same amount of work, it's more lucrative to bid for the larger dollar amounts than the smaller ones. The RFQs for a single Federal Supply Classification might total as much as $920,000 a month, so businesses were eager to pay extra for information that might help them win these lucrative contracts.

But GovCon went a step further. While publicly available, the RFQ awards were supplied in a separate document that lists the RFQ by number along with the dollar amount, making it difficult to cross-reference this material. GovCon did the cross-referencing to match up the RFQ numbers, the contractors who received the awards, and the dollar amounts involved. This cross-referencing provides important historical information to subscribers.

GovCon also provides an analysis of the data in the form of an executive report issued periodically that lists the top twenty federal supply categories, the top twenty federal supply groups, the most active agencies, and so on.

The subscription service has been very successful. While GovCon still accepts advertising, it also has the second revenue stream of the subscription base to work from.

The subscription base, along with information about visitors who sign up for the free information, provides GovCon with strong demographic information to attract advertisers. To be sure that the e-mail list the company has is complete, GovCon sends a welcome notice to every visitor who signs up. If the welcome e-mail bounces, GovCon immediately deletes the name and the related information from the list. In this way GovCon assures advertisers that there's been some verification of the company's demographic profiles.

Edward said GovCon's demographics show that 35 percent of users are coming from large companies who have over 500 employees, while the next largest segment of 29 percent is from very small companies who employ fewer than 10 people. Fifteen percent are from companies with 11 to 50 people, and 6 percent come from companies with 51 to 100 employees.

GovCon also offers a self-published book for sale titled *The Art of Winning Contracts*. The first four chapters of the book are available without charge on-line, the service takes credit card orders for the $60 book through a secured server, and the author prints the book himself and handles shipping it out to those who order. Edward said the service hopes to capitalize on the need for information in this market by offering similar books and resource products to visitors.

GovCon plans to expand in a venture with the National Association of Manufacturers to do a GovCon just for manufacturers. Manufacturers have a different set of criteria from other types of government suppliers, so GovCon hopes it can expand by reusing the search engines and capabilities it has already developed.

How to Sell in Cyberspace

Now that you've seen the type of goods and services that fare well on the Web, let's look at how to sell successfully in cyberspace. Selling in cyberspace is work, no matter how you slice it. But so is selling anywhere else. The difference between those who've sold successfully on the Internet and those who haven't is more than just the amount of work put into the project. It has to do with knowing who your customers are, making the shopping process easy for them, providing good-quality images, and establishing yourself as an expert.

Know Your Customer

Lots of successful sales on the Internet start with entrepreneurs asking themselves what would make *them* buy. This practice has a long history in every business environment, not just in cyberspace. In her book, *CEO: Building a $400 Million Company from the Ground Up,*[2] Sandra Kurtzig recounts how engineers William Hewlett and David Packard, founders of Hewlett-Packard, developed products using the "next bench syndrome." The team searched for and tried to develop products that the engineer at the next bench would want or that they would want themselves if they were working at the next bench.

The most famous example of the next bench syndrome was in 1972 when Bill Hewlett got tired of his slide rule and decided it would be more accurate to have a hand-held calculator he could put in his pocket. The market research department at HP said no one would pay $400 (for that is what it would cost) for a calculator he could put in his pocket when a perfectly good slide rule was available for only $40. Hewlett made them build the hand-held calculator anyway, saying he didn't care if anyone else wanted one, *he* wanted one. Hewlett's invention not only made history; it also put the slide rule into the ranks of museum artifacts.

[2]Sandra Kurtzig, *CEO: Building a $400 Million Company from the Ground Up* (New York: Norton, 1991), pp. 68–69.

Like the site of consultant Bruce Clay of @bruceclay.com, most successful Web sites are built as a result of saying "Why would I want to come to this site, buy this product, or subscribe to this service?" Bruce aimed at people like himself who were interested in building successful Web sites, and he provided compelling information on that subject. Knowing your customer can have a lot to do with knowing yourself.

Ann Withey, of Annie's Homegrown, knows that her customers are affluent people who have an interest in nutrition and the environment and who also have young children and are short on time. So it's no mistake that she mentions on her site that her main competitor for fast-to-fix pasta dinners is the Kraft brand, owned by Philip Morris—the largest manufacturer of cigarettes worldwide. Annie's point, stated so subtly, is that it's obvious that Philip Morris doesn't care about health or nutrition. In fact, those long, slender macaroni pieces may look like small cigarettes to Mom and Dad next time they think about a Kraft dinner for the kids.

John Wells, of Netstores NW, knows that his customers are fanatics about certain television shows or movies. What John looks for are movies or TV shows that attract the interest of a large number of avid fans by searching the Internet to see how many Web sites have been put up voluntarily by fans of hit movies and television shows. While John's interest is in retailing movie memorabilia, he's also something of a movie buff himself, and he follows with care the giant promotional machines that he sees behind productions coming out of Hollywood to see if he can leverage off those marketing efforts. Customers are emotionally involved and feel an intimacy with the characters from these Hollywood productions, and John's product offerings allow his customers another way to express that emotion. John also discovered early on that doing cross-promotion with other sites started by movie fans brought him the most business.

Paul Graham of ViaMall told us Frederick's of Hollywood found out the hard way that large numbers of visitors don't necessarily equate to lots of sales. Frederick's, a ViaMall customer who offers women's lingerie, paid to post advertising on the *Playboy* site on the Internet. While Frederick's got a huge number of hits from the *Play-*

boy site, the number of visitors converted to sales was dismal. The site attracted lookers, not buyers.

So one of the important features that Paul uses to sell ViaMall to stores is the reporting capability of ViaWeb to tell customers who's visiting their sites, which sites those visitors come from, and who's buying. That's how Frederick's knew that the large increase in visitors was people coming from the *Playboy* site and that those visitors weren't the ones buying at the Frederick's site. This reporting capability is an important aspect of selling on the Internet, and it's one you should look for when deciding who should host your Web site on the Internet.

What to Do If You Don't Know Your Customer

As we've seen, you can aim at customers who are like yourself, if you're offering something you're interested in. You can also look at where customers are coming from to get an idea of who they are. Or you can look at the competition to see the type of customer they're attracting and try to do something different. But what if you don't know your customers or don't know as much about them as you'd like? There are still things you can do. The first is find a partner who does know the customers, and the second is to ask potential customers what they want.

In the case of GovCon, Raj Khera didn't know much about the government contract industry; but he understood business, and building the Business Resource Center Web site brought him a client that understood government contracting. The resulting GovCon site attracted customers like his client Freidman Fuller who were interested in government contracts. However, Raj didn't know customers were interested in more specific information until his customers suggested the idea to him. That leads us to the next point, which is that customers will tell you what they want if you're listening.

Take the GovCon example. Raj hadn't planned to offer a subscription service, and it cost him additional resources to do so, but it became a lucrative opportunity to produce additional income for the site. In addition, it allows customers who become regular visitors to the site to become further involved with the company on another level. This allows for a personal relationship—so important in cyberspace—to grow even stronger and provides it with somewhere to go beyond the initial interaction. Selling additional products to the same customers offers a way to produce additional income at a lower cost per customer, since you have already gone to the expense of serving the customers you have.

Rick and Ralph Fazio found themselves asking what customers wanted when they launched a Flamingo Surprise operation in Atlanta, Georgia. Rick said he ended up traveling to Atlanta because the business didn't seem to be going as well there as it had in other cities, like Cincinnati and Chicago. To find out why, Rick talked to customers and potential customers mostly over the phone, made adjustments to the Atlanta operation based on his research, and business began to take off. What Rick discovered was that customers in Atlanta weren't interested in a lot of information about the service before they bought, but they were interested in doing what was "in," so Rick changed the way customers were handled and the marketing efforts in the city to reflect that this was *the* thing to do. While the Atlanta customers are still referred via the Internet site, they are handled differently from the company's northern customers, who want a lot more information before they purchase the service. Rick said he knew that the business would sell well in Atlanta because the service practically sells itself, but it was just a matter of talking with customers until he found the right approach.

The Internet makes it easy to ask for and get customer feedback, so using its unique interactive capabilities is a great way to get to know how you can serve customers better. Don't worry if the feedback comes in the form of complaints instead of carefully worded compliments with suggestions included. Complaints mean that customers are paying attention and want to do business with you. In fact, it's been said that if you're not getting any complaints, you probably aren't doing anything people are interested in. You can get input by providing your e-mail address and inviting responses, posting a questionnaire, and offering choices of topics or information to view and recording which ones visitors select more often.

Images Are Important

Cyberspace is a visual place, so images are important. Your site expresses who you are and what you can do. While time-consuming images and animations that take forever for customers to see are not what customers want, they do want to see fairly simple but elegant visual images that convey that what you offer is important.

If you're selling something tangible, images are even more important. We talk about the mechanics of building a Web site and the resources for doing so (including imaging) in part II of this book, but for now an important consideration in selling on the Web is to realize that customers probably aren't going to purchase items they cannot see.

Besides product images, visual representations that answer customer questions about your product can boost your profits. For example, Mike Smith placed an illustrated overview of how wood trim kits for cars are installed as well as images of the wood types and, as a result, significantly cut his expenses on presale customer support. Illustrated explanations also boost your credibility.

CASE STUDY

John T. Wells
Netstores NW Inc.
Oregon City, Oregon
http://www.moviemadness.com

John Wells says his favorite type of business is selling something that allows him to leverage off someone else's promotional efforts. He's always worked in retail sales, first as the owner of a clothing store. Later he went to the University of Oregon for a while, then he dropped out and started a business doing slide advertising and movie trivia questions as prefilm entertainment. It wasn't a new idea—slides had been used before World War II to entertain audiences waiting for the start of movies, and they were being shown on the East Coast when John started doing it in Oregon.

Since his business frequently took him into movie theaters, he noticed the popularity of the *Star Trek* movies and happened to have a friend who owned a *Star Trek* paraphernalia store. So John bought some inventory and set up a *Star Trek* table in movie theater lobbies to offer the items to people who came to see the science fiction movie.

John said the problem with the *Star Trek* paraphernalia was that he ended up with too much inventory. But he liked the idea of leveraging off the huge promotion engine that's behind the movie industry. So John and his wife decided to try selling the *Star Trek* paraphernalia on the Internet.

The obstacle to setting up a store on the Internet was the cost. John said he'd heard stories about people spending $7,000 to $8,000 to pay someone to build their first Web store, and he'd also heard that over 50 percent of the on-line stores were failing. Rather than spend that kind of money, John heard about ViaWeb, an on-line electronic mall where he could set up his store for $100 to $300 a month to start with no lease or long-term commitment. ViaWeb also offered the advantage of allowing John to display his products without knowing how to program HTML. All John needed was Internet access, which he had through Microsoft's MSN service, and he could design his Web store while on-line.

So in 1994, John went to work to test his first "beta" store. Even though the ViaWeb site was inexpensive, John needed images and descriptions of the products to place on-line. John got most of the images of products from the vendors. To find the vendors, John went to the studios, who provided him with a licensee list of companies who had acquired the rights to design "branded" merchandise. John then contacted those companies and made deals to buy the merchandise from them.

To keep his inventory low, John tried to make sure that he only bought merchandise he already had orders for. This meant people had to wait two to four weeks for shipping, but the customers were so fanatical about the movies and there was such a lack of merchandise that John found it worked out fine.

The problem for John in the beginning was that he didn't know how to market his site. He said he spent the first year and a half doing minimal business while he learned how to get people to come to his Web site. He listed his site with the search engines and bought banner ads, and although he got traffic, he didn't get sales. John said he purchased a banner ad on CompuServe and got thousands of people to come to the site, but only saw a 3 percent increase in his sales volume. Through trial and error, he discovered that the key to selling his merchandise on the Internet was to get to know his customers.

For John, knowing his customers meant he had to find products from movies and television shows for which fans have high levels of fanaticism—fanaticism strong enough so that large numbers of them built Web sites around their interest. *Star Trek* is like that, and John found he needed to go to *Star Trek* sites and make arrangements with the site owners to link to their sites if they'd link to his. This reciprocal linking is what drew the fans who were interested enough to actually buy the merchandise. John also started advertising his site in publications like science fiction magazines and newsletters that are aimed at those fans.

Since that slow start, John has built over a dozen specialty merchandise stores. Some are based on other television shows such as *The X-Files, Friends,* or *ER*; others are based on popular movies like *Men in Black* (MIB); and others are stores he runs for other Web sites on the Internet.

ViaWeb allows him to build stores that have the look and feel of another Web site, but he can reuse the images and merchandise descriptions from a product line he already markets. Since he can control access to and from the store, the customer never knows he's left the original Web site. And building a store using ViaWeb is easy enough so that while John asks that his costs be reimbursed, all he requires from a potential Web site is a percentage of the sales of the new store. John says this helps him sell stores to other sites because it's essentially a no-risk proposition to them.

These other stores offer another advantage to John. Not only can he reuse the images; he can also increase the volume of products he buys from his suppliers (for better price advantages) and discourage competition. It may look as if there are several stores out there marketing *Star Trek* merchandise, so to a competitor the market seems to be already saturated. "What they don't know is all those stores are really me," John maintains. He can also boast that he's the largest provider of movie paraphernalia on the Internet.

John has 800 numbers for most of his stores, but he discontinued the toll-free line for *X-Files* because those fans were so fanatical they would call just to stay on the line and talk with the operators about the show. Plus, *X-File* fans would call several times a week to check on their orders, whereas a *Star Trek, ER,* or *MIB* fan would call only if an order was late. "We couldn't afford it," John added.

Advantages to running an on-line store include flexible hours, low overhead, and the ease of customer service via e-mail, John said. The biggest disadvantage is the absence of walk-in traffic. "It's like having a store that is essentially in the middle of the desert. On-line you have to do more work to get and educate the customer to come to your site," John added.

John says his biggest mistake in the beginning was assigning every item its own stock-keeping unit (sku) number. After a while, he said everything got so confusing he felt as if he needed a "Little Orphan Annie decoder ring" to figure out which numbers belonged to which products. So he changed the system and just started using the manufacturer's numbers exclusively, which made everything a good deal easier.

Customer orders come in on reports generated by ViaWeb, and John has to process the credit card orders just as he would if the orders had been mailed to him. One of the first things he does is address verification on an order through the credit card company using special software. If the credit card address and the address on the order don't match, John doesn't ship. Also, he pays less for his merchant account because he uses the address verification software, since the credit card companies feel the practice lowers their risk, so it actually pays for itself.

On international orders, John can't verify addresses. Although he has been the victim of a small percentage of credit card fraud, John says he hasn't stopped shipping internationally because the average overseas order is two and a half times the amount of the average U.S. order. It's just too lucrative a market to ignore.

Like the owners of most mail-order businesses, John complains that every dispute regarding a credit card is settled in the customer's favor. One of the reasons for this is that he doesn't always have time to provide proof of an order during a busy period, like Christmas. If he doesn't answer a challenge in a certain amount of time, the customer gets credited and John loses out. Also, credit card companies will cancel a company's merchant status if the charge backs reach more than 1 or 2 percent of the total credit card volume.

To improve his stores, John is reshooting the photos of the merchandise, since some of the vendor photos were not of very good quality. On other photos, he's rescanning the image and making the background transparent to give them a better look on-line.

Interestingly enough, while mail-order companies are trying to get on-line, John believes his Internet-based company should enter the mail-order market. He says there's lots of customer demand for him to print a catalog and do the same business through the mail that he's now doing in cyberspace. His plan is to study successful mail-order companies like L. L. Bean first, however, before he makes the plunge.

Be an Expert

Credibility is an issue when selling on the Internet, so it's important to be as well versed in your subject as possible. In fact, it would be safe to say you want to be an expert. Referrals from other sites on your subject, lots of information about your product, and publicity about yourself and your site all add to your credibility. For example, if you were selling, say, toasters, you'd want to have as much information on your site about toasters as possible. You'd want to have the history of toasters, photos of toasters, recipes that involve using toasters, and tidbits like the most unusual way to use a toaster. Your site should be *the* place to go if you need information on toasters.

We simply threw this out as an example, but as you can guess, a search engine query using the term *toaster* brought us a number of toaster sites. Among them we found toaster collectors and the Toastmaster Company, which makes toasters and other appliances. The Toastmaster site offers recipes, troubleshooting tips, and toaster history. (Did you know the first pop-up toaster was introduced in 1926?) This illustrates our point, but it also shows that anyone wanting to start a Web site should do his or her homework before jumping out there.

Dennis Fett has managed to become an Internet expert on peacocks, or peafowl, as the birds are more scientifically known. Peacocks have an immediate visual appeal, so publicity has not been difficult to get, but Dennis and his wife, Debra Joan Buck, have worked tirelessly to learn about and provide information on these birds. The effort is made easier for them by the fact that they like peafowl and enjoy collecting every piece of information they can.

Marc Andreessen is credited with being the key cog in the development of the Internet browser that changed the world, now known as Netscape. As a computer science student at the University of Illinois, Marc got acquainted with the Internet in the physics lab. He spent some time during 1990 and 1991 in IBM's facility in Austin, Texas, working on a graphical project for workstation computers. When he returned to the university, Marc decided he was interested in a branch of the university known as the National Center for Supercomputing Applications, or NCSA.

When Marc arrived in 1992, networking computers was an important project at the NCSA. In fact, the Internet backbone developed by the National Science Foundation was originally built for the supercomputer centers run by the NCSA.

Marc says his role was putting together the pieces that were already there in an Internet browser that would combine networking, multimedia, and the hypertext markup language (HTML). Marc and fellow student Eric Bina spent about three months writing the first version of Mosaic for the PC in the programming language C.

Once the browser was developed, Marc and Eric started giving it away on the Internet. The idea was to get as many people using it as possible, so in March of 1993 the browser was released. The excitement over Mosaic was contagious, and other companies saw a business opportunity and approached the NCSA about licensing Mosaic. Government funding was limited, so the NCSA was motivated to find a way to garner funds for something developed in-house. The NCSA version was still distributed without charge and, at one point, 100,000 copies a month of NCSA Mosaic were being downloaded from the university's computers.

Marc eventually became dissatisfied with the way things were going and, in the shuffle over this hot new technology, lost control of Mosaic, so he looked for a job outside the Midwest. He graduated in December of 1993 but never attended his graduation ceremony, nor did he pick up his diploma. He ended up going to work for a small company in Palo Alto, California, called Enterprise Integration Technologies but only lasted there a few months.

It was then that Jim Clark, founder of Silicon Graphics, Inc. (SGI), was leaving SGI and invited Marc to start a new company to build another Web browser. Marc had wanted to rebuild a new browser from the ground up and saw this as his opportunity. This time he called the browser the Netscape Navigator but named the company Mosaic Communications. The company name didn't last long.

Marc and Jim decided that, like Mosaic, Netscape would be freely distributed, but on an evaluation basis to individuals and without charge to educational institutions. The pair were betting that Netscape would become as popular as Mosaic. Once the University of Illinois heard of Marc's plans, they forbade him to use the Mosaic name. So in midstream and after lots of publicity, Marc and Jim renamed the company Netscape Communications.

Netscape Communications not only distributes browsers to end-users but also develops server software for business use, including secure server software for credit card acceptance. It was Marc, as chief operating officer of the company, who invited Stanford graduate students David Filo and Jerry Yang to move their newly developed Yahoo search engine to Netscape's servers.

Netscape Communications went public in 1995, and by the fall of that year Marc was twenty-four years old and worth over $70 million. In an interview with *Smithsonian,* Marc said that in ten years, as uncertain as this business is, he could be "bagging groceries at Safeway." However, his plans are to continue to attempt to shape the mechanisms and the technology behind computing to make it even more compelling for consumers in the future.[3]

How to Sell to Corporate Clients

Marc Andreessen, founder of Netscape Communications, said in a *Smithsonian* interview that he talked partner Jim Clark into giving away Netscape to individuals and educational institutions as a means

[3]David K. Allison, "Marc Andreessen," *Smithsonian Institution Oral and Video Histories* (June 1995): http://www.si.edu.

of getting into the corporate market. Jim agreed to the giveaway because Marc told him about how, with Mosaic, companies were attracted because of the broad user base. Marc attracted corporate clients by attracting individuals.

Marc said his discovery with Mosaic was that companies do not want things for free; they *want* to pay. Companies wanted to reach that huge user base Marc established by giving away Netscape, and Marc was able to create a demand for Netscape-compatible products, such as secure server software aimed at business users. Giving away Netscape also allowed Netscape Communications to demonstrate that it could deliver on a large scale.

Why do companies want to pay for items instead of getting things for free? There are lots of reasons. Let's take free software as an example. While individuals are happy to use items they get for free, companies are made up of individuals whose future may be riding on the software about to be implemented. In addition, free software can cost companies more than software purchased from reliable sources in terms of hours spent on support and possible system malfunctions caused by conflicts, bugs, or other unforeseen problems. A few hours or days of even one employee's time are more expensive than paying for software that comes with customer support. In addition, companies have found it is difficult to hold someone responsible for the performance of something that was obtained for free.

Sandra Kurtzig said that what you're selling when you sell in the corporate market is yourself. Sandra, who founded the software company ASK and who was the only woman CEO of a technology company for many years, said in a personal interview with this book's authors regarding her autobiographical book that what makes a difference is not how big you are or how many resources you have at your disposal. According to Sandra the real issue is Can you convince the people making the decisions that you can deliver the goods? Sandra should know, because she convinced hardware giant Hewlett-Packard to take a chance on her fledgling company to develop critical software applications for the HP minicomputer platform.

Summary

As we've seen in this chapter, successful cyberbusinesses selling goods and services take specialization to a razor's edge with unique and compelling products aimed at specific niche markets. These businesses know their customers, take advantage of the lower costs of cyberspace to sell at a discount when competitors loom on the horizon, and emphasize service and convenience whenever possible. These businesses operate using the four principles that we outlined in the beginning: specialize, keep up with your e-mail, provide a reason to return, and give something valuable away. The only exception are Web stores who have products so compelling, convenient, or attractively priced that no giveaways are necessary.

While pricing varies from business to business from several thousand dollars a year to under two dollars an item, the low cost of doing business in cyberspace is a factor in each business. In some cases, the low cost of business in cyberspace is the only reason some of these businesses have survived.

In the next chapter, we'll talk about Web sites that offer free content to visitors but make a living via advertiser support.

Chapter 4

Advertiser-
Supported Sites

Every time a message seems to grab us, and we think,
"I just might try it," we are at the nexus of choice
and persuasion that is advertising.

—Andrew Hacker,

professor of Political Science,
Queens College, New York

When you stop talking, you've lost your customer.
When you turn your back, you've lost her.

—Estée Lauder,

cosmetics executive

 Advertising is the openly sponsored promo-
tion of goods, services, or ideas using any medium of
public communication. The United States is number one worldwide in money spent on advertising to
the tune of billions annually. In fact, the name of a street in New York
City where several major advertising agencies traditionally had their
headquarters has come to stand for the advertising industry as a
whole. The street is Madison Avenue.

The first site to officially adopt advertising on the Internet was the
electronic magazine *HotWired,* on October 27, 1994. Because until
then the Internet had been largely "free," early Internet users, who

were mostly government- and university-related individuals, felt a certain disdain for commercial ventures.

But Madison Avenue was eager to get into cyberspace. Fourteen companies advertised with *HotWired* that October, and one agency—Modem Media, of Westport, Connecticut—was so eager it took the risk of buying space for its client AT&T before it consulted the client. *Advertising Age* quoted Modem Media partner G. M. O'Connell, who said, "There was no guarantee, and we didn't care."[1]

What Is an Advertiser-Supported Site?

An advertiser-supported site is a Web site that makes money by selling space on the site to those interested in promoting other sites or goods and services, while offering its services without charge to site visitors. The key to advertiser-supported sites is either the number or the type of visitors it attracts.

As we noted in chapter 2, advertising on the Internet is experiencing an exponential climb. In the first six months of 1997, Internet advertisers spent $217.3 million, an increase of more than 250 percent over the first six months of 1996 when advertisers spent $61 million, according to Stamford, Connecticut–based market research firm Cowles/Simba. The firm predicts that Web advertising expenditures will reach $2.46 billion annually by the year 2000.

Since *HotWired* pioneered Internet advertising, the practice has become a part of the medium. However, advertisers and advertising agencies are no longer eager to jump blindly into cyberspace advertising. As the medium matures, there are definite characteristics for sites sought by advertisers. We'll share those characteristics with you, but first, it's important to understand a little background information.

---

[1]Debra Aho Williamson, "Web Ads Mark Second Birthday with Decisive Issues Ahead," *Advertising Age On-Line* (October 1996): www.adage.com.

A Short Discourse in Web Page
Advertising Terminology

In order to understand what advertisers are looking for, you have to know some of the terminology used in Web page advertising. A short tutorial on Web page terminology follows.

How Web Page Traffic Is Measured

There are several ways to measure traffic to a Web site, including hits, impressions or page views, and click-through. Each of these terms describes a way in which the demand for individual components on a Web site is measured, but there are significant differences in each one. To understand the differences, you need to know a little bit about how a Web page is built.

Remember how we said in the beginning that the Internet is simply the world's largest word-processing application? Well, now is the time when that information becomes important. Each Web site is a document, built just the way any other document is built in any word processor. That's why Web sites are often referred to as "Web pages."

Each Web page, or document, is made up of elements that usually incorporate text and graphics and can also incorporate sound, animation, and even video. Each of these elements is stored in a separate file on a computer (or server) connected to the Internet. When a user "travels to a Web site," what is really happening is that a request is made to the server for all the files or elements that make up the Web page the user wants to see. In the text file, or HTML file, is a set of instructions for how to assemble all the elements that are to be displayed on the user's computer. Those files are sent across the network, or "downloaded," one at a time to the computer that made the request. The Internet browser software constructs the files based on instructions transmitted along with the files into the proper sequence and displays the page.

When you're surfing the Internet, you can see this process happen, as you'll receive part of the page and see the rest of the page coming in, displayed a piece at a time on the monitor. Sometimes this process happens so quickly that you're not aware of it. At other times—depending on the amount of demand on the server, the speed of the server, the size of the files, and the traffic on the network—it can seem like a very long time until the entire page is completed.

How Hits Are Measured

Each time a file that makes up a Web page is sent to someone wishing to view it, that's called a "hit." Let's say a single Web page could be made up of two graphic files, a text file, and the instruction file (HTML file) for how to put it all together. That's four elements, so a request for that Web page would be counted as four "hits." The server computer is aware of how many times it sends out each element and keeps a count, which is easily accessible and usually provided without charge to the Web page owner by the owner of the server.

How Impressions, or Page Views, Are Measured

Another way to measure Web site traffic is to count "impressions," or "page views." Each time all the elements of a Web page are transmitted to a user counts as a single "impression." Obviously, tracking impressions is a little tougher than simply tracking hits because you have to correlate the information about each page more carefully. But from an advertiser's perspective, counting page views is a more meaningful indication of how many people will see an advertisement.

What Is a Link?

Web pages can (and should) be designed so that the user can select another Web page from the one he or she is currently viewing. Computers have the ability to track where the user's mouse is at all times; and when the user's mouse is over a certain portion of text or a graphic on the screen and the mouse button is clicked on, a request is sent to a server for a new Web page. This is called a "link." A link is usually indicated to the user by words that are set off by underlining or a different color, or it can be a graphic image that the user is encouraged to click on. The link can be to a Web page that resides on the same server as the referring page or to another server altogether. Often advertisers pay to have links to their own sites placed on active Web sites to encourage visitors.

How Click-through Is Measured Using Links

The number of times that visitors click on a link on the Web site is called the click-through. Click-through numbers are considered the most valuable information to advertisers because they represent active requests for material and therefore show more involvement on the part of the person visiting the site.

Types of Web Page Ads

Advertising on Web pages falls into several categories, with more being added on a regular basis. The most popular are: banner ads, in-line ads, and pop-up ads. We'll take each of these one at a time.

What Are Banner Ads?

A banner ad is usually rectangular in shape and is inserted as a graphic at the top of a Web page. It can include animation, and it does include a link to another Web page where more information about the topic of the ad is available. Banner ads are popular because they load fast, are easy to design and to change, and are easily inserted into a Web page.

What Are In-line Ads?

In-line ads appear in a column down the right- or left-hand side of the Web page and usually take up the entire length of the page. In-line ads can also be a graphic and contain a link, or they can be text and contain hypertext links set off by underlined text or text that is a different color, or both.

What Are Pop-up Ads?

Pop-up ads are separate from the Web page. These ads are separate windows that open over information displayed initially. Some people find these ads intrusive because they cover a portion or all of the Web page underneath.

What Is Sponsoring?

Sponsoring is when an advertiser takes credit for supporting a chat group, contest, or some other form of information or entertainment on a Web site. The sponsor may have any one of the above types of ad in the forum, but in addition, the Web site will probably post notices showing which business sponsors the site or particular activity. The sponsor is usually the exclusive advertiser. Sponsorship implies a closer relationship, like an endorsement, to the Web site on the part of the sponsor.

What Are Advertisers Looking For?

In a nutshell, Web advertisers are looking for traffic, or "eyeballs." The most successful advertiser-supported sites have a lot of visitors. Advertisers are also looking for demographic information about who is visiting the sites.

The Rules for What It Takes to Attract Advertisers

Advertisers and advertising agencies say they're looking for sites that are six months old that are receiving at least 500,000 impressions per

---

QUICK REFERENCE

Web Page — A document made up of an instruction file in HTML code. Can include a number of other elements such as graphics, sound, animation, and even video files.

Web Site — One or several Web pages available on the Internet

Hits — The number of times each file is sent out by the server. Note that Web pages can be made up of several files.

Server — The computer that stores the Web pages and is connected to the Internet.

HTML — Hypertext markup language: the instructions that tell the Internet browser software how to display the Web page and all the elements.

Elements — In our context, elements are the individual files that make up each Web page.

Link — A request to a server for download of another Web page. A link can be a graphic or hypertext.

Click-through — The number of times a user clicks on page elements that are linked to other Web pages.

month. They say they want to see promotional and marketing plans for now and the future designed to attract Internet traffic. In addition, agencies tend to avoid sites with "adult" material or sites that have the appearance of having been built by amateurs. Agencies will also tell you that it is necessary to pursue Internet advertisers to attract them to your site. Both advertisers and agencies would like to see demographics about who is visiting your site as well.

Rules Are Made to Be Broken

For every example of someone following the ad agency rules for how to attract advertisers, there is an example of someone who is breaking the rules and still attracting the funds he or she needs. Here are a few examples of sites that follow the rules and sites that don't.

The Happy Puppy offers reviews of computer games and new games for sale, and it meets the advertising agency criteria. This advertiser-supported site records millions of hits each month. In fact, on September 14, 1996, the site boasted that it had a high of over 4.6 million hits and 57,000 visitors in a single day.

Phil Margolis of PC Webopaedia, an on-line computer terminology reference, said that his site started getting attention from advertising agencies when the site's hit rate reached a million a month. It is a widely held opinion that 13 percent of the number of hits in a month will give you the number of visitors to a site, although this statistic has not been seriously tested. Using this statistic in Phil's case would mean that Phil was getting about 130,000 impressions a month.

Aliza Sherman's Cybergrrl site, which provides information and issues aimed at women, attracts advertising and sponsorship from very large companies like IBM. But Aliza was able to attract advertisers and sponsors when her site reached 250,000 impressions a month.

Dr. Cliff Kurtzman of the Year2000 Web site said in 1997 that he had 140 advertisers, all of whom have come to the site unsolicited. He says that the site receives 200,000 impressions a month, yet at this advertiser-supported site there's enough income to support a staff of over a dozen people.

The popular search engine Yahoo is an example of a site built by amateurs. David Filo and Jerry Yang were Ph.D. candidates in electrical engineering at Stanford University when they started Yahoo. The service has always had a "cut to the chase" approach, offering little in the way of bells and whistles but emphasizing ease of use. It was still an amateur operation when a venture capital firm backed it and Netscape offered the students space to house Yahoo. Today Yahoo is the number-one search engine on the Internet.

C A S E   S T U D Y

DAVID FILO AND JERRY YANG
YAHOO
SANTA CLARA, CALIFORNIA
HTTP://WWW.YAHOO.COM

David Filo and Jerry Yang discovered that they had a common interest. While each one found the Internet fascinating, both were keeping a private list of the sites they found the most interesting along with descriptions of each site. This was at a time when Web sites were as often located by entering a long string of numbers and periods as they were by entering letters.

The pair, each using his own personal computer connected to the Internet via Stanford, decided to make their lists public in 1994 and call this service to the Internet community Yahoo, for "Yet Another Hierarchical Officious Oracle." The PCs that first supported Yahoo were named after legendary Hawaiian sumo wrestlers: the list of sites resided on Yang's student workstation, "akebono," while the search engine for digging out what people wanted from the list of sites was on Filo's computer, "konishiki."

Yahoo became popular quickly, and Stanford was beginning to get concerned about the amount of traffic that this free service was generating for the university's Internet connection. Filo and Yang also found that they were spending all their time keeping up with the demand for site listings.

Things had reached a crisis point in early 1995, when Marc Andreessen, co-founder of Netscape Communications in Mountain View, California, offered to house Yahoo. Filo and Yang took notice when *HotWired* offered advertising and for the first time thought that might be a way they could finance the running of Yahoo. A venture capital firm, Sequoia Venture Partners, was interested in Yahoo. Filo and Yang had to have a business plan and a proposal, so they got a how-to book, developed the material they needed, and got the funding from the venture capital firm. In 1996, Yahoo went public, and by 1997 the company was reporting profits to shareholders.

Yahoo started by individually viewing each site and still does so. Sites can be entered by those interested in being listed by Yahoo, and a real person views each site before listing it in the Yahoo database. As an advertiser-supported site, Yahoo offers companies the ability to display banner ads to customers who enter search terms related to the ad to further target potential clients for advertisers. For example, if a visitor enters the search term *doll*, the visitor will not only get sites specific to that term but could also see a banner ad from Mattel about a new collector's edition of Barbie.

Yahoo offers sponsored advertising as well and has teamed up with companies not traditionally known for involvement in cyberspace, such as fashion designer Guess! and American Airline's SABRE travel network. The company has also worked to help nonprofit groups such as the Children's Miracle Network.

Yahoo is now a brand name. The company has expanded to include sites in Europe, has its own chat room, customized news pages for frequent visitors, a magazine, and financial and other services almost too numerous to count.

Filo and Yang advise people who want to start an Internet business to find their "value proposition." They ask themselves each day, "What is the real value we're providing?"[2]

As you can see, there are no hard-and-fast rules, but there are guidelines that can help you build a successful advertiser-supported site. We'll cover those next.

Characteristics of Successful Advertiser-Supported Sites

Most advertiser-supported sites tend to be search engines, technology publishers, and consumer/news organizations. However, that's still pretty general information. After looking at literally

[2]Rhonda Abrams, "Coffee Talk with Experts," *Idea Cafe* (1995): www.ideacafe.com.

hundreds of sites, we've come up with a list of four things that successful sites have in common. Successful sites provide compelling content, have a high incidence of visitors, and know the demographics of their visitors; and most offer advertisers a guaranteed number of impressions.

Compelling Content

The most important element of an advertiser-supported site is content that the cybercitizen finds compelling. This means a focus on the information offered by the site, a task that requires constant maintenance on a daily basis. The content can vary from tips and reviews of the latest games, as evidenced by the highly successful Happy Puppy Web site, to the serious local and national news presented by the Web versions of city newspapers.

Time-sensitive content is especially good for advertiser-supported sites. For example, the Year2000 Web site was built around the problem of electronic devices and software that were not designed to roll over from 1999 to 2000. The thing about a site like this is that, one way or another, the problem gets solved because action is taken or because time simply takes care of it. While the Internet is a great medium for time-sensitive subjects, and a big problem like this is going to get lots of national and international publicity for several years before and maybe even a couple of years after the event, there's not much to build on once the problem has been solved.

High Incidence of Visitors

As we've already said, advertisers are looking for eyeballs. The way to get people to view the site is to have a reason for them to come, which usually translates into a reason for them to come back. In the case of search engines like Yahoo, the reason for coming and coming back is to find other Web sites on topics the visitor is interested in. Sites like Cybergrrl constantly change their focus to whatever is interesting to their audience of women between the ages of eighteen and thirty-five. The PC Webopaedia serves visitors by offering definitions of computer terms and sites where they can find additional information concerning those terms.

News sites are popular, as are weather and other sites that focus on information that is constantly changing. Newspapers are popular on the Internet. However, news about specific subjects can also be a source for getting visitors to return. Electronic games are always changing, and it's been a favorite practice since the first computer games came out for gamers to supply hints and tricks to one another. In fact, Nintendo's popular Mario Brothers games had hidden passages and secret "tricks" that gamers only learned from one another and from "insider" publications. Building on that tradition, Happy Puppy offers gamers the latest tips and tricks for favorite games. Since games are always changing, either with new versions of favorites or new games altogether, there's always more material available.

Sites aimed at performing services for Internet visitors are favorites for advertisers. Netscape leverages off this with its Web browser. It offers a version of the browser without charge, but the browser is set to load the Netscape homepage first. While users can change this setting, millions don't know how, and so they come to the Netscape homepage each time they log on to the Internet. Microsoft has done the same with its Internet Explorer product. Most ISPs purchase copies of a browser to distribute to users just so that they can set it to focus on their homepage and reap the benefits of selling impressions to advertisers. America Online, Prodigy, and other services have practiced the same theory in selling ad space to advertisers for years.

Other Internet services have figured out that a captive audience is worth advertising dollars. A number of free e-mail services are popping up, like Juno. Funded and developed by the New York investment bank D. E. Shaw & Company, Juno does not charge fees to subscribers for either its software or its free mail service. Juno's support comes from advertising. Each time one of the millions of Juno users logs in, along with their mail, they download advertising.

For users with Internet access where they cannot get personal mail, there are Internet services that are providing e-mail accounts. The user has to have access to the Internet, goes to the Web site of the e-mail provider, and enters his or her name and password to receive any mail that has come in. As with Juno, there are no charges or limits to the number of e-mail messages or the number of times a user can check for e-mail each day. But again, users are required to fill out a marketing survey, and each time they check in for mail, advertisers have a chance to get exposure.

Demographics

Advertisers expect Web sites to know who is visiting and why. The more you can tell advertisers about the average age, income, interests of your visitors, and where your visitors come from (both on the map and on the Internet), the more advertisers you can attract.

Sites that claim they don't pursue advertisers do plan carefully to attract them. They do this by posting demographic information about their visitors or information from which anyone with half a brain can reason out the demographics. Aliza Sherman is a prime example. She succinctly outlines in three sentences in a special section the characteristics of her visitors—that they're women, their ages, their education, and their interests. She does this with statistics that appear to be even more authoritative because they're precise—for example, saying "33 percent" rather than "under 35 percent."

The Year2000 site does something similar. It's obvious that people who visit this site have software and systems problems they're trying to solve, which places them in positions of influence in corporations or government installations. So rather than list statistics on visitors, the site's builders display a three-dimensional graph in a section they call the Access History of the Site. The graph shows the number of visitors for each month from the site's inception in May 1995 to the present month. What becomes obvious in looking at this graph is, first, that the site has been around since 1995 and, second, that the number of visitors has been growing exponentially as the year 2000 approaches.

In both cases, these sites that haven't pursued advertisers have presented compelling reasons for advertisers to pursue them. Also, both sites made the critical information available by a single click at the bottom of the homepage near the copyright and contact information for the site.

Sites like Juno offer even more detailed demographic information.

The service requires users to fill out a detailed survey of their household income, preferences, and habits. The service then sells the marketing information and advertising space to investors. While sites like Cybergrrl are more subtle, asking users to "tell us about yourself" down in the site at a more comfortable point, services like Juno put their demographic questions right up front as part of the cost for installation of the software. Users feel that they're getting something, so they'll tolerate the intrusion.

In this way, Juno not only has the name, address, and phone number of each user; it can also match demographic information based on the neighborhood and area of the country where the user lives. This allows for a checking system, so Juno can tell advertisers how accurate its demographic information is.

CASE STUDY

ALIZA SHERMAN, PRESIDENT
CYBERGRRL
NEW YORK, NEW YORK
HTTP://WWW.CYBERGRRL.COM

The Cybergrrl Web station is aimed at issues of interest to women on-line.

Aliza (pronounced "a-leez-a") Sherman considers herself a shy person. Her father was in the military, so she moved every two or three years. As a consequence, she says, she's not the sort of person who will go start a conversation with someone at a party. She'll hang back and munch on snacks until the event is over, then leave without ever having met anyone unless someone speaks to her first. But she found the virtual environment of cyberspace appealing. "On-line it's cool," she says.

Aliza was in the music business for a couple of years, doing public relations, marketing, and promotions; then she ran a nonprofit organization aimed at helping victims of domestic violence. She bought a computer to do word processing, and a neighbor showed her how to go on-line. At that time the on-line world consisted mostly of local bulletin board services (BBS) and non-Internet services such as America Online.

Once Internet access was available, Aliza got an account with a local ISP and in January 1995 decided to start a Web consulting and on-line marketing business. She created the Cybergrrl site as a sample and ran it for her own personal enjoyment.

But a surprising thing happened. Cybergrrl became a popular site on the Web. Aliza credits part of the success of the site to timing, since the site was introduced at a time when there wasn't much out there. As the popularity of the site increased, companies started approaching her about advertising and sponsorship. While she'd like to have someone devoted to sales, Aliza said Cybergrrl has been able to get the advertising support needed to be profitable without pursuing it.

For example, IBM wanted to promote a new shopping mall called World Avenue (which later failed) and sponsored a section on Cybergrrl for Mother's Day. The Mother's Day section, "branded" especially for IBM, encouraged visitors to submit their worst gift ideas and displayed the best of the worst gift ideas. There was also a family-matching contest where visitors were challenged to match a celebrity mom with her family.

Like any good marketer, Aliza knows what types of people are visiting her site. She collects the information voluntarily by encouraging visitors to the site to provide information about themselves. The site is aimed at women from the ages of eighteen to thirty-five because over 62 percent of the female visitors to the site are in that age range. However, 34 percent are between the ages of thirty-five and fifty-five. An increasing number of women younger than eighteen are starting to visit, and there are male visitors as well.

Of the women, 33 percent have a bachelor's degree, 23 percent have a master's, and 24 percent are still in school. Of the site's female visitors, 38 percent make over $30,000 and 15 percent make over $50,000 per year. This is individual income, so Aliza said the household income of these women is much higher.

Aliza said she measures page views rather than hits. At the time of the interview, Cybergrrl was getting about 250,000 page views a month and selling lots of 50 to 100,000 views per advertiser.

At first, Aliza said she was afraid to offer banner advertising because she thought it might put people off; but instead, she got a positive response. People who were regular visitors to the site were saying things like "We're glad you're finally making money doing this."

The Cybergrrl site contains almost 10,000 pages of material on topics ranging from book reviews, to travel, to business, to category links to other sites. Some of the content of the site is created by the Cybergrrl staff, and other content is submitted by the visitors themselves. There are chat forums, and a Cybergrrl Web News publication is regularly e-mailed to those who sign up to receive it.

While she claims she doesn't start or predict trends, Aliza says she seems to end up on the cutting edge. For example, she created a book site for women, and now there are a whole bunch of book sites for women; then she started featuring travel, and many other sites started doing that too. Aliza says she does what's interesting or cool to her, and it seems to be what is interesting to others as well. She says, "Our personal ideas have to come through because this could be a very cold medium. That's why people keep coming back—because they feel connected."

One of the surprising things that's happened is that journalists ask her, "How do you feel about working in a male-dominated field?" Aliza said she hasn't noticed any bias but finds it disturbing that such questions so frequently assume there is one. She said, "While I'm sure that experience exists, I wish the media wouldn't perpetuate it. It can become a self-fulfilling prophecy."

Aliza has a dozen people working for her and runs her own servers that support the site rather than having an ISP host Cybergrrl. Her future plans for expansion include offering more material and separate forums for the increasing numbers of visitors under the age of eighteen who are coming to the site.

Targeted Advertising

A more powerful technique for attracting advertisers is targeted advertising. A good example of this is Phil Margolis's PC Webopaedia site. Phil has designed the site so that banner ads are targeted to specific words chosen by the advertiser—when the definitions for those words chosen by the advertiser are displayed, the banner ad is also displayed.

Yahoo is targeting advertising in a similar manner but also displays ads based on the last e-mail address or the last location on the Internet that the visitor came from. This information can sometimes reveal the area the user is from, since some ISPs only operate in certain areas of the country. Also, if the user just came from a site about France, a travel ad or an ad about a French language course will have a better chance of attracting the attention of this person than just any visitor. Obviously, Juno and similar services that collect more detailed demographic information target advertising as well.

One of the big concerns for advertisers is the increasing number of "spiders" or "robots," which are automated programs that go from page to page cataloging material based on the text and the links on each page for listing in search engines. Advertisers do not want to pay to have robots view their banner ads, which the automated search engines are designed to ignore anyway.

Using targeted advertising, advertisers get more of what they want, which is less of a random approach and more assurance that their advertising is being viewed by the people it is intended for. Target advertising goes hand in hand with guaranteed impressions, which we discuss next.

Guaranteed Impressions

Some sites are offering a guaranteed number of impressions to their advertisers along with targeting who the potential visitors are that see the advertising. This is attractive to advertisers for several reasons, one of which is that banner ads, which are considered graphic elements by the browsers, are not always displayed by the user.

Graphic elements do not get downloaded because users have figured out that they can turn off the ability to display graphics in their browser. The browser never requests the graphics described in the HTML document, so the graphic files are not downloaded by the server when the accompanying page is displayed. One of the reasons for turning off graphics is to speed up access to information. Web pages display faster without graphics, since graphics are usually the largest files and take the longest time to download.

As users get faster and faster Internet access, the issue of the download time for graphics files will become less of a problem. However, advertisers have a valid concern that they get what they pay for.

A guaranteed impression count means advertisers can be assured they will get the full number of impressions for the visitors they target.

CASE STUDY

PHILIP E. MARGOLIS
SANDY BAY SOFTWARE
ROCKPORT, MASSACHUSETTS
HTTP://WWW.PCWEBOPAEDIA.COM
OWNER OF THE PC WEBOPAEDIA SITE

Philip Margolis has been interested in creating reference guides ever since he was a child. He said his first major project at age eleven was writing an encyclopedia of Greek mythology. He used index cards for each term back then. Later, he went to Hampshire College, an experimental college where instead of grades there were advisor evaluations, and his advisor said of him, "Phil has a very ordering mind." He says his favorite activity is to condense information into a few key sentences and break large subjects into little pieces.

In order to use this talent, Phil became a writer, publishing two reference books with Random House. After the second book, he "got caught up in the entrepreneurial storm" on the Internet and decided he could put the terms from the Random House book in an electronic form up on the Web. So he worked out a deal with Random House.

To finance the project Phil sold some stock to friends and family, and he invested his personal money as well. Work started on the site in July of 1996, but Phil said it took three months of pure development until the site was ready for public access at the end of October. It was the summer of 1997 before the site started to show a profit.

Users visiting the site enter a term and can then see a definition of the term. To take full advantage of the interconnectivity of the Internet, Phil started adding relevant links to other sites that have information on the topic the user is seeking. In this way, the user sees not only the definition but also other sites on the Internet relevant to the definition he or she is looking for. There is also a form of the PC Webopaedia available on the site that users can download to their own PCs.

Phil says that for the Webopaedia he concentrates on sites that have to do with computers, and he or his staff personally visit the sites and write reviews. They also attempt to directly reference the actual part of the site that's relevant by linking to the specific page with the information. In this way, the user doesn't end up at a homepage and have to figure out where the relevant information is on an unfamiliar site.

As the Web grows, it'll get tougher and tougher for users to find what they're looking for using search engines, Phil asserts. Using a search engine, "you may find 10,000 sites for your term and the one you want is on page 55. Long-term, the ability to quickly home in on the handful of homepages that have the answer you're looking for will be valuable. Compared to search engines like Excite, there's no substitute for a real person looking at your page."

The way Phil has made the site profitable is by offering the information to visitors for free to attract advertisers. But it took some time to get to the point where advertisers were interested. To get the kind of advertisers he was looking for, Phil decided to go through an agency. There are Internet advertising agencies, such as Double-Click and Softbank, but these companies require a certain number of hits a month before they will consider working with a site. The agencies encouraged him to increase his hit rate to attract advertisers. "A million hits a month—that's the magic number where people start noticing you," Phil added.

When the site was launched, Phil looked for low-cost or free ways to promote the site. One he used was Internet Link Exchange where he was able to barter a banner ad for his site to other Web sites in exchange for displaying their banner ads.

He also made sure his site was listed in all the search engines. To maximize the site's exposure in search engines, Phil created a separate Web page for each term and listed each page separately with the search engines. This was a lot more work, but he feels it has brought him a lot more visitors. After all, if visitors are looking for specific terms in a search engine, he wanted them to find those terms on his site.

By listing in the search engines and bartering, his site began to be known, and it started to win recognition. *Netguide* gave the site an award and *PC Magazine* honored PC Webopaedia as one of the top-100 Web sites.

At the time of the interview, Phil said PC Webopaedia gets 10,000 hits a day. He did mention that one week when Netscape listed PC Webopaedia on its Web page, the hits jumped to 30,000 a day.

One of the selling points of the site is that it is tailor-made for producers of hardware and software. For example, if a company that manufactures monitors wants to advertise on the site, Phil can set up the advertiser's material so that whenever a visitor requests a term having to do with any aspect of computer monitors, the monitor manufacturer's material is displayed along with the definitions.

Phil said there's no way to measure the effectiveness of an ad. But here the monitor manufacturer can be sure that the audience viewing the ad has an interest in the product. Just as in television advertising, companies are looking for "mind share."

To attract advertisers, Phil carefully tracks information about visitors. He knows, for example, that PC Webopaedia is popular at universities because he gets reports from the server who hosts his site of the "domain," or the last part of a user's e-mail address and the last site a visitor came from. He also places a "cookie" on a visitor's computer so he knows when a visitor comes back. In addition, Phil builds an e-mail list of visitors to whom he periodically sends news about new terms or new items on the site.

Phil says he spends "a good two hours a day" answering e-mail. The mail includes suggestions for new terms, error reports, and generic feedback. One of the things he feels makes the site special is that he replies to everyone. Although mail is sure to increase as the number of visitors to the site goes up, Phil says he intends to keep answering it personally.

Even though Phil hired a professional graphic designer to build the site and has a handful of researchers working for him, he still writes new definitions himself. He found it just took too much time to explain everything he knows to someone else, especially material about other terms on the site, and his doing the writing helps the site maintain continuity. He calls his company Sandy Bay Software, a virtual company. Although he currently has just a handful of employees, they work out of home offices from Canada to Hawaii.

As for the future, Phil is thinking about other Webopaedias, like one for travel. He is also working on new ideas like word link, a service to dynamically link one Web page to another one.

How to Get More Information

With the information you've garnered here, you're prepared to go out on the Internet looking for more information. The most reliable way to get current information on advertising is to visit other sites and look for their advertising information and to employ the search engines using the keywords *advertising* and *entrepreneurial*. Web sites and forums that discuss these issues will offer helpful hints and up-to-the-minute resources. Now you have the background information you need to hold an intelligent discussion and come away with information you can use.

Summary

We've seen how advertiser-supported sites use compelling content, a high incidence of visitors, demographics, targeted advertising, and guaranteed impressions to attract advertisers. It's important to note that compelling content is the most important element of an advertiser-supported site. Yahoo founders David Filo and Jerry Yang understand this approach and advise those interested in starting business on the Internet to be sure they're providing value to visitors.

Advertiser-supported sites also follow the four principles set forth in chapter 1, which are to specialize, keep up with your e-mail, provide a reason to return, and give something valuable away. As we've seen, advertiser-supported sites specialize in a particular type of information for a particular audience, and they have both the audience and the information well defined. These sites also keep up with e-mail from visitors, and some use the e-mail as a means of finding new subjects of interest or of allowing the site's visitors to aid in the development of the content on the site. This content development is one of the main ways advertiser-supported sites provide incentive for return visits. And finally, information is the valuable resource that visitors come back for and the main item advertiser-supported sites provide as a giveaway.

In the next chapter, we'll examine a different category of business that's making money in cyberspace—those who offer support to others doing business in cyberspace through content development.

Chapter 5

Content
Development

In the business world, everyone is paid in two coins:
cash and experience. Take the experience first;
the cash will come later.

—Harold S. Geneen,

former chairman,
International Telephone and Telegraph

Before the year 2000, the estimated number of words on the Internet is expected to be more than every book ever printed in the history of mankind.[1] Someone has to write that material, put it into a form that can be displayed on the Internet, and help other people find it. That's the essence of the three types of content development opportunities in cyberspace:

> ➤ *writing for publication on the Internet (or writing Web content)*
> ➤ *designing Web sites*
> ➤ *selling services to those who develop content for the Internet*

---

[1]Evan I. Schwartz, *Webonomics: Nine Essential Principles for Growing Your Business on the World Wide Web* (New York: Broadway Books, 1997).

As you might expect, writing Web content tends to be less lucrative than designing Web sites or selling services on the Internet. We found people making from $30,000 annually to more than six figures, but the higher incomes were in Web site development and selling services. We'll take a more careful look into what's involved in each of these types of content development opportunities next.

Writing Web Content for Pay

Being published on the Internet is a lot like being published anywhere else; however, the demand for content on the Internet is high and is bound to continue to rise as sites attempt to attract repeat visitors. Most writers currently working on the Internet write for Net publications or start their own Web sites and provide material for the sites themselves.

Writing Articles

The most traditional type of writing on the Internet is the traditional outlet of writing for a publication, which then publishes the material in the form of articles or serialized material on the Internet. On-line magazines are a prime example of this type of writing. The writers who tend to be successful at article publication are the ones who have developed a combination of expertise both in writing and in some other area of interest to others such as art, photography, gardening, home repair, computer upgrades, music, etc. This skill is commonly known as technical writing.

A writer might combine writing with other creative skills like art or photography and illustrate his or her own material. For example, a writer might take photographs of a travel destination or of local events for an Internet publication. Since the Internet is a visual environment, the ability to provide illustrations is an attractive plus.

Making Electronic Submissions

For a writer to make a go of it in cyberspace, an additional skill is needed. Writers on the Internet are expected to know how to use e-mail both to submit ideas for consideration and to submit completed work. Writers can also garner additional interest from a publisher if accompanying material such as slides, photographs, or illustrations can be submitted in an electronic format the publisher understands and can use with little or no modification. Submitting material electronically means knowing something about the file formats generated by word processors and the various graphical formats for photos and illustrations in use on the Internet. Texts on file formats include the books *Internet File Formats,* by Tim Kientzle, and *PC File Formats and Conversions,* by Ralf Kussmann.

Querying to Attract Interest

Most first contacts between writers and publishers start with a "query." The query is a short, to-the-point e-mail message that explains one or several article ideas. If the publisher is interested, the writer might be encouraged to call or submit further material. It is always best to send a query, even if an article has already been written, because it shows consideration for the time and workload of the editorial staff involved. It is the mark of an inexperienced writer to send a full article without a query first. Queries should be submitted to an editor or assistant editor by name. Many Internet magazines will ask for article ideas and list an e-mail address for submissions, so that's the place to start.

An effective query could be a short list of three to five ideas for articles, with an introduction of who you are, and then a numbered list of article ideas expressed in one to three sentences each. Your contact information should be at the end of the query, listing an e-mail address and a phone number. Good queries are an art in themselves, and some writers spend as much time on their queries as they do on writing the article. Many writers keep a running list of ideas so that, if they get a response from an editor but the editor cannot use any of the ideas they submitted, they can quickly come up with another query while they have the editor's attention.

Editors expect writers who are submitting queries to be familiar with the format and content of the magazine. This is universally true whether the publication is put out in cyberspace or is sold on a newsstand.

Building a Track Record

In order to be paid to write on the Internet, you'll need to develop a track record of material you've written in order to show your skill to an editor. This means you may have to write without pay for a period until you've built up a sufficient volume of material to convince an editor that you can deliver high-quality articles. There are plenty of opportunities to write without pay in cyberspace. Many upstart magazines specifically state that the form of payment is a by-line (your name on the article as the author), and on-line forums of all kinds are looking for content; however, just writing your opinion in a chat room doesn't constitute writing. You need to have a number of pieces in an article format with your name on them as the author.

Be prepared to send a résumé and writing samples on paper or electronically to an editor who requests them. Since material on the Internet appears and disappears rapidly, you will probably want to print out any article with your by-line that appears in cyberspace so you'll have it to send to an editor. It's important to get the name of the publication and the date the article appeared on the copy if possible. Most browsers, like Netscape or Internet Explorer, will print the URL and the date at the top of any page printed from the Internet.

Book Writing

Book writing takes two forms on the Internet. One is writing a book that is interactive, meaning the work is published and built on the Internet. While some of this is going on, for this type of writing to succeed, the topic has to be very compelling or the writer very clever. Like Internet magazine publishers, book projects on the Internet can become advertiser-supported sites, funded by the publisher to draw a crowd or by companies whose products or services are aimed at the type of people drawn to the site. This sort of project tends to be an attention-getter but, usually, is more of a labor of love than a real moneymaking activity.

The second way to have books on the Internet is to publish them in the traditional way (on paper) and then use the Internet as the marketing vehicle. One author at GovCon, a site aimed at U.S. government contractors, sold a book on writing government contracts.

Three chapters of the book were offered on-line as a sample to elicit orders for the printed version. GovCon takes the payments, keeps part of the profits, and sends the order information and the remaining balance to the writer, who is responsible for shipping the book.

Self-publishing

Self-publishing is a time-honored way for authors to get books into a market that mainstream publishers have ignored. Publishing on your own works best with books that have too small or narrow an audience to be profitable for large publishers but that still have a unique appeal. For example, Debra Joan Buck self-published her father's writings about World War II after his death and sells the book via the Internet. The well-known *One-Minute Manager* by Kenneth Blanchard was originally a self-published book before a publisher bought it. So were *What Color Is Your Parachute?* by Richard Nelson Bolles, and *The Christmas Box,* by Richard Paul Evans. An excellent text to help you get started is *The Complete Guide to Self-Publishing,* by Tom and Marilyn Ross. In their book, the Rosses outline such basics as how to get an International Standard Book Number (ISBN), various bindings, paying someone else to publish your book, and ways to promote your book through traditional distribution channels such as book wholesalers.

Making Your Book Stand Out

One of the most important aspects of book writing is being able to differentiate your book from the others in the market. If your book is the only one on the subject, that helps, but the only way to know how many competitors you have is to do some research. The most obvious place to look for possible competing works on your subject is your local library, where you can look through *Books in Print* and *Forthcoming Books in Print,* published by the R.R. Bowker Company. Bowker's *Books Out of Print* reference might also be helpful for finding out what books didn't make it, or you may access Bowker on the Internet at http://www.bowker.com.

To make your book stand out, you need to have a one-to-three-sentence synopsis of what your book is about and how it is different. If you want to sell your book to a publisher, you will need a proposal.

A book proposal addresses market research issues, such as why the book is needed, who the audience is, and how the book is different. It also provides a tentative outline of the contents and usually two to three sample chapters.

If you're going to self-publish, you will still need to do market research to sell the book to the public. You must be prepared to answer the question: What compelling reason do people have to purchase your book? In developing a Web site to sell your books, you will also need to answer that question, although you can do it in a subtle way. Let's look at an example. In the case of Dennis Fett's books, *The Wacky World of Peafowl, Volumes I and II*, the subject is compelling, there are not many books in his subject area, and he demonstrates his expertise by selling peafowl and by the publicity he gets. If you plan to buy peacocks or peacock eggs, it makes sense to get a book that will help you be successful. In the case of the book on writing government contracts sold on the GovCon site, the reader only needs to see the large dollar amounts of contracts awarded by the government to see why such a book would be advantageous. Still, the author sells the book by offering the first three chapters for viewing on-line to whet the reader's appetite.

If you decide to sell your books on the Internet, you can design your Web site yourself; however, offering your book on another site lends credibility to your project. If you do decide to learn to design your own Web site, you can also earn income by designing Web sites for others. We'll cover that next.

Designing Web Sites

One of the easiest cyberbusinesses to start is designing Web sites on the Internet. This business requires slightly more investment than writing content for the Internet because, typically, Web site designers need additional computer hardware and software. Web site designers often have optical scanners for converting artwork or photographs into digital images that can be displayed on the Internet. In addition, they own graphics software for modifying or converting digital images. The most popular software packages include Adobe's Photoshop or Corel's series of products bundled together that include the graphic design program CorelDraw and CorelPhoto-Paint, a tool for modifying digital images. Additional larger hard disk storage space is needed for manipulating and storing Web site pages and for storing digital images.

The advantage of designing Web sites is that each site you design will probably become an ongoing project. Web sites need constant change in order to stay current and the demand for them is high, so this moneymaking activity can provide a continual source of income.

What You Need to Know to Design Web Sites

In order to successfully design Web sites, you need to learn HTML and know something about computer file formats.

HTML

The most basic aspects of Web site design involve learning Hypertext Markup Language (HTML). HTML is the "language" used to author documents on the Internet.

HTML is not hard to learn, and there are no secrets. On any page you can view using an Internet browser like Netscape or Internet Explorer you can see the underlying HTML code just by entering a keystroke or two. One of the ways some people have learned the language is by surfing the Web, then using their browser to look at pages that they like to view the underlying code using an edit document command. It is not unusual for people to simply copy and modify pages they like by inserting their own graphics and text in place of the graphics and text in the page that they copy. HTML is based on technology that has been available for many years—all the way back before the first IBM PC was available on the market—so it is reliable, if somewhat tedious. (For those of you who remember, HTML will remind you of the text you might see using the Reveal Codes function in the word-processing program *WordPerfect* or codes used for special formatting in the even older word-processing program *WordStar*.)

There are also software programs that will allow you to put together a Web page without knowing HTML, such as Microsoft Front-Page. Those who develop Web pages say those programs are helpful to speed up page development, but there comes a point on almost every page where to get what you want you simply have to know HTML. This is especially true if you are developing pages for someone who plans to accept advertising.

Self-study materials are also available. A number of books offer lessons on HTML, and your local library is a good place to start looking for these books. The Internet itself has a number of HTML forums and sites that will help you learn HTML. Developments in Web site design change at a rapid rate, so to get the most up-to-date information, you'll need to do a keyword search using the terms *HTML* or *Web site design* in one or several of the search engines listed in the appendix to get the most current material.

In addition, Microsoft offers a course called Mastering Internet Development that offers interactive lessons you can practice at your own pace at your PC. The course is inexpensive and could work as a springboard to help you get started.

File Formats

In order to successfully design Web sites, you also should be able to understand and work with various file formats. File formats refer to the way information is put together into groups called files. The format provides specific information to the computer about the type of data in the file, such as whether the file contains text, a picture, a digitized sound, an animation, or a video; how the file is to be displayed; what programs can display the file; and how the file should be printed if it is printed.

For example, if someone has a company logo and brings you the artwork in an electronic format on a diskette, you need to be able to look at the file name to tell if you can use that file as it is on their Web site or if you have to convert the file into a format that can be displayed on the Internet. If you decide to add an optical scanner to your computer to scan photographic images for display on the Internet, you'll need to know what graphic file formats work on the Internet and how to scan the files in the most efficient way to maximize their effectiveness in cyberspace. (We address many ways to maximize your Web site images, information on file formats, and other tips and tricks in part II, chapter 7.)

You can pick up expertise in file formats and working with visual information by learning about word processing and basic computerized graphic design. You can usually find courses on these subjects in the adult-education department of your local community college, or you can purchase software that offers tutorials you can do on your own computer.

CASE STUDY

CRAIG HICKSON
HOMEPAGE MAKER
HURST, TEXAS
HTTP://MEMBERS.AOL.COM/HOMEPGMAKR
WEB SITE DESIGNER

Craig Hickson had a background in accounting but wanted to start his own business, so he began a desktop publishing business. He wanted to expand his operation but didn't have any good ideas until he went to an event that focused on home-based businesses, and someone there suggested that he look into Web site design. Craig's objection was that he didn't want to buy a lot of books or expensive tools, so the suggestion was made that he simply get Internet access and a browser and use the edit mode of the browser to teach himself HTML. It just isn't that hard, he was told.

So Craig tried it and discovered he could indeed teach himself HTML. He used the Notepad program in Windows on his PC to write the code and started by putting up his own Web site on America Online (AOL). "I started looking at the code behind Web pages. Even now, when I see one I like, I save it and look at the source code later. A lot of times I just copied the code and modified it for my own use," Craig said. He also discovered there was a lot on the Web about HTML coding, so he started looking up references to the language in search engines to find more information. He also is an avid reader of *WebMaster* magazine, published by CIO Communications of Framingham, Massachusetts, now renamed *WebBusiness* (http://webbusiness.cio.com).

To generate business, Craig went through the AOL member directory and picked out people to contact in his local area. That's how he got his first customer. "I wanted local customers because I felt that there was more of a connection," Craig added. He does have customers as far away as Hawaii, but he still feels that local businesses are his core clientele.

Craig's business is aimed at people on low budgets who want to put up a Web site for the first time. At his Web site, Craig encourages customers to take a look at his work. He also offers ideas for what can be done and before-and-after examples.

Craig still uses Notepad for generating his HTML code, Netscape as his browser to view Web pages, CorelDraw to create images, Paintshop Pro to make images transparent, and the shareware utility GIF Construction Set to create animated images. One thing he says he's discovered is that no one tool will do everything.

Selling Yourself to Clients

While Web site design is an easy field to enter, the downside is there's lots of competition, so you'll need to differentiate yourself from the pack if you want to stay in business. We'll spend this section talking about ways in which you can sell yourself to clients and how to set your services apart.

Setting Up Your Own Web Site

The most common way for Web site developers to attract business is to create their own Web sites as samples and showcase their work to clients. Some fledgling developers have offered to set up Web sites at a reduced rate for new customers in order to get their businesses off the ground. That was the case with the Web site development company that built Mike Smith's Joshua Tree Wood Trim site. The company gave Mike a significantly reduced rate and used all the resources at their disposal to make his site look good in exchange for the ability to show off the site to other potential clients. The tactic worked, and Mike said the Web site development company is now designing sites for art museums in Boulder, Colorado.

Meeting Potential Clients

While advertising to businesses, printing fliers, and other ways of letting people know you're in the Web site design business seem to be obvious ways of getting clients, several Web site designers told us they met most of their clients on the Internet. There are forums and discussion groups on business issues on the Internet where you can meet people. This is usually done via e-mail. For example, if you were interested in attracting local business, you could join discussion groups on local issues in your community. Of course, it's important how you come across in these groups. The best advice is to remember how personal a communication channel cyberspace is and win people over based on the amount of good information you offer in a helpful and friendly way without being in a hurry or appearing to be pushy.

CASE STUDY

BRYCE MCGUIRE
SATELLITE CONSULTANTS, INC.
WATAUGA, TEXAS
HTTP://MEMBERS.AOL.COM/SATCONN/
SATELLITE SALES AND SERVICE

Bryce McGuire worked for over a decade for satellite dish manufacturer Uniden as a manager in customer support before he started his own company, Satellite Consultants. When America Online started offering Web pages, he wanted to have one for his company. "I sell state-of-the-art equipment and I want to look state of the art to my customers," he said.

While lots of people approached him about doing a Web page, Bryce said he shopped around for someone local to his area, near Fort Worth, Texas, and decided to work with Craig Hickson of HomePage Maker. "It was easy to meet with him, and it was easy to convey my ideas to him. I felt that he was someone I could work with," Bryce said. Most of Bryce's business comes from referrals from Uniden, although he's done a lot of work for members of the Dallas Cowboys football team based on referrals from former coach Jimmy Johnson.

He offers information on his site about the various satellite systems and answers technical questions that sometimes result in sales. He says his background in customer support makes it easy for him to diagnose problems and offer alternatives. To promote his site, he "works" the Web by going to on-line discussion groups, but he admits he finds it hard to do as much promotion as he'd like.

Bryce gets several e-mails a day and is collecting a base of e-mail addresses. In the future, he hopes to be able to e-mail everyone who has contacted him when new products become available or when suppliers offer discounted pricing.

Setting Yourself Apart

Web site development, at its most basic level, is so easy nearly anyone can do it. In fact, several companies told us teenagers and college students were the first to design their Web sites. This leaves someone who wants to make a serious business out of Web site design the problem of differentiating him- or herself from the crowd. There are several ways you can set yourself apart. One is to pick a field or a certain aspect of Web site design and focus on that, while another is to set yourself up as a complete marketing and promotion company with Web site design as a function of the overall picture. Let's examine each of these.

Specialize in a Type of Web Site

Many Web site designers pick a field, or a type of Web site, to specialize in. For example, Don Dowell specializes in developing sites for golf courses. This gives Don the ability to sell himself to new clients interested in developing sites for their golf courses by focusing on looking at golf-related sites and learning what is out there. Don has coupled his interest in and ability at golf with his Web site designing skill in order to capture a unique portion of the Web site development market.

Some Web site developers have focused on their local market. While anyone can do business anywhere on the Internet, a lot of companies prefer their Web site developers to be within easy commuting distance. Being close can be a selling point as it allows for face-to-face communication. Also, the Web site developer can offer the client more personalized service, such as pickup and delivery of materials to be made into images for the site.

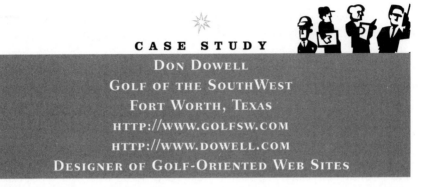

CASE STUDY

DON DOWELL
GOLF OF THE SOUTHWEST
FORT WORTH, TEXAS
HTTP://WWW.GOLFSW.COM
HTTP://WWW.DOWELL.COM
DESIGNER OF GOLF-ORIENTED WEB SITES

Don Dowell was a business major at Texas Christian University (TCU), and while in school he ran a small marketing and direct-mail business. It was during that time, he says, that he learned about word processing and databases. Once he was out of school he decided to go to graduate school, and during that time he worked for his family's printing business. Don said he was able to use his familiarity with computers to get the family business into prepress work, optical scanning, and computer graphics.

When Don was deciding what type of work to do on the Internet, using the skills he already had, he went looking on-line to find help. One of the sites he found helpful was Paul and Sarah Edwards's Working from Home forum on CompuServe. Don said the most helpful information he got was from contacting Paul directly via e-mail with specific questions on the type of business he could start.

Once he decided on Web page design, Don decided he needed practice. Don had always been interested in sports and had contacts at TCU, so his first Web site design work was doing a sports site for TCU. Through his work on the sports site, Don was able to get a speaking engagement where he met the president of the Texas Professional Golfers Association (TPGA), Kim Brown. Brown was the one who suggested that Don check into golf sites, as at the time no other sites on the topic were available. So Don did just that.

At the same time, Don decided to try developing sites for bed-and-breakfasts. He approached potential customers with a six-month free-trial offer, based on what he saw happening in cyberspace. "A lot of people who have been successful on the Internet, like Yahoo and Netscape, have gotten market share first before they actually started making money," he said. But doing both golf sites and bed-and-breakfast sites didn't seem to be working, so he chose the market he had a more personal interest in, which was golf. The free-trial approach didn't work well either: "In my market, I did better when I started charging for Web design services," he added.

Don said there are distinct advantages to specializing in development of Web sites for a particular market. "When I design a Web site, no matter what industry it is, I want to go look at all the other Web sites. I want to learn about their particular industry from their standpoint. This will take a lot of time. If you don't do it, you're at a disadvantage as you need to evaluate their competition. When I do a golf course now, I don't have to look at another site. I can say, 'We can make your site different. Here's what you're not doing that you can do. Here's how other courses have gotten people to interact with the site.'" Another advantage is that Don likes to play golf, so he often gets an expenses-paid trip to the golf course in question to play the site and take photos.

To promote his Web page design work, Don maintains the Golf of the SouthWest site. The site has won several awards. It includes links to golf courses and practice facilities, golf businesses, products, tournaments, associations, and an "Ask the Experts" section where visitors can get help from golf pros. The site is advertiser supported as is a printed newsletter published quarterly, which also promotes the on-line version. Don also hired a couple of part-time people to sell advertising for the site.

Don tracks hits to his site and the Internet locations where visitors come from, called the referring page. However, he's found that only 50 percent of his visitors have referring page information he can obtain. After some research on his part, Don believes that people come to his site as a result of seeing his URL in the printed newsletter.

Don said that in getting started he found it took longer to get business and develop a name than he expected. He attributes part of that to the golf industry, which is slower and more conservative than other businesses. It also took time for him to learn the golf business. He works about half of his time promoting his services and networking and the other half actually doing the design work. One of his avenues for promoting his work is getting publicity from regional publications and speaking at golfing events and association conferences.

As for trends, Don notes that his advertisers are getting a lot of business from people in small towns who wouldn't necessarily have access to a golf store. He says people come to his advertisers, often traveling to do so, when they want to purchase equipment. While the golf pros who provide golf tips pick up some extra lessons, Don says advertisers of golf equipment tend to benefit the most.

Although Don's done Web sites from all over the country, his plans are to work more on nearby business relationships, doing other sports-related sites. "I think as time goes by people will want local businesses to develop their Web sites, and that's where I plan to focus."

Specialize in a Certain Aspect of Web Page Design

Another option for differentiating your Web design business is to focus on a particular aspect of Web site development, like animation or banner design. Then you can sell your services to agencies, corporations, or individuals looking for expertise in your field. Laila Rubstein and Eugene Yushin of Artec International offered their expertise in animation to corporate Internet clients in order to provide additional income to make their electronic greeting card company work.

Offer Marketing and Public Relations Help

Starting a business that incorporates Web design into an on-line marketing and public-relations service has the greatest income potential. These businesses specialize in helping large companies develop a presence on the Internet the way an advertising agency might specialize in helping a company develop brand loyalty using television. Developing an expertise in Internet marketing and public relations can be a natural outgrowth of garnering expertise in Web site development.

Developing marketing and public relations expertise requires a commitment to keep up with the latest trends and developments. Keeping up means following analysts' predictions, tracking what is successful with your own clients, and reading about and watching for new developments in software and hardware technology in cyberspace—in other words, making yourself an expert. (More information on promoting Web sites is found in the section "Services That Promote Web Sites" later in this chapter.)

Using the make-yourself-an-expert principle, Cliff Kurtzman, Ph.D., built Tenagra, a successful marketing and public-relations company that develops Web sites. Tenagra is a partner in the very visible Year2000 site, which deals with the information technology problem of rolling over computer-based systems into the next century. The company also hosts the On-Line Advertising Discussion List, which is an advertiser-supported e-mail-based exchange of ideas on marketing and public relations issues. Both the Year2000 site and the discussion list allow Tenagra, and Cliff, to keep abreast of the latest technology and serve as a friendly showcase for the company to demonstrate its expertise.

Selling Services to Web Sites

Selling services to Web sites and to people who spend a lot of time on the Internet is lucrative but requires experience and expertise both with computers and in cyberspace. Popular services include those that promote or enhance a Web site, "turnkey" business sites, and setting up Web servers.

Services That Enhance Web Sites

Services that promote or enhance Web sites range from offering maps to people who are developing Web sites so that customers can find a physical location in a city to offering automated tools that allow Web site developers to track the validity of links on their site. As the number of Web sites on the Internet increases, the demand for services to help people enhance their sites also increases.

For example, John Moen of Graphic Maps offers custom maps to Web site developers. The maps are in a digital format so they can be easily displayed on the Internet and are often custom-designed to help potential customers of the Web site find the physical location of the business. One of the ways John garnered customers when he started his business on the Internet was by approaching real estate sales sites using e-mail to encourage them to purchase a custom map of the locations of the properties being advertised.

Matt Freivald and his family also started with an idea to help Web sites and Web surfers track when other Web sites change. Web users register sites with URL-Minder, a service from Matt's company Net-Mind. An advertiser-supported service, URL-Minder notifies users by e-mail when the sites they registered have changed. This is especially useful to Web site developers who can register all the site links and then be notified if a linked site has changed or if it no longer exists.

Other Web services allow developers to check how long it takes a Web page to load, try out color combinations, supply a counter for those who cannot get a visitor count from their Web server, and a host of other functions. In each case, the service solves a problem for the Web site developer, a task that requires knowledge of the problems developers face. Interest in services for Web site developers is high and the more attractive services, such as LinkExchange or Web counters, tend to get lots of word-of-mouth exposure.

Database programmers are also finding profitable avenues into the Internet. Many sites that rely on providing information in a look-up type format need programmers who can write custom applications to present the data. Also, sites need programmers who can help the site make use of demographic data from on-site visitor surveys. A common and relatively low-cost tool for this type of application is the database development tool from Microsoft called Access, although larger companies tend to go with products aimed at professional developers such as Powersoft's PowerBuilder.

CASE STUDY

MATT FREIVALD
NETMIND SERVICES, INC.
MOUNTAIN VIEW, CALIFORNIA
HTTP://WWW.NETMIND.COM
FREE URL TRACKING SERVICES FOR THE INTERNET

Matt Freivald says his family has always been Internet savvy, but it was Matt and his brother who came up with the company's flagship service, URL-Minder. Matt graduated from the Rochester Institute of Technology and went on to get a master's degree in business administration from

San Jose State University. His background also includes operating a computer bulletin board service (BBS).

Since the most popular application on the Internet is e-mail, it made sense to Matt to come up with an idea that incorporates the use of e-mail. Matt had been on the Internet for at least ten years and was looking for a business idea that would enable him to establish a long-term one-to-one relationship with people. "The Net is not really a mass media; it's a mass *customized* media. Everyone is there for his or her own specific reasons. [This] brings an unprecedented level of interactivity," according to Matt.

One problem on the Internet is that Web sites change rapidly, which makes it tough for individuals who follow certain topics to keep up. Rapid change also creates a maintenance problem for Web site developers who have links to other Web sites. A big complaint on the part of Web users is finding links to pages that don't exist anymore or pages that no longer are valid for the subject at hand. One day when he was thinking about the link problem, Matt said the concept for URL-Minder came to him like a "lightning bolt."

An advertiser-supported service, URL-Minder enables cybercitizens to register an unlimited number of URLs. Matt's company, NetMind, has programmed its computers to check a URL when it's registered, then check back on a regular basis. When the URL changes, e-mail is generated to notify cybercitizens. The advertising is added to the e-mail notification, and that's how the site generates revenue. The site was developed by the Freivald brothers in the programming languages C and C++, and the scripting language Perl. The site uses the Web server Apache running under the Linx operating system on Alpha computers made by Digital Equipment Corporation.

Matt said the hardest part of the service is that he can't give every person the attention he'd like to. At the time of this interview, Matt said the company's user base was in excess of a million people and growing. NetMind incorporated in 1996.

NetMind offers other services as well, such as E-Minder, a service to remind someone of a calendar date, and Reference.com, which does searches of Usenet News groups on a keyword selected by the user and then sends the results of the search via e-mail. NetMind's plans for expansion include taking advantage of HTML e-mail for advertisers and coming up with new services to attract cybercitizens.

Java Programming

Java is a high-level, object-oriented programming language developed by Sun Microsystems. The appeal of Java to businesses lies in the fact that code developed in Java can run on any computer. Companies like Java because it can be used as a front-end development tool so that legacy systems such as mainframe computers can exchange data with mini-computers and personal computers. Almost anything that can be written in C or C++ can be written in Java, without the hassle of figuring out the quirks of each operating system and hardware the application will run on. On the Internet, it's Java "applets" that are making a stir. Java applets are small software programs that can perform functions such as the display of animation or for interactive Web site applications. (You do not have to use Java to get animation or interactivity on a Web site, but Java is a popular tool for performing these functions.)

Programming Java takes time and training, although you can teach yourself. Java is much more difficult to learn than HTML, but programming in Java can get you a job making $50,000 to $70,000 a year in the corporate world. Or you can get work as a contract programmer writing Java code for $65 to $80 an hour. The place to start investigating Java is at the Sun Microsystems Web site, at http://www.sun.com.

CGI Programming

It's easy to mistake CGI, which stands for the Common Gateway Interface, as a programming language. It is not a programming language. CGI is a standard for developing forms on the Internet. A CGI application can be written in any language as long as it accepts and returns data according to the CGI specifications. The idea is to be able to use the Internet as an interactive tool to collect and transmit data. This is attractive to large companies and to sites that want to collect information from visitors.

CGI is also used to display information stored on various types of computer systems to Web site visitors. For example, if a company has a database on a Unix server and it wants people on the Web to be able to search the data, then a CGI program is needed. The CGI program would run each time a query was made, the search would be submitted to the database software (engine) that controls the data, and the resulting data would be displayed back to the Internet.

Developing CGI applications and other standards similar to CGI for Internet Interactive forms development can make you marketable in both the corporate sector or as a contract programmer. Salaries are comparable to those of Java programmers (see above). The National Center for Supercomputing Applications (NCSA) at the University of Illinois at Urbana, near Champaign, Illinois, is a good place to start looking for information on how to develop CGI programs. You don't have to travel there, however. You can visit the NCSA Web site at http://ncsa.uiuc.edu.

Webmaster

A busy Web site needs a Webmaster. The Webmaster is the person who handles the day-to-day operation of the site, deals with technical problems, answers e-mail, and generally keeps an eye on the operation. As the number and size of Web sites increase, Webmaster jobs are more and more in demand. A Webmaster usually knows a lot about HTML, e-mail, and setting up Web servers. Corporations like to employ people with computer science or telecommunications degrees, but experience is the most important factor in this new field. Webmasters can make between $50,000 and $80,000 annually in the corporate environment. For more information on becoming a Webmaster, a good place to start is at the Webmaster Guild site at http://www.Webmaster.org.

Services That Promote Web Sites

Promoting a Web site can be a daunting task, especially to someone who hasn't ever done it before. Services that offer promotion ideas and help are popular in cyberspace. For example, Scott Banister and Bill Younker started SubmitIt to address the problem of listing a site in the wide variety of search engines on the Internet. SubmitIt offers free advice to visitors about how to get their sites listed in search engines, but the company generates income by actually performing the listing work for sites that don't have the time or the expertise to do it themselves.

Bruce Clay of @bruceclay.com has built his entire consulting business around helping people promote and market their Web sites and products. Part of the way he attracts consulting clients is to offer a free consultation concerning how a site can be improved so that it will be listed higher in the more popular search engines. A typical search on a common keyword in a search engine may generate thousands of possibilities, but users are likely to limit themselves to the first one or two pages of listings. Getting a search engine to list your page higher, and thereby have a higher "ranking," is an issue of importance to Web sites. Bruce also offers to visit any site without charge and offer free advice as to how to improve the site.

Another popular service, LinkExchange, was started by Sanjay Madan and Tony Hsieh in March 1996. This membership service brokers banner ads as a means of generating Web traffic to its member sites. LinkExchange says it places five million banner impressions a day on over one hundred thousand active member sites. Members of the service either pay to have their banner ads placed or barter placement of their banner ads in exchange for displaying ads for other members.

These are just a few examples of the wide variety of Web site promotion services offered on the Internet. Other ideas include new search engines that specialize in certain categories of site listings and services that send subscribers e-mail to promote sites.

"Turnkey" Business Sites

Some enterprising entrepreneurs have turned their computer expertise into a way to provide "turnkey" business sites. "Cybermalls," groups of stores on the same Web server, are no longer the rage everyone thought they would be in the beginning, mostly because cybercitizens are not bound by geographical limits. What is becoming popular are services that do the programming for businesses, so all the business has to do is use a browser to create and maintain store stock in a Web "store." ViaWeb is such a concept, started by four Harvard graduate students who decided that businesses shouldn't have to go to the trouble of knowing how to code HTML in order to have an Internet store.

We expect this trend to continue with services aimed at novice Internet businesspeople. Just as there are services aimed at providing complete phone systems or computer networks, we expect there to be businesses providing a complete Internet business setup aimed at people who understand the products and services they want to sell but don't want to learn the technical details of doing business in cyberspace.

CASE STUDY

PAUL GRAHAM
VIAWEB
CAMBRIDGE, MASSACHUSETTS
HTTP://WWW.VIAWEB.COM
TURNKEY INTERACTIVE INTERNET STORES

Paul Graham was one of four Harvard graduate students who were sitting around one day trying to come up with an application for doing business on the Internet. The group agreed that an on-line mall was a good idea, and that an application could be built so that potential mall merchants wouldn't have to know HTML code to have a storefront on a cybermall. But the magic moment came when someone suggested that stores could be built interactively, so the user needed nothing more than a PC with Internet access to create his or her own cyberstore. "That was when we knew we had to do it," Paul said.

In the beginning, the students started ViaWeb on a Pentium PC in someone's living room. To attract the funding they needed to keep the project going, the team sought out venture capitalists to drag into the living room and see ViaWeb in action. ViaWeb became a two-part project: ViaMall, an Internet mall where cybercitizens can shop, and ViaWeb, the interactive engine that allows merchants to build their ViaMall sites. All that is required of the merchant is photos in an electronic format that can be transferred to ViaWeb (uploaded) as the site is built and descriptions of the items for sale.

In July 1995, ViaWeb was ready to go. To attract merchants, Paul said pricing was set aggressively with no leases or long-term commitments. The company also set up an interactive demo so that users visiting the ViaWeb site could practice setting up their own store—they just couldn't save it. In addition, ViaMall supplies merchants with an easy-to-read report available anytime that contains a complete listing of information on the visitors to their site. The report includes hit rates, click-through, the last Web site the user came from before entering the store, and how much each individual purchased. By tracing the last Web site and the purchase amount, vendors can find out which Internet advertising is working and which isn't.

Orders are taken via credit card and stored on a secure server. Merchants can get their orders at will, and Paul said that most stores download their orders several times a day. Merchants are responsible for verifying the credit card information, confirming the orders with customers, and filling the orders, just as they would if they were running a mail-order business.

ViaMall has attracted an impressive list of merchants, including Dean and DeLuca, Frederick's of Hollywood, and *Rolling Stone* magazine. Because each site can choose its foreground and background colors, use its own graphics, and select fonts, each store can have a unique look and feel characteristic of the image the company wants to build.

Paul says the successful companies in ViaMall are selling as much as they would with a store in a regular shopping mall, some as much as $180,000 a month, but without the mall overhead. Stores can register a domain name (like www.moviemadness.com) and have the domain name linked to the Via-Mall site, so visitors to a site don't even have to know they visited ViaMall.

While other malls on the Internet are borrowing huge sums of money to outdo the competition, Paul said ViaWeb has chosen to keep costs low and borrowing at a minimum. ViaWeb has not put huge amounts of money into advertising campaigns or merchandising pushes, but the site has gained attention by winning several awards from magazines such as *PC Computing, PC Magazine, Internet,* and *Forbes. Business Week* reported that a Columbus, Ohio–based chiropractor who sells vitamins on the Internet spent a month putting up a Web site using HTML but later switched to ViaWeb and had a site running in just two days.

ViaWeb only succeeds when the merchants succeed, so the company is eager to give advice to new vendors. In addition, Paul has seen a lot of businesses succeed and others fail, so he offers what he considers to be expert advice to newcomers. His advice includes the following tips: find a niche you can dominate, work hard to keep your site looking good, promote your site, make it easy for customers to navigate your site, start out with as many products as possible, emphasize service, keep prices as low as possible, and change your site regularly.

Setting Up Web Hardware

Helping people set up Web hardware, Web servers, or even becoming an ISP are other profitable services for those in cyberspace. In order to be successful at these services, technical expertise with both the Internet and computer hardware is needed. That technical expertise can be garnered by working for an ISP, setting up hardware for yourself to gain the experience to do it for others, and taking courses at a local community college or adult-education program.

Setting Up Internet Video

Being able to display live video or capture still images at regular intervals is a continuing trend on the Internet. Video is used on the Internet for everything from enticing visitors to vacation spots to allowing parents to supervise children in a day-care setting from their computer at work. In order for the video to be displayed, there has to be hardware installed in conjunction with a computer so the video can be converted into a format that can be displayed in cyberspace. For the convenience of a customer, you can make video on the Internet a turnkey operation so that all they need is a telephone line and a grounded electrical outlet. The installer offers his or her expertise in Web development, sets up an account with an ISP, and provides a computer with a video card, a color camera to capture images, proprietary software such as Web-Cast from Galacticomm, wiring, and a modem.

ParentNet, an Atlanta, Georgia–based company, provides day-care centers with video feeds of classrooms to the day-care center's homepage on the Internet. Jack Martin of New York–based Simplex runs I See You, a service that allows parents to log in and see a live picture of their child's classroom, updated every thirty seconds. Parents must have a password to get a video picture, but once they have access, they can choose one of several rooms in the day-care center to view.

Usually child-care centers pay for the service as an added feature to attract parents.

Martin also offers Cybermourn, a service for viewing the funeral of a friend or loved one on the Internet. Like I See You, Cybermourn updates the images of the service every thirty seconds in one window, while other surrounding windows contain the name of the funeral home, the name and dates of the departed, and space for an obituary or comments from mourners viewing the scene.

Setting up video on the Internet begins with finding the right software, as the software determines what hardware is needed. The company that makes the video software product will print on the outside of the box or on its Web site the components and capacity needed to run its software. Since software requirements change rapidly and new versions of software packages can be released several times a year, it's important to see what's needed at the time you plan to set up the video operation.

Setting Up Web Servers

Setting up a Web server requires knowledge of computer architecture, server software applications, telephone connections, and the mechanics of how the Internet works. A Web server is a computer connected full-time to the Internet that serves up Web pages for Web sites. A Web server may be operated by an ISP who sells space and access to others for a fee or by a private company who wants complete control over its Web pages, including control of the server that houses the information. IBM-compatible personal computers or Macintosh computers can be Web servers, but many servers are based on the faster Reduced Instruction Set Chip (RISC)–based machines that normally run the operating system UNIX, such as workstations made by Sun Microsystems, IBM, Hewlett-Packard, and other companies.

Web servers require special software, some of it available as shareware. Netscape Communications and Microsoft also make Web server software. Because the companies make popular Internet browsers and have considerable market share, they can attract corporate customers to these more expensive products.

There are several books available on setting up a Web server, some of which contain the shareware versions of the Web server software. One such book is *The Web Server Handbook*, by Pete Palmer et al., which contains information on setting up a very basic IBM-compatible or Macintosh-based Web server and has a CD-ROM containing several shareware Web server software titles.

In addition to the hardware and software, setting up a Web server requires a certain amount of knowledge of telephone connections and optical data lines, such as Integrated Service Digital Network (ISDN) lines or T-1 lines (often referred to as "leased" lines). While the telephone company will set up these lines for anyone wanting to pay for them, the connection between the computer and the telephone lines will have to be made by the person who sets up the Web server.

Becoming an ISP

According to *Boardwatch*[2] magazine, which did a survey of all ISPs in the U.S. (as well as a detailed diagram of the Internet, if you're interested), ISP revenue in 1996 was $131 million monthly or about $1.5 billion annually. In about two and a half months in 1996, the number of ISPs in the U.S. increased 59 percent or at the rate of about seventeen new ISP businesses per day. In the same period, only fifteen went out of business.[3]

While the potential for profits is there, being an ISP is a competitive business that can be expensive to start. However, most ISPs cut costs by starting out of their garages and doing the work themselves. This is how Robert Maynard of Dallas, Texas, started Internet America. Working in his garage in a Dallas suburb in January 1995, Robert has built one of the largest ISPs in the country and has branched out from Dallas into a number of other U.S. cities.

Unlike installing computer hardware for someone else, for which you can get money up front to purchase supplies and materials, becoming an ISP requires you to front the start-up costs. Users then pay for the service on a monthly or an annual basis. Start-up costs are $20,000 to $50,000.

---

[2]Jack Rickard, "Editor's Notes," *Boardwatch On-Line* (July 1996): http://www.boardwatch.com.
[3]Jack Rickard, "So . . . You Want to Be an Internet Service Provider," *Boardwatch On-Line* (June 1996): http://www.boardwatch.com.

The business model of a low-cost, flat-rate unlimited-access account for users is highly debated. The debate centers on the issue of cost because the expense involved in having enough phone line connections so that all users can have access cannot be met if each customer pays only $20 a month. So services have to come up with a way to add features to get customers to pay more, limit the number of hours available for $20 (and charge by the hour for additional time), offer low-cost but attractive premium services that users can opt to subscribe to and hope users want to do so, or find some other way that customers will pay more than $20 a month for unlimited local access.

In addition, telephone companies are starting to figure out that they can rather easily become ISPs. Phone companies need a lot less capital to set up access for subscribers than independent ISPs, who have to pay phone costs at commercial rates. Most independent ISPs have survived because of customer service. According to *Boardwatch*,[4] only one in ten typical computer users can get themselves on the Internet without help, and that's where the local ISP, who is service oriented, makes a splash.

However, the more lucrative opportunities lie in becoming an ISP in a rural area. Rural areas have a high demand for ISPs but are usually poorly served, and therefore customers will pay more for Internet access. Phone companies have little interest in providing Internet access to rural areas because they think in terms of large numbers. However, the costs of becoming an ISP in a rural area are not much different from those involved in providing similar services in a large, metropolitan area—and there's less competition. Successful rural ISPs tend to take on a local flavor, becoming a clearinghouse for news and events of interest to the citizens in the area.

If you're interested in more information on what it takes to be an ISP, we recommend visiting the *Boardwatch* site on the Internet at http://www.boardwatch.com. The trade show arm of the magazine, One, Inc., also hosts the annual ISP convention, ISPCON, each summer. This ISP trade show features guest speakers on subjects such as raising capital, legal concerns, and technology issues. In ad-

---

[4]Philip L. Becker, "Net Profit," *Boardwatch On-Line* (April 1996): http://www.boardwatch.com.

dition, this is a place to see a number of Internet and Web server–
related software and hardware products all at the same time. The
show is an information-packed event for the newcomer and pro alike.
More information is available on-line at the *Boardwatch* site.

CASE STUDY

CLIFF KURTZMAN, PH.D.
TENAGRA CORPORATION
HOUSTON, TEXAS
HTTP://WWW.TENAGRA.COM
AN INTERNET MARKETING AND PUBLIC RELATIONS AGENCY

Cliff Kurtzman, founder of Tenagra, got his Ph.D. at MIT in aeronautical
and astronautical engineering. Cliff originally started building a company
by joining an "incubator" at the National Aeronautics and Space Administration (NASA) in Houston. NASA's incubator program encourages the found-
ing of new companies by placing start-up companies in a building together
so that they can interact with one another. And the agency provides MBA
students to help the new businesses get under way. NASA's idea in doing
this is to create a nurturing environment where start-up companies can
grow large enough to spin off jobs and technology for the agency.

Cliff's first effort was to start a company developing aerospace software.
During this time, he was in a position to watch NASA make a move to communicate with the public on the Internet, and the space agency's efforts
drew his attention to cyberspace. Cliff said he could see the aerospace software market dwindling, but the Internet looked like a market of great
growth. So he decided to start a company to do Internet marketing and
public relations for companies wanting to do business in cyberspace.

Tenagra was one of the first Internet marketing and public relations agencies. Cliff got the company name from a *Star Trek: The Next Generation* episode
entitled "Darmock." In the episode a legend is told of how two warriors, Darmock and Jilad, both learn to work together to defeat a common enemy on
the island-continent of Tenagra despite the fact that the warriors did not
speak the same language. Cliff decided that the Tenagra legend is a metaphor

for the way people communicate on the Internet and that his company of the same name could facilitate successful on-line communication.

To promote itself, Tenagra runs a number of Internet activities, including a tennis site (www.tennis.com); the Tenagra Internet Marketing Excellence Awards held each year since 1993; and the On-Line Advertising Discussion List, an advertiser-supported sharing of ideas via e-mail among business-people trying to solve Internet marketing problems. One of Tenagra's most visible Web ventures is the Year2000 site. Like most start-up marketing and PR companies on the Internet, Cliff felt Tenagra needed a sample of a successful Web site to show potential clients. The way Cliff got the opportunity to partner with the profitable Year2000 site is a typical example of the nature of the Internet.

It started with Peter de Jagar, who is considered one of the foremost experts on the Year 2000 problem. Beginning in 1991, de Jagar started speaking on the problem, also known as the Millennium Bug. The problem centers on the fact that many software systems were designed to record the year using only the last two digits. This means that when the year 2000 comes, these systems will think the year is 1900, 2001 will then be 1901, and so on. The problem is expected to cost millions to solve and is a source of concern for many Information Systems (IS) professionals worldwide. Peter has co-authored a book on the problem, *Managing 00*,[5] and speaks several times a month at conferences worldwide.

Peter decided that the Year 2000 problem would make a very profitable advertiser-supported Web site, but at the time he didn't have the money to have the Web site built or the time to do the work himself. So he sent an e-mail to every company he could find who might be capable of the job, which at the time, with so few people on the Internet, ended up being about fifty companies. Cliff described the first e-mail as obviously a mass mailing, poorly worded and arrogant, about this great business opportunity doing a Year 2000 site. In other words, a spam. Cliff later received a second e-mail from Peter, complaining that no one had responded and again emphasizing the opportunity.

Cliff decided to write Peter back, telling him why no one would respond to a spam. "We argued via e-mail for a while, but then we both started to

---

[5]Peter de Jagar and Richard Bergen, *Managing 00* (New York: Wiley, 1997).

see that maybe we should work together," Cliff said. The resulting Year2000 site serves well the purposes of both companies. "The Year 2000 community thinks it's his [Peter's], while the Internet marketing community thinks it's ours," Cliff added. The site is advertiser-supported, and Cliff says Tenagra has yet to actively pursue advertisers as companies come to the site and ask about becoming involved.

All of Tenagra's activities put the company in a position to meet and get to know potential clients for its marketing and public-relations services. "We do zero advertising and nearly zero direct sales. We get work because people see what we do on-line or read about us in the paper. I [also] do a lot of speaking," Cliff said. While Web site development and ISP services are not what attracts customers, Tenagra tries to provide above-average levels of service, especially in providing information to clients. Cliff sees the information provided as essential to a successful marketing effort. "No one would come to us just for Web site development, but we give our clients very detailed information on what happens on their Web sites. We've written our own systems to provide this information," Cliff added.

As for the site ending around the year 2000, Cliff maintains he can see other information technology problems being discussed on the site that will allow it to continue well into the twenty-first century. One is the Euro2002 problem, which deals with the concept of rewriting all the financial systems worldwide to handle a unified European currency scheduled for adoption in 2002. Another opportunity Cliff foresees is the 2040 problem, which is the same as the year 2000 problem but only affects UNIX-based computers. "After that, we're confident other information technology issues will arise that we can address," Cliff said.

Providing Intranet Services

Intranets are like the Internet, but they are private corporate networks. Usually these networks also provide access to the Internet for corporate employees, although they certainly don't have to. Corporations, especially those spread out over a large area with many employees, are the most likely candidates for an Intranet. Existing ISPs have taken to providing Intranet services, but some businesses specialize in Intranets.

The most important aspect of an Intranet is providing timely information to employees. This information can include a summary of employee benefits, company policy manuals, listings of phone numbers and contact information for individuals within the company, and even forms that have to be filled out internally. Changing and printing paper documents for hundreds or thousands of employees can be an expensive and time-consuming process that can be avoided using a company-wide Intranet.

Essentially, the same technology that enables Internet access can be used for these internal corporate networks, but with the added benefit of preventing unauthorized access. Because of the speed of such networks, other functions such as meeting scheduling and project collaboration can also be accomplished using the Intranet.

A Web server is required to set up an Intranet. For users, the software is the same as if they were accessing the Internet in terms of browsers and Web page–creation tools. Like the Internet, Intranets are also cross-platform, meaning various and formerly incompatible types of computers can be connected to share information with ease.

The *Wall Street Journal*[6] reported that car maker Chrysler Corporation found its Intranet to be a success after only a year. The report said Chrysler did not have to purchase a new computer system company-wide but found instead it could quickly, conveniently, and inexpensively link its personal computers, workstations, mainframes, and supercomputers using the Intranet. If companies can use existing computer hardware to accomplish project monitoring, information flow, and data searches, selling an Intranet is an easy proposition indeed. The process is called "repurposing" and often involves building new "front-ends" or user interfaces that work on the Intranet that allow data input or display of information using the existing software applications running on the old hardware.

To make an Intranet work, there have to be people who understand the system, can install and run a Web server, can install software on individual computers, and make the communication connections work. In addition, someone has to mind the server as an "in-house ISP." In addition, there have to be programmers and Web page designers.

[6]Joseph B. White, "Chrysler's Intranet: Promise vs. Reality," *Wall Street Journal* (May 13, 1997): pB1(W) pB1(E) col 3 (22 col in).

Predictions are that new corporate departments of "internal ISPs" will spring up, since some corporations like to control everything they use. What is more likely is that there will always be services who are contracted to run the Intranet and companies who decide to develop an in-house Intranet staff—just as there are companies who have their own print shops and companies who contract out printing services.

Providing Intranet services is not work a company is likely to give to an inexperienced business. However, anyone who wants to sell him- or herself as an Intranet service provider will need a track record of running such systems. A track record can be established by working with an ISP, doing work for a company who installs Intranets, or by being an ISP.

One further application of the Intranet is called the Extranet. An Extranet is an Intranet that is used by more than one company. An Extranet allows companies to share the costs and the benefits of an Intranet and works well for companies that use similar types of business applications.

Conclusion

We've seen how the demand for content on the Internet is driving the creation of new business opportunities for both creating the content and for housing and maintaining the content once it's been created. As we've seen, these opportunities range from writing content, to creating Web pages, to creating services for those who write Web pages, to setting up hardware for the storage and distribution of Web content.

This leads us to the next chapter, where we'll look at how existing businesses have successfully entered cyberspace.

Chapter 6

Take an Existing Business into Cyberspace

The Internet is the most exciting innovation
to impact U.S. businesses since the
invention of the telephone.

—New York–based
Market Analysts FIND/SVP

 One of the ways to measure the potential of
a new consumer-oriented electronic medium is to
look at how long it takes that medium to penetrate
50 million U.S. households. Radio reached this
landmark in thirty-eight years. Television took thirteen years. However, the New York–based investment firm Morgan Stanley predicts
that, at its exponential rate of growth, the Internet will penetrate 50
million U.S. homes in only five years. The Internet provides a powerful, efficient new channel for retailing where, by the year 2000, an estimated 150 million Web users will be "just a mouse-click away from
consummating transactions twenty-four hours a day, seven days a
week."[1]

But gains to be made are not just with consumers. According to

---

[1]*Internet Retailing Report,* Morgan Stanley, U.S. Investment Research Division, New York (May 28, 1997): http://www.ms.com.

analysts at Cambridge, Massachusetts–based Forrester Research, the total value of goods and services traded among companies in cyberspace will reach $327 billion by the year 2002. With growth potential like this, what business wouldn't want to get in on this growing consumer and business segment?

In this chapter we'll look at businesses that have successfully entered cyberspace, ways an existing business can gain a presence on the Internet, and the most common mistakes businesses make when entering cyberspace.

> **TIP**   *If you've turned to this chapter first, we'd encourage you to finish it, then go back and look over chapters 1 through 5. The information in those chapters will help you define what type of Web site you want your business to have and will bring you up to speed for entering part II of the book, where the focus is on actually getting started on the Internet.*

Existing Businesses Succeed in Cyberspace

Even though the Internet is in relative infancy as a communications medium, existing businesses are starting to see results from marketing in cyberspace. Internet sites started by existing businesses generate additional profits and, in many cases, allow businesses to cut costs.

Existing Businesses Generate Additional Profits

Name-brand stores can gross as much from their virtual mall sites as they do from physical mall stores. Paul Graham of ViaWeb, the Cambridge, Massachusetts–based virtual shopping site, said some Via-Mall stores are doing as much as $180,000 in sales each month. That's as much or more business than a physical store does, but without the overhead of mall rent, merchandise display furniture, salesclerks, inventory, security, and losses due to theft or damage.

Model horse marketing company Cascade Models of Edmonds, Washington, says since putting up a Web site in 1995, business from

Internet visitors went from nothing to one-third of gross revenues in two years. Cascade, a mail-order company offering everything from plastic model horses to fine porcelain collector horses, said business became especially brisk when the major on-line services, such as America Online, allowed members Internet access. Their business from the Internet has been increasing ever since.

Dave Dickstein, co-owner of Pacific Partners Mortgage Corporation of Woodland Hills, California, says his Internet site generates substantial revenue for his $600,000-a-year mortgage brokerage firm. The site is convenient for his market, which is the "Generation X" age group of twenty-five- to thirty-five-year-olds who are first-time home buyers. Pacific Partners' Web site, available to Net surfers twenty-four hours a day, seven days a week, generates four or five requests for loan preapprovals a day. Those requests turn into an average of one extra loan a week of additional business for the small brokerage firm.

Mail-order-catalog company Fingerhut Corporation started a Web site for the purpose of solving the problem of what to do with obsolete merchandise. The site, called Andy's Garage Sale, is aimed at reducing unwanted stock while getting more for the merchandise than the company could through its normal liquidation channels. Quantities are limited, stock is rotated quickly, and when it's gone, it's gone. Using the Internet, Fingerhut has not only found a way to solve one of its challenges in the direct-marketing business, but it has also created a profitable site with content that changes constantly and a strong base of new customers.

CASE STUDY

DAPHNE AND DUNCAN MACPHERSON
CASCADE MODELS
EDMONDS, WASHINGTON
HTTP://WWW.AA.NET/~CASCADE

Daphne Macpherson calls model horse collecting "the underground hobby," because thousands of people around the world do it, but few people know about it. In fact, there are model horse shows with class categories much like real horse shows. The model horses are judged and the winners are awarded trophies. In Daphne's opinion, much of the interest in the hobby has come from the move to urbanization, which has forced people who like horses but don't have the room or the resources to keep them into collecting model horses.

Daphne got into the hobby in 1977, and several years later she was approached about selling by an individual artist who was making collector-quality model horses. Daphne became a representative for the artist's models, and a few years later when the artist stopped making horses, Daphne wanted to stay in the business. So she decided to sell models made by mainstream companies like Breyer, Peter Stone, Winner's Choice Micro-horses, and the Best Collector Company. Her business has been mostly catalog sales, although Daphne is well known on the model horse show circuit where she regularly displays her products.

Meanwhile, Duncan, Daphne's husband, was an aircraft engineer in charge of new business development for Lockheed. Born in Woking, England, Duncan joked that he was the "only English contract engineer in Seattle who never worked at Boeing." One of his accomplishments was to design and patent a power roller for the cargo handling system used on the Boeing 747 plane, and at the time of this writing it was still in use.

But at age forty-eight, Duncan found himself with a serious heart condition, about the same time the aircraft company was downsizing. So he took early retirement and started looking for something less physically taxing to do that would keep his mind occupied. Drawing on his background in computers, he got involved in Daphne's business, by writing database applications to track her customers.

It was Duncan who decided in October of 1995 that the company should have a Web site. Duncan is a self-taught Web designer, who started by copying bits and pieces of Web pages he liked in order to learn to create his own site. The company now has hundreds of images of model horses available on the Web site, which customers say is their favorite part. When the major on-line services, such as AOL, provided their members with the ability to surf the Net, Cascade noticed an immediate benefit in terms of increased business, Duncan said. Orders now come in from all over the world, from places like Brazil, Sweden, Norway, Hong Kong, the Philippines. The Web site has brought new customers and boosted profits, accounting for a full third of Cascade's gross revenue.

Daphne and Duncan expect to spend time with customers, and they devote several hours a day to answering e-mail and their toll-free phone line. Duncan said that, at first, everything he put up on the Web site seemed to get misinterpreted by someone. "Clarity is God on the Web," he quipped. The company also tries to keep up with what's going on but stays behind the curve on implementing the latest advances in Web page technology, such as the latest animation techniques or image design. "Most of our customers don't have the latest technology available, so we don't do the latest stuff because our customers can't see it," Duncan added.

Daphne emphasizes the importance of knowing your customers. For example, the average age of the model horse collector is thirty-five, not the teens as many people would guess, even though the company does special promotions aimed at 4-H clubs. Two-thirds of the company's U.S. customers are east of the Mississippi River, and two-thirds have rural addresses. Daphne says it's important to her customers that they receive orders quickly, so the couple makes a point of keeping stock current and shipping orders the same day they're received. "Depending on where the order is shipped to, some customers can call on Monday and get their order on Wednesday," Daphne said. "Our prices are not the lowest. Our business is built on service," Daphne added. The couple estimates that their current customer base is about twenty thousand.

Many customers are long-term, some ordering regularly for over ten years. Orders come in on-line and on the toll-free number, even though some people see the products first on the Internet. In order to protect the interests of customers, Duncan came up with a system that assigns each new customer a unique ID number that can be used for on-line ordering. That way, customers can simply send an e-mail with their name, ID number, and what they want and the order can be automatically billed to their credit card, so there's no danger of someone else getting a credit card number.

The company promotes its Web site in magazine ads in horse magazines and in promotional magazines put out by model manufacturers as well as by direct mail. With such a large amount of information available about model horses, the Cascade site is listed high in many search engines. This allows Casade to get a lot of business from people who use search engines to find model horse sites.

Duncan said selling on the Internet is "apparently a very narrowly known secret. The whole thing is so simple, it's laughable. All you need is a Web page and a product and you can make more money than you ever dreamed of." Duncan does advise offering a very specific product. The other ingredients are "hard work, ingenuity, and a willingness to learn and keep up with technology," he added.

Daphne and Duncan say their future plans are to attempt to interface electronically with suppliers to speed shipments and reduce inventory, continue to expand the product line, and move more into the higher-priced collectible model horses.

Internet Allows Businesses to Cut Costs

In addition to finding new customers, cost cutting is a big part of profits for businesses on the Internet. Su Penny of Canadian-based competitive pricing service PriceCheck said that, in addition to opening new markets for her firm, having a Web site allowed her company to make significant savings in data entry costs along with lower error rates. Using the Internet allowed PriceCheck surveyors across North America (and eventually worldwide) to enter data themselves, eliminating retyping errors and speeding the entire process. The bottom line is that PriceCheck can get more accurate information to customers in less time.

Mike Smith of Joshua Tree Wood Trim says the Internet provides him with the maximum profit by allowing him to sell wood trim kits for automobiles for less than he can using the telephone or the mail. Rather than spending money paying for a toll-free phone call and sending out product literature, Mike advertises in strategic publications and makes sure his URL is in the ad. The Web site then provides information to handle the customer education necessary to make the sale. Customers can get all their questions answered by seeing step-by-step installation photos, looking up their own automobile make and model to see what kits are available, and complete the order paperwork right on the Internet.

Palo Alto, California–based Killen & Associates predicts that an increasing number of automobile loans will be made using the Internet. In fact, the group predicts on-line auto loans will account for as much as 20 to 30 percent of the overall auto loan market by 2001, with everyone involved in the loan process coming out ahead finan-cially. One of the cost-cutting benefits of getting auto loans through cyberspace is the reduction in errors from reentering data. Cus-tomers can enter data themselves into a form that takes several steps out of loan processing. In addition, the paperwork can be done at the customer's convenience instead of spending long hours in a car dealer's showroom.

Direct marketers also expect a significant portion of their future sales to be from the Internet. According to a recent report from For-rester Research, direct-marketing companies predict that 36 percent of sales will come from the Internet by 2001, up from 7 percent re-ported in 1996. Rather than placing orders in more traditional ways, such as over the telephone, direct marketers are hoping customers will enter their own orders over the Internet, thus reducing labor and phone costs. "Direct marketers are being drawn to the Internet by ac-cess to a worldwide audience, the ability to form deeper customer re-lationships, and the promise of cheaper marketing," says Bill Bass, senior analyst with Forrester's Media & Technology Strategies ser-vice. "Direct marketers see the Internet as a dream come true, a way to grow the customer base and improve customer service while si-multaneously cutting costs."

Book retailer Barnes & Noble has energetically begun on-line book selling, obviously in an attempt to garner some of the market Amazon.com found selling books exclusively in cyberspace. Ama-zon.com reported just under $30 million in sales in its second quar-ter of 1997, up 74 percent from first-quarter sales and up 1,168 percent over the same period in 1996. Operated from the fourth floor of an old Seattle office building, where desks are doors mounted on two-by-fours, the company boasts it is the largest elec-tronic bookstore with 2.5 million titles available at discounts as high as 40 percent.

CASE STUDY

Su Penny
PriceCheck
Ontario, Canada
http:// www.pricecheck.com

Su Penny was managing two large hardware stores when she saw a need for competitive pricing information. "I hated doing the pricing surveys and ended up thinking, 'There has to be a business that will do this for us,' but there wasn't one," she said. So Su decided to start one herself. The business, PriceCheck, simply went into stores and checked prices on comparable items each month.

Su said she started checking two hundred items in seven hardware store chains each month. The business "exploded in popularity," Su said. She soon expanded to checking prices of eight thousand items at seven grocery store chains in fourteen markets each week. Once Su had information for across Canada, she said PriceCheck put together a system whereby businesses could check prices worldwide. The company had clients, franchisees, and surveyors worldwide. But, as in any business, there were problems.

One of the main problems in Su's type of business is getting the prices. Price checkers, called "surveyors," are not welcomed in stores and will often get thrown out. Successful surveyors are often a "tag team," according to Su. "One person goes in as sort of a wounded duck and is very obvious, and the other one is subtle. The manager throws out the obvious one and the subtle one stays and finishes the survey."

Another problem was getting surveyors to markets where Su saw opportunities to sell information to clients. Often surveyors had to be flown into markets they weren't familiar with. "If we had a client who wanted chewing gum prices in Russia, we'd have to fly someone in, or the manufacturer might have to fly in a sales representative," Su said.

The third most pressing problem was the integrity of the data. The surveyors' handwriting wasn't always legible, and even when it was, errors in the data entry were common. Su said in 1987, incoming data from surveyors was "touched" as many as seven different times and each touch meant introducing errors into the data.

Then Su discovered the Internet. She estimated it was either 1992 or 1993 when she started using a Web site to solve two of her three business problems. Once PriceCheck was on the Internet, surveyors could type in their own data and send it via e-mail. "They can read their own handwriting," Su quipped. Sending the data in an electronic format meant the elimination of error-producing extra handling and at the same time sped up the process.

Not only did using the Internet save time, but it significantly reduced labor costs in another area. Obtaining information from international markets became a much less challenging and costly process. Su said she was now able to use the Internet to find someone who already lived in the area to do surveys. "We were able to reduce our costs in obtaining the information, and so we've passed the savings on to our clients," Su added.

Without doing anything, Su found that the search engines were listing PriceCheck. "If anyone typed 'check prices' or 'price check' they got my site," Su added. But this was early in the development of the Internet, and Su said that the guys at Yahoo and some of the other search engines said to her, "Why don't you become a search engine for checking prices on the Internet?"

So Su decided to look into the idea. "When we looked more carefully at our visitors, we found we had thousands of hits from people interested in checking prices on the Internet." She also did some market research and discovered that, at the time, there was no dominant site strictly for checking prices. "So I asked some of the Internet gurus who work with me to create a site that would allow people who have commerce Web sites to link to us," Su said.

Su said that North American banks, stock markets around the world, automotive companies, and major clothing manufacturers are just a few of the companies who have signed up to be on the PriceCheck site. "We have them fill out an application to be part of our site—we don't pursue businesses—and we have thousands on our site," Su maintains.

In part, PriceCheck is advertiser supported. Su picked up her first multinational advertising client on the site without a public-relations agency, although she plans to use an agency in the future. "Being your own PR agent is like being your own lawyer. You should never do your own stuff because even if it looks bad, you'll think it looks good," Su added.

Su's not worried about charging for access to the site, since the site pays for itself with the reduced costs it provides for PriceCheck. Even with lowering her prices to clients, Su says she sees a nice profit from maintaining the site since maintenance expenses are low and the site helps her cut costs. Su's future plans for PriceCheck include adding a fee for being linked on the site if she feels her market will bear the charge. Su says one of the careers she sees a future for in cyberspace is the Internet "librarian." She's struggled with organizing the information on her site and believes someone trained in library science could have made a big difference organizing the mountain of information so that it's useful.

How to Move Successfully into the On-line World

While almost any business can move into the on-line world, there are important decisions to consider. The first is to make sure you know your goals for being on-line, and the second is to be sure you're prepared to devote resources to your on-line presence. Let's look at each of these individually.

Know Why You're On-line

As is true of any business venture, making a successful foray into the on-line world requires a specific goal and a way to measure whether you've reached your goal. Having a presence on the Internet is a way for a business to say it is up-to-date and technology aware. However, a Web page can and should be more. The most common goals businesses have for being on-line are to increase sales, cut costs, and promote the business. Increasing sales by having a Web site depends on the type of business. Selling tangible products people can feel and touch has more obvious potential, but you can also increase sales of intangible items such as legal services, counseling, entertainment, vacation information, self-help, and other services. Whether you can cut costs by being on-line depends on the type of business you're in as well as the type of costs your business has. If you're looking for "mind share" or consumer awareness of your company, you could benefit from having an effective Web site. Or you may want to consider advertising on a Web site developed by someone else that reaches the customers you're interested in. Here are some questions to help you determine a specific goal for your Web site or other Internet presence.

> *What are the characteristics of the customers your business serves?*
> *Do you want to attract international business, regional business, local business, or does it matter where customers are located?*
> *What are the biggest costs and problems your business faces?*

Once you know the answers to the above questions, you can start determining what you'll need to create a successful Web presence for your company. We've already seen several examples of how businesses have asked themselves these questions and used the answers to come up with an effective approach on the Internet. When the Audit Department of Aetna Life Insurance Company decided to put up a Web site, looking at the goal for the site was their first step. According to *Internal Auditor* magazine, the Aetna Audit Department had this to say concerning defining content for the Web site:

> *Our biggest lesson learned from this stage of the work was that time spent at the beginning of the project to clearly define content is extremely valuable.*[2]

As we mentioned in chapter 1, an effective approach to developing a goal for your Web site is to consider how you'll incorporate the four principles of success on the Internet into your plans. Again those principles are: specialize, keep up with your e-mail, provide a reason for visitors to return, and give away something valuable. In order for you to be sure your site effectively meets your goal, and to get ideas

[2]Serge Beaulieu, et al., "On the Net: How Aetna's Internal Audit Department Has Built a Home in Cyberspace," *Internal Auditor* (August 1996): v53, n4, p30(5).

you feel you can modify and implement, it is also important to do research to see what the competition is doing.

C A S E   S T U D Y

JANE WESTLIND
MANAGER OF ELECTRONIC COMMERCE
ANDY'S GARAGE SALE, A FINGERHUT COMPANY
MINNETONKA, MINNESOTA
HTTP://WWW.ANDYSGARAGE.COM
A MERCHANDISE LIQUIDATION COMPANY

Imagine a corporate vice president and a group of other high-level managers sitting around after hours with their feet up on the desks, kicking around ideas for how to solve the marketing "challenges" of a multimillion-dollar direct-mail company. One of the biggest challenges discussed was the problem of getting stuck with oddball merchandise, such as twenty sets of pink bath towels or odd clothing sizes, and having to take a beating on the excess inventory through the company's standard liquidation channels. The items, the group decided, were stuff fit for garage sales and swap meets.

That's how Senior Vice President of Fingerhut Marketing Andy Johnson and his staff came up with the idea of having a garage sale on the Internet. According to Fingerhut's Manager of Electronic Commerce Jane Westlind, the idea was a simple one—offer excess inventory Fingerhut was unable to sell through the catalog at an on-line garage sale with the intention of recovering more for the merchandise than was possible through normal liquidation channels. In that vein, the group decided the electronic garage sale should have a cast of characters and a homey approach, just like any real garage sale. The beauty of the idea is it leveraged off Fingerhut's marketing apparatus, which meant there was already a mechanism in place for order fulfillment and credit card acceptance.

So Andy's Garage Sale was born. Using a title based on Andy Johnson's first name was perceived to be an advantage because *Andy* begins with the letter *A* and Web sites are often alphabetically organized in search engines. The company was set up as a separate legal entity, although it is dependent on resources and expertise from Fingerhut. It was important to Fingerhut that Andy's Garage Sale operate in a much different way from the catalog sales company. Fingerhut catalog customers receive their products and try them for thirty days with a no-questions-asked return policy. But the discounted Garage Sale items would be sold on a first-come, first-served, no-returns, cash-and-carry basis.

Like Jack of Jack in the Box, the imaginary character Andy was to be the focal point of the site. Soon, a family was "born." Andy needed a wife, so the group came up with Gert, Andy's imaginary counterpart. Together Andy and Gert are the main characters in Andy's Garage Sale, which takes place in a town called South Branch. Back in 1995, a handful of people were assigned the task of creating the electronic garage sale. Along with marketing the merchandise, the writers started creating life situations for Andy and Gert. It was important to the staff to maintain continuity in the characters, according to Jane Westlind, who said, "We were asking each other stuff like 'Would Andy really say that?'"

The site was first launched at Marketplace MCI, a cybermall, in October 1995, but MCI dropped the mall. So by March 1996, the company decided to bring Andy's Garage Sale in-house. The site now has its own server and a small staff that includes writers, customer-support personnel who answer Andy's e-mail, Web administrators, marketing staff, and others who maintain and support the project.

The story line at Andy's Garage Sale has expanded significantly over time from Andy and Gert to their three children, some of whom are married and have kids of their own, a dog, and a variety of neighbors and friends. On the site, Andy provides his "top picks" of liquidation merchandise, a section where visitors can read homey stories about Andy's "life," and a joke section where visitors are encouraged to copy or e-mail favorite jokes to friends.

Early on, it was decided the site was loading too slowly for the average visitor and was too difficult to navigate, so a complete overhaul was done. A single image on the left side is the navigation signpost, and it appears on every screen so users can choose to go to any location on the site from any other page. Since the navigation graphic appears on every screen, it only has to be downloaded to the user once. In addition, the site dropped a background color, going to white instead, and changed the format of the images from the GIF format to the JPEG format, which allows for smaller files that load to the user faster.

Since a lot of people asked questions before ordering, Andy's Garage

Sale realized early on that answering e-mail is important. So e-mail is answered in one business day (no weekends). There's also a frequently asked questions (FAQ) section available on the site.

The e-mail has been surprisingly personal, Jane added. People actually invited Andy and Gert to come visit them when the imaginary couple announced vacation plans. One woman sent an e-mail to Andy asking for help in locating the child she gave up for adoption three years ago.

To promote the site, the company has purchased banner advertising on the Internet. The company has also done some direct mailing and print advertising, and even television advertising. While Andy's Garage Sale wouldn't release sales figures, Jane says the site is meeting the company's marketing goals. She emphasizes the importance of a goal for putting up a Web site. "There has to be a reason for having something on-line. There has to be value added rather than just slapping up a site."

Check Other Web Sites in Your Business Arena

If you haven't done so already, you need to look at what your competitors are doing on the Internet. Since cyberspace is relatively new territory, you may be the only business in your field that you know of who is preparing to enter the Internet. But before you devote time and money to building a Web site, it's important to do a thorough search of the Internet to find out what other, similar businesses are doing. This can be accomplished using search engines and keywords that describe your business. A list of search engines is available in the appendix.

Your research may turn up information that will require you to go back to the drawing board and come up with new ideas. This happens often and, in fact, you may have to go through several ideas before you hit on one with the potential for success. The easiest sites to promote on the Internet are ones with new ideas that no one has done yet, so if you can come up with an idea that is fresh, it will make getting publicity for your site a lot easier. Either way, doing your homework first, no matter how discouraging, will save lots of money and time later on. (See chapter 8 for more information on promoting your Web site.)

Devote Resources to Your On-line Presence

Once you've determined what you want to do, it's important to re-member that you'll need to devote resources to your Web presence. Starting and maintaining a Web site can be a full-time business in it-self, as you've seen from reading about the experiences of others in this book. Even if someone else does your Web site development, as we've seen from previous chapters, entrepreneurs on the Internet can spend two hours a day just answering e-mail.

If your business is not prepared to devote ongoing resources in the form of time and personnel to keeping up your Web site, then adver-tising on someone else's site may be your best option. Once you've determined the characteristics of the customers you have, you can use that information to find a Web site that attracts that type of cus-tomer and advertise there. It's possible, depending on the size and complexity of what you want to accomplish, that advertising on the Web could be cheaper than starting your own Web site. Chapter 8 of-fers more information about advertising on the Web.

The Biggest Mistakes Businesses Make Entering Cyberspace

Since mistakes in cyberspace can be costly, it makes sense to learn from others how to bypass the most common mistakes. Here's a list of mistakes you'll want to avoid when entering cyberspace for the first time.

Lack of Coordination

If no specific person or team of people within your company assumes the task of coordinating the Web site development effort, problems can arise and your plans may never get off the ground, according to Cliff Kurtzman, CEO of the Internet marketing firm Tenagra. Even if an outside firm is hired to design and manage the Web site, you or someone inside your company will need to be responsible for it. In large companies, a related problem is getting backing from key management people. The Web site coordinator will find him- or herself having to get other departments within the company—such as marketing, advertising, public relations, and customer support—to sign on to support the project. Without the support and acknowledgment of key management people, getting sign-on from other departments, who probably have other priorities, is going to be difficult, if not impossible, to accomplish.

No Internet Marketing Research

We've already talked about doing a search on the Internet when a new Web site is being planned, to see what is already being done. Surprising as it may seem, there are lots of businesses and individuals who start a site without looking at all to see if anyone else is doing the same thing.

No Plan for Promoting the Web Site

Without a promotion plan, your Web site may just sit there costing money. Putting up a site without promoting it is like building a billboard in your basement—no one will see it. There needs to be a plan in place for how the site will be promoted on an ongoing basis. As we've said, it is much easier to promote a site that is the first of its kind, and that should be a consideration. But however fresh an idea for a site is, there still needs to be a plan in place to make sure people know about it and will be attracted to it. Promoting your Web site is the subject of chapter 9.

No Objectives or No Criteria for Knowing If Objectives Are Met

How do you know if you have a successful Web site if you have no objective or no way to determine if you met your objective? Jane Westlind, manager of Electronic Commerce for Fingerhut and Andy's Garage Sale, says, "There has to be a reason for having something online. There has to be value added rather than just slapping up a site."

Inadequate Allocation of Resources

Many companies fail to count the cost of having a Web presence. For example, companies put an e-mail address on their site without taking into account the fact that someone will have to answer the inquiries that come in.

Failure to Design for the Medium

Designing for screens delivered over a modem is a different task than designing for print. Many companies fail to take into account the amount of time it will take the average Internet user to receive the screens on the Web site or put up a site that looks amateurish, which doesn't project the proper professional image for a company. Cliff Kurtzman said, "Web design is like photography. Anyone can buy a disposable camera at the store and shoot pictures for Grandma, but you wouldn't do that with a company brochure."

No Preparation for Dealing in an International Market

It's a common mistake to overlook the fact that the Internet is an international market. So companies often fail to have any plan in place to handle the problems that go along with attracting even unintended international business. So, for example, when the first order comes in from Kuwait for 100 gizmos or an inquiry in French, you have a crisis on your hands. It's important to decide if you want to do business internationally and to have thought about the answers to the following questions.

> ➤ *Are there laws against shipping our product outside our country's borders?*
> ➤ *Are there import or export duties due, and who pays those duties?*
> ➤ *Who ships to this place, and what do they require in terms of packaging?*

➤ **What about payment or a return policy for international orders?**

➤ **Where can we find translators who can answer e-mail in other languages?**

Conclusion

Most businesses with an eye to the future have heard that the Internet is the future for business. We've seen how growth of the Internet as a communications medium makes getting on-line attractive to business. And we've also taken a look at a variety of businesses who have generated additional income and cut costs by moving into the world of cyberspace. We've also noted the importance of having goals for why your business is on-line and criteria for knowing when you've reached those goals, doing market research to find out what others are doing on-line, and allocating resources for the company's Internet presence. In addition, we've noted the most important mistakes businesses make when entering the Internet.

But by now, you probably want more specific information on exactly how these Internet feats are accomplished. How do you deal with issues like Web page design, promoting your Web site, getting paid, and so on? Not to worry—the answers to those questions and lots more are all in part II of the book, which follows.

AUTHOR'S NOTE *Several months after our interview, Duncan Macpherson of Cascade Models passed away from congestive heart failure at age sixty. Besides his wife, Daphne, he is survived by a son, Kevin, daughters Shauna and Lindsay, and four grandsons. Daphne told us he lived ten years longer than predicted. It is our hope that others who find themselves forced by circumstances into a life they would not otherwise have chosen will find strength in Duncan's courageous example.*

Part II
How to Get Started

Chapter 7

Building a Successful Web Site

To the uneducated, an A is just three sticks.

—Eeyore,

from Winnie the Pooh

 Fortunately, Web site development can be a very fast and relatively inexpensive process. You can have a Web site up in less than a week working part-time, even if you have never done this before. But getting your site up is just the beginning. Ask anyone who is doing Web site development, and they'll tell you it is an ongoing process. And it should be. The most successful sites are updated often so they look and feel current to the people who visit—not like some forgotten closet where advertising materials are kept.

In this chapter, we'll explain how to build your Web site, direct you to many fine materials and products that will help you accomplish the building of it, explain some design considerations, and give you practical tips to make your site a satisfying ongoing experience for your visitors.

Six Steps for Building a Web Site

Building a Web site is more like putting together a jigsaw puzzle than building a skyscraper. The six steps to building one are:

> ➤ *define your content*
> ➤ *do the appropriate research*
> ➤ *determine who will be involved*
> ➤ *build and test your site*
> ➤ *promote your site*
> ➤ *maintain and update your site.*

While we present these steps in what we believe is a logical order, in practice the construction of a Web site is more dynamic than just checking items off a to-do list. For example, you may find that you've gotten to the point of building your site only to discover that you need to go back to the research stage because unforseen questions have arisen that you hadn't thought of when you were doing your initial research. So now you need to see how other people have handled this particular problem. Or you may get your site built, start to update it, and determine that you need to do further research or even tear down and rebuild the entire site to get the results you intended. So don't be surprised if you find yourself moving in a circular fashion between steps on the list during the building of your site. Now let's look at each step individually.

STEP 1: DEFINE CONTENT

You probably already have some idea of what you think you'd like to do on your Web site. (If not, keep reading, because there are more case studies and ideas that will help spark your imagination as we go along.) But you need to make a concrete plan as to what information you want to present because this will affect how you build your site and who needs to be involved. For example, if you plan to offer goods on the Internet and you can already accept credit cards, you may want to use a mall like ViaWeb where you don't need to know about programming HTML and can get a lot of help in creating and maintaining your site. If you want to offer information that people look up and plan to have advertisers support your site, you probably wouldn't want to choose a cybermall storefront. Instead you most likely would want to choose a fast ISP. In other words, your content determines almost everything else about how you set up your site.

As we hinted at earlier, it's also important to remember that this is a dynamic process, so you may come up with an idea for a content, take the next step, which is doing research, then scrap all or part of your original content idea. You may find yourself going around and around for a while in this manner from determining content to research, over and over, before you hit the right combination. Time spent at this stage of the game is very important and will pay off later.

STEP 2: RESEARCH

We covered this briefly in chapter 6, but it bears repeating. Research is one of the most critical steps in building a Web site. You need to know who else is doing what you think you'd like to do and how you can make your site different. The search engines are the places to start your research. You may also want to look at sites that interest you as well as those that have won awards or appear on lists as top sites. Many of the search engines, Internet sites, and on-line publications feature interesting Web sites. In the appendix, we have provided URLs of search engines, sites that give awards to other sites, and other lists of sites for you to visit.

Here are a couple of points to remember while you're doing your research. One is to bear in mind that you don't have to do everything at once. You can start a site and build it, gradually adding pages as you get experience. So you don't need to feel overwhelmed when you visit sites that have tons of information and resources. Second, you'll want to take into account how much time you want to spend on your site. Try not to choose an idea that requires several hours a day of updates if you cannot make that kind of commitment either yourself or by hiring someone else to do so. Finally, keep in mind that if you can be the first with an idea, it makes promoting the site a lot easier.

Once you know what you want to do and have done the research, you need to determine whom to involve to make your site happen. Hopefully, you already have access to the Internet either through an ISP, an on-line service, or some other means, but now you need to determine who will host your Web site. Again, if you choose to go with an on-line mall, the decision is made for you, as the on-line mall does the hosting; but if not, then you need to determine if your current Internet access provider should host your site or if you should shop elsewhere. Most services that provide Internet access also provide a few megabytes of disk space without additional charge on their server for you to put up a Web site. Most people starting small see this "free" disk space as a real money saver in getting their site off the ground. Certainly, this is an inexpensive option, especially if you're planning a small site, but there are both pros and cons to consider.

One of the cons to putting up your site in the disk space provided along with your Internet access is that these services rarely offer reporting facilities on the number of visitors, where the visitors came from (referring pages), what files they received, and so on. (There are third-party hit counters that are free or that charge a few dollars a month to report to you the number of times a file on your site was loaded. See the appendix for a list.)

Reports on the activity on your site are extremely important in making advertising decisions and can play an important part in determining whether or not you can attract advertisers to your site. (If you'll remember from chapter 4, the referring page information is how John Wells of Netstores NW discovered that the majority of visitors to his Movie Madness site who made purchases came from sites created by movie fans.) There is software available for servers that will prepare detailed reports on activity for each site on the server, but this costs the server extra so you can expect those costs to be passed on to you. Some ISPs choose to write custom programs to generate their own reports for sites, and cybermalls regularly offer complete reports to participants. When determining who will host your site, you may want to comparison-shop for reporting capability as well as price and other services.

Next you need to determine whom to involve inside your organization. Do you want to build your site yourself or have someone else do it for you? Like Phil Lipton of the IBDA, you may decide you'd rather save money by doing it yourself. Or like Bryce McGuire of Satellite Consultants, you may decide that you want to hire someone who already has the equipment and the know-how. If you want to do Web site design work as a career, then of course you'll want to make your Web page a showcase for your work in order to attract customers. In addition, you may need to have photographs or artwork done for your site, and now's the time to start thinking about that.

You'll also want to think about the involvement necessary to maintain the site. Will you be managing the site? Will an existing employee be in charge, or will you be hiring someone?

If you are in a larger organization, you may find yourself needing help and resources from systems, database administrators, marketing, public relations, and other parts of your organization. Of course, the best time to get their input is in the planning stages when you're developing the content and doing the research, but we mention it here because it's not until this stage that you're likely to think of others in your organization. These groups may have critical input that will change the content you will want to feature, so having them involved from the beginning will help cement their commitment to the project. If you haven't already, you may need to go back a couple of steps and ask for ideas or go ahead and present your plans as a springboard, then ask for input.

STEP 4: BUILD AND TEST

The plans are made, the content is ready, and now it's time to build the site. (We talk about the tools you need to do it yourself later in this chapter.) This process can go very quickly, depending on the size of the site. However, it's important that testing be done frequently and by a number of other people both inside and outside your organization before the site is announced to the public. Testing will give you the opportunity to see what works and what doesn't and will help you build momentum when it's time to promote your site. It's tough to get people to look at a site again when they've had an unsatisfying experience, so make your first shot as good as you possibly can.

Part of your testing should include thorough spell-checking. You can run a spell-checker from a word processor over your HTML code, although it can be a tedious process due to all the "code" the spell-checker won't recognize. But you should also have other people proofread your Web pages. While proofreading seems like an obvious point, you'd be surprised how many people don't do it and then find themselves embarrassed later.

STEP 5: PROMOTE

It is important to take into account how you plan to promote your site during the planning stages before you build the site. There are techniques for building your site that will help you promote it and that will help you get help promoting the site from search engines, which is one of the key ways people will find your site. Promoting your site is so important that we spend an entire chapter, chapter 8, on how to do it. We recommend that you read chapter 8 on promoting your site before you start designing it, as you will find information there that will probably change your plans.

STEP 6: MAINTAIN AND UPDATE

In chapter 6, we identified one of the biggest mistakes that businesses make in building a Web site is not allocating resources to the site once it's been built. Besides making sure someone answers the e-mail, it's important to design your site so it has something people come back for, and that means there have to be maintenance and regular updates on the site. Nothing generates less interest than a stagnant site where nothing is happening. So it's important to consider the cost of regular maintenance and updates as an ongoing cost of having a Web site. For the purposes of estimating, you can figure you'll spend between 10 and 20 percent of the cost of building the site per year to maintain it. Tools for building the site and updating those tools are part of the maintenance cost of the site we'll cover next.

Tools You Need

For the purposes of addressing the widest possible audience, we're going to talk about tools you'll need from the point of view of those who are building the Web site themselves and hosting that site using an ISP. While some companies, such as Amazon.com, have spent upwards of $20 million developing a Web site, we're going to limit ourselves to what can be done for a few thousand dollars. Obviously, if you're not coding HTML, developing graphics, or preparing photos for display on the Internet, then you won't need the tools we'll talk about. But a look at this section will help you better understand what your developers will be doing.

Software

While you might think we'd start with buying computer hardware, then talk about purchasing software, the smart thing to do is just the opposite. You need software to develop a Web page. While it is possible to use software, such as a text editor, that is already included with a computer, most beginners buy software to generate the HTML code for them. In addition, there is software that will help you create graphic images and modify photos for use on your Web site.

There seems to be no end to the number of products on the market to lay out Web pages, then generate the HTML code for you so that all you have to do is upload or transfer the HTML files created by the program to the host computer (a task known on the Internet as "ftp"). Some HTML-generating programs will even help you with the ftp. Many HTML generators are available for under $100. The most popular for the Intel-based PC platform include Microsoft's *FrontPage* and Sausage Software's *HotDog*. For the Macintosh, expect to pay under $200 for the most popular titles such as Adobe's *PageMill* and Claris's *Home Page*. These products will help you create Web pages quickly, but don't expect that you'll be able to do everything automatically. Almost every Web page designer we talked with said that although authoring tools helped, they invariably had to make changes in the HTML code themselves in order to get exactly what they wanted.

As for developing graphics and modifying scanned photos, favorite graphics software tools include Adobe *Photoshop* (available for both the PC and the Macintosh platforms) and *CorelDRAW!* But expect to pay in the $500-to-$1,000 range for these graphical software tools. For animation, you can use the tools that you use in developing graphic images. After all, animation is simply a number of images displayed quickly one after another to produce the illusion of motion.

TIP *You can often get expensive software bundled with hardware for less than you could buy both separately. For example, we've seen examples of Adobe's* Photoshop *packaged with an optical scanner used for scanning photographs.*

If you want to build Web pages that include sound or video, there are a number of tools available. In order to offer sound or video to your visitor, you must first record the sound or video, then translate it into a digitized format so it can be stored on the hard-disk drive in files. The next step is to encode the file into a format that can be played by visitors to your page, and then the file can be referenced in your HTML document. The advantage of sound is that you can record sounds using your PC or Macintosh, so they're already digitized, but digitizing video requires special hardware added to your PC so you can hook up video input from a VCR or video camera.

The most popular software for sound is *Real Audio,* and there's a version of *Real Audio* for video playback as well. Other popular formats include the *Media Player* built into Windows or Apple's *Quicktime* for both the PC and the Macintosh.

Software is constantly being updated, so the smartest thing to do is to go looking for a software package that will do what you want to do, then buy the hardware to run that software. Software packages list hardware requirements for both the minimum computer system needed to run the software (often referred to as the "required hardware") and for the hardware configuration that is easiest to use (often referred to as the "recommended hardware"). We recommend that you get the hardware that's listed as "recommended" rather than the minimum requirements because it can be difficult and frustrating to work with the minimum hardware necessary to perform a task, especially if you happen to be new at this. If you already have a computer, look for software that will run on the computer you have. If you've purchased your computer within the last two years, it's a pretty safe bet the computer you have will run the software you can buy for Web page development.

Computer System

The most obvious item that you need to build your own Web site is a computer system. It is not practical to build and maintain a site without one. What we mean by a computer system is a computer with a CD-ROM drive, a modem, an optical scanner, and a printer. You can expect to pay about $2,000 for a computer that will meet your needs in setting up a site, and most computers you can buy in the average consumer retail outlet will work just fine. In most cases, you can expect to have to add an optical scanner for digitizing photographs and a printer to the package price. If you just bought a computer for the first time, be aware that you will need to spend some time learning your way around the computer before putting up your Web site, so allow yourself that extra time.

Although it's okay to purchase a Macintosh computer for your Web site development, we recommend an Intel-based, IBM-compatible PC because the cost of ownership is less and it's more widely supported. But either will work. What you end up with will depend on your personal preferences.

If you plan to take photographs with a camera to put up on your Web site, you'll need either a digital camera or an optical scanner. A digital camera allows you to take photographs in a digital format and import the photos directly into your computer for placement on your Web pages without chemical developing of the images first. There are inexpensive digital cameras available that produce quick, low-quality images. If you're looking for sharp, clear, professional images, the digital cameras that produce those types of images cost thousands of dollars, but may be worth it for your application.

An inexpensive digital camera and a full-color optical scanner cost about the same—you can get either one for under $200. You may want to purchase both or just an optical scanner if you already have a camera or existing photos or artwork you'd like to use. An optical scanner takes any image on paper and uses light to scan the paper to create a digitized copy of the image that is then stored on your computer. Some scanners can be installed by connecting to the outside of your computer, to the parallel port, the way your printer connects to your computer. High-end optical scanners require installation of a special "card" or circuit board into your computer that helps the scanner translate the images into a format your computer can store. Installation of an optical scanner usually requires some knowledge of how computers work and can probably be done at the store where you purchase your computer. If you're interested in learning more about doing computer upgrades yourself, including information that will help you add an optical scanner, check out *Upgrade Your Own PC* by this book's co-author, Linda Rohrbough.

Once you have your computer software and hardware, you're ready to go to work building your Web site. The next sections focus on practical tried-and-true advice for making your site attractive to visitors.

C A S E   S T U D Y

PHIL LIPTON AND LORNE NIELSON
INTERNATIONAL BELT SANDER DRAG RACE ASSOCIATION
(IBDA)
POINT ROBERTS, WASHINGTON
HTTP://WWW.BELTSANDER-RACES.COM
PROMOTES THE HOBBY OF BELT SANDER DRAG RACING

Phil Lipton, a cabinetmaker, Lorne Nielson, co-owner of a lumber yard, and some friends were having drinks at Kiniski's Reef Tavern in 1987 when they started comparing notes on how a belt sander can get away from you. The conversation never died, and in 1989 a small group gathered behind Nielson's Lumber in Point Roberts, Washington, to see whose belt sander actually got away the fastest. "We started just for fun—just did it for a stupid thing to do," according to Phil, co-founder with Lorne of the International Belt Sander Drag Race Association (IBDA).

Now belt sander drag racing is catching on all over the U.S. and Canada. And the Nielson Lumber race is an annual event where five hundred to seven hundred people gather to watch up to forty participants drag-race belt sanders. The HWI cooperative of hardware stores has a contract with the IBDA to sponsor race days at participating hardware stores, which have also been well attended. In addition, power tool manufacturers Bosch, Makita, and Shop Vac sponsor the events and provide prizes for contestants. Hardware stores sign up to become a member of the IBDA for a fee and get an entire marketing in-store promotional program that includes everything from the dimensions of the track to a promotional how-to list.

Phil, who believes Web sites are the future of business because "eventually everyone will have a computer," came up with the idea of the site to promote the sport and to offer listings of events nationwide. "Getting stuff printed is very expensive. You can spend two thousand dollars to three thousand dollars printing one thousand brochures, and in a year those brochures are outdated and have to be thrown out." Instead of paying someone to build his Web site, Phil decided in 1996 to invest a little time and patience to learn how to do it himself. "I'd rather invest the money in the hardware that I can play with than pay someone," Phil added.

He bought an Intel-based PC with a modem, Microsoft's *FrontPage* and *Publisher* software, and an optical scanner that came bundled with Adobe *Photoshop*. By early 1997, Phil had the IBDA site up, and he learned how to put Quicktime movies on the site using a video camera, a video capture card for his PC, and *MGI Video Wave* software.

Phil said he learned by doing, but one of his toughest challenges was understanding how to make his Web site work. One of the things he had trouble understanding was that the pictures and videos on his homepage were each a separate file and each file had to be ftp'd (transferred) to his server. "I would test my page and see the graphics, like the movies, were missing. I thought that because I could see the graphics in *FrontPage,* that those graphics were automatically part of my HTML document. Fortunately, my ISP at iplus.net was small enough that I could call and ask him questions. He helped me get it right," Phil added.

Phil promotes his site in a number of ways, including an ad on the back cover of *Fine Woodworking* magazine. He started by publicizing the URL assigned by his ISP, www.iplus.net/ibda/. The uniqueness of the races got the site a lot of attention and several awards. For example, Yahoo, one of the largest search engines on the Internet, listed the IBDA site as one of its "Weekly Picks." Later, Phil got the IBDA its own domain name, www.belt-sander-races.com, and linked the old domain name to the new one. But he wishes he'd done his own domain name right away. "I would have definitely set it up right the first time had I had the forethought and known that this was going to be the success it is." In fact, Phil said the experience made him book a domain name for his own personal cabinetmaking business site several months before that site was available.

The IBDA is growing and races are being held all over North America. Phil said one of the functions of the site is to help promote the sport by listing a schedule of races including the city, location, and time. In fact, belt sander drag racing has become so popular that Phil and Lorne have already realized their dream of an annual event. Winners of local races are eligible to attend the IBDA world championship, held each year in Indianapolis.

Stuff You Need to Know

Before we get into design considerations and tips on developing your Web site, we need to cover the basic mechanics of what occurs when you develop a site and some information on the types of files that it contains.

The Mechanics of Your Web Page

When you develop a Web site, you generate HTML code in the form of one or more files, which together make up your Web page. The server is a computer connected full-time to the Internet on which your Web page is stored. If you do not own the server, you must transfer a copy of your Web page to the server. This practice is referred to as "sending up," "uploading" or "ftp-ing" (pronounced "f-teepee-ing"). The acronym ftp stands for file transfer protocol.

You'll probably need special software for this task, such as WS-

FTP for the PC or *Fetch* for the Mac. These programs and others like them are available on the Internet. You'll enter your name and a password into the software. Once the software establishes communication with the server, it will show you the contents of both the server and your hard-disk drive. Most programs let you use your mouse to drag and drop the icons representing your files over to a window that represents the host computer, then your computer will make a copy of those files on the server. The Webmaster on the system where your site is stored can give you more detailed information on how to ftp your Web page to the server.

Once your Web page files are available and a request has been made from the Internet to your server for your Web page document, the HTML file is sent first. Usually this file is called INDEX.HTML. If you added pictures, graphics, sound, animation, or video to your Web page, that data is stored in separate files that are referenced in the first HTML file. Once the initial HTML file has been delivered, your computer looks at that file and sends requests back to your host server for any other files that are mentioned in your initial Web page document.

File-based Mechanics

The other files used for your Web pages for graphics, photos, animation, sound, and video will have filename extensions that indicate the file type. The extension isn't the only indication of the type of file. There are clues at the beginning of files that indicate to the programs designed to use them what type of information is in the file (so you can't just rename a file and make it a different type of file). However, filename extensions are a good indicator.

> **TIP** *While UNIX and the Macintosh allow four character extensions for filenames, Intel-compatible PCs allow only three-character filename extensions. So you'll often see Web page files named like this: index.htm. This is still an HTML file, but it was developed on an Intel-based PC.*

The table in Figure 7-1 gives you a list of filename extensions and the type of file that extension indicates for the most commonly used

FILE EXTENSION	FILE TYPE
html, htm	HTML
jpeg, jpg	photo or graphic
gif	photo, graphic or animation
wav, ra, au, aiff, midi	sound
avi, qt, rm, ram, mov, moov, mpeg	video

FIGURE 7-1: *A table of typical filename extensions and the file types they represent.*

files in Web pages on the Internet. There are issues involved in developing Web pages that have to do with file formats such as using software to generate certain types of files and the fact that some formats are smaller than others (which makes these formats faster to transfer across the Internet).

Fortunately, there are software programs to help you with all this, so you don't have to be an expert on file formats, uploading, or servers in order to set up a Web page. You will find, however, that the more you know about file formats, the easier it will be for you to understand what you're doing. We encourage you to investigate file formats further if you plan to develop your own Web pages by using the resources we've listed for you in the appendix.

Design Considerations

We could write an entire book (and many people have) on Web page design. However, since this is a book about doing business on the Internet, we're going to limit ourselves to what we feel are the most critical and practical points—considerations that affect your bottom line. These points include ways to make your site easy for visitors to navigate and practical points that will keep you from making obvious and amateurish mistakes.

Tricks Visitors Use That Affect Your Design

It's important to keep in mind when building a Web site that users on the Internet are in control and they make all the choices. If a site loads too slowly, a visitor can simply "click off," which means he or she stops the process by clicking on a "Stop" button at the top of the Internet browser. The visitor is then free to type in another URL, go back a page and take a different route to another site, or whatever.

The other option Web surfers have, and one that is damaging to advertiser-supported sites, is to simply turn off the graphics. Most Internet browsers have an "Options" menu that allows users the option of turning off the automatic loading of graphic images (sometimes called the "Show Pictures" option). This means banner ads, as well as any other image, won't be loaded after the HTML file is received. If users decide the graphics on a page are worth seeing, they can simply change the option to automatically load graphic images, then click on the reload option to ask for the page to be sent up again. For those with a slower Internet connection, turning off graphics makes Web surfing much faster, as there's no waiting for large images to load. (We give tips on how you can make your images load faster in the Practical Tips section later in this chapter.)

How do these visitor tricks affect your Web design considerations? Well, for one thing, you need to hold the visitor's interest, grabbing it with something interesting as quickly as possible. In addition, you need to decide what audience you're aiming to attract. If you want to talk to the masses, then you need to design your site so it can be successfully navigated with graphics off or minimize the graphics so the user who decides to turn graphics back on doesn't get frustrated while waiting and go elsewhere. Sound, animation, and video also take time to load, so adding these files, unless you've hooked your visitor into waiting, will also prove frustrating.

If you're aiming at a higher-income visitor or a highly motivated group of people seeking special niche information, you can get away with including more bells and whistles. But the safe place to be is behind the curve. Whatever speed modem is the latest on the market, you can figure your average user has half that speed and the masses are probably at a third to a fourth of that speed. So, for example, if a 57,600 bps modem is the hot one, then half your visitors will probably have 33,600 bps, and the majority will be at 28,800 bps. So it's important to know whom you're aiming at and design accordingly.

Help Visitors Navigate Your Site

If you've been surfing the Web, then you soon realize how frustrating it is to visit a site, click around, and suddenly realize you don't know where you are or how to get back. You look at the bottom of the page you're on, but there's no clue how to get back to where you started or how to get anywhere else. If you're a savvy user of your Internet browser, you can work your way back using the history (or cache) the browser keeps of where you've been, but this is inconvenient and interrupts the flow of surfing.

As someone responsible for the Web site design, you should make sure visitors have an easy time getting around your site. One of the

FIGURE 7-2: *The Pacific Partners homepage* (courtesy Pacific Partners Mortgage Corporation).

best ways to do this is to provide a navigation graphic on the left side or the top of each page of the site that tells the visitor where he is now and where else he can go. The Pacific Partners site, whose homepage is shown in Figure 7-2, is an example of how this can be done. The company starts with these images on the opening page, which it then revamps as a navigation tool for subsequent pages, as shown in Figure 7-3. Navigation tools are always on the left side of any particular page. The beauty of this concept is that it also speeds access to the individual pages of the site for the visitor, as many of the graphics can be downloaded once initially and then reused for each page.

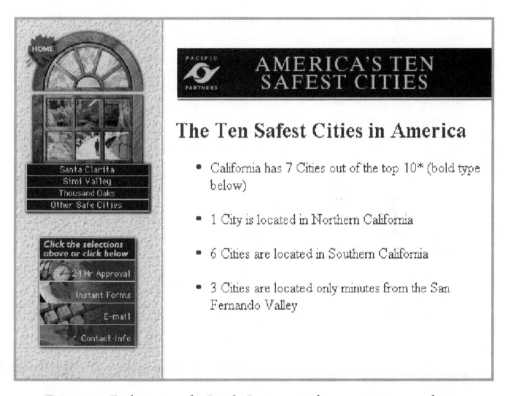

FIGURE 7-3: *Each page on the Pacific Partners site has a navigation graphic on the left side that makes the site easy for visitors to use[1] (courtesy Pacific Partners Mortgage Corporation).*

---

[1]The site credits a 1996 Crime Report and the U.S. Census Bureau for the ten safest cities information.

> **DISCLAIMER** *Web sites are subject to constant change, so don't expect to go to the Pacific Partners Mortgage Corporation site and see the exact same pages you see reproduced here.*

Another point that goes along with helping visitors navigate your site is to avoid long pages of text to be scrolled through. Unless there's a compelling reason not to, information should be divided into categories and subcategories that visitors can choose from at will.

CASE STUDY

DAVID DICKSTEIN
PACIFIC PARTNERS MORTGAGE CORPORATION
WOODLAND HILLS, CALIFORNIA
HTTP://WWW.PACPARTNERS.COM
MORTGAGE BROKERS

David Dickstein was a University of Southern California graduate in business who'd spent seventeen years in the mortgage business, moved up to the senior vice president level, then decided to open his own mortgage firm. He brought in as equal partners his wife, his daughter, and her husband and formed Pacific Partners Mortgage Corporation in 1996. The company grew to ten employees with annual revenues of $600,000.

Being a forward-looking kind of guy, Dave decided the firm needed a presence on the Internet. "I'm convinced if you don't get involved in the Internet now, you're going to be way behind trying to catch on later. By that time, the pioneers will be getting the ultimate efficiencies from the system," Dave said.

So Dave set up a site, but to his dismay, the site produced a few inquiries but no significant responses. "So I spent about four months checking out all the sites the mortgage lending publications said were productive." Dave said he found the good sites had good graphics that loaded fast and they were designed like electronic magazines with a table of contents on every page.

"I realized our original site had way too much text and scrolling. It was kind of an ego trip for us. We had all kinds of background information we thought people would be interested in—but they weren't. We didn't know our audience," Dave added.

But Dave found out about his audience. He discovered that those who visited his site were Generation X-ers, ages twenty-five to thirty-five, college educated, earning $65,000 to $75,000 annually. So Dave asked himself, "What is it about Generation X that's important?" and looked to demographic studies for the answer. "I found sources that said Generation X is a bright group that doesn't want to work forever for a single company. They don't like waiting, tend to be independent, hate glitz and gimmicks, and don't like to be pushed into decisions. Also, they're often first-time home buyers and the majority of first-time home buyers are in California, where we are.

"We wanted to stay away from the markets the banks were after and focus on special-needs people like first-time home buyers, because that's where we felt we had a shot at developing business. In niche marketing, the Internet levels the playing field," he added.

Once Dave had a definition of his audience and research to guide him in overhauling the site, he decided to cut down the amount of text by eliminating it or dividing it into sections. In addition, he included specific information important to first-time home buyers, like the "safest cities" section. And he determined that interesting, high-quality graphics that loaded fast were important. Those graphics, he decided, were the only way he could communicate that Pacific Partners is a top-quality company people can trust.

So Dave contacted a friend who had a graphics studio and expressed his desire for good graphic design without compromising navigation speed and his idea for the "magazine" approach. Dave defined the magazine approach as the ability to get quickly to an index from anywhere on the site in order to go directly to the topic of interest. He also wanted visitors to be able to fill out a short, preapproval loan form right on the site, send it in instantly, and get an answer back within twenty-four hours. But Dave specifically determined to avoid cute animation or any other "fun" stuff that doesn't get customers closer to getting a loan.

The new site was a success right away. Dave said Pacific Partners gets three to five requests a day for loan preapprovals that convert into about one new loan a week. Four to five extra loans a month, without the overhead of paying sales commissions, is "gold," Dave added.

As for the future, Dave plans to leverage his site to produce even more business by developing relationships with professionals who can help his company sell loans. For example, the safest cities section lends itself to links with real estate agents in those areas who can help busy potential buyers find suitable homes.

Browser Compatibility Issues

As you might expect, people who aren't using the latest hardware to surf the Internet are also usually not using the latest Internet browser. This happens for lots of reasons. For example, if the latest browser requires Windows 95, and the user's machine won't run Windows 95, then they're going to be forced to use a browser that's not as up-to-date. The more up-to-date browsers allow Web page designers more options for doing "fancy" stuff.

In addition, there are browser wars going on, so incompatibility may be purposefully introduced between browsers made by two different manufacturers. Unfortunately, what's compatible and what isn't and what browser supports what features change all the time. You have a couple of options for dealing with this challenge. You can write two (or more) versions of your site and then query users as to which version of which browser they have before you send the pages (and this can be automated). The easiest thing to do is to stay behind the technology a year or maybe even two years, so you can be assured your page will be visible by almost anyone who comes to your site.

Make It So That Visitors Can Order or Make Inquiries On-line

If you're offering something for sale or expect visitors to contact you, create ways for them to do so on-line. Most people who run Web sites have several telephone lines as do many businesses, so it's easy to forget that the average person has a single phone line. If they're visiting your site, that phone line is already in use. So if you offer a toll-free number or a fax service, your average visitor will have to get off-line to contact you. That means either getting off-line right then to call or leaving the computer to find a paper and pencil to make a note of your product, company, and telephone number and trying to remember to call later. Either way, you risk losing that customer.

The best answer is to allow customers to fill out a short form on-line that you can process the next business day. Be sure to follow up so their effort in providing you with information is rewarded and if there's an order, be sure to confirm the order. Some sites provide a frequently-asked-questions (FAQ, pronounced "fak") section to handle the most common inquiries, and this is an excellent idea. However, we've been told over and over in interviews that visitors will make a couple of e-mail inquiries before they actually order just so they can feel comfortable that real people are on the other end. So expect inquiries that may have already been answered in the FAQ or are just trivial questions, but answer all such e-mail questions promptly and courteously.

If you can't let visitors order on-line because you can't take credit cards or you want to use the personal touch of one-to-one telephone communication, let visitors give you their contact information and times when they're available as an additional option to calling a toll-free number. Then you can make a personal call to them at their convenience or send them materials by using regular mail (or "snail mail," as it's known on the Internet). Be sure to print on the outside of the mail piece or say in the beginning of the conversation that your follow-up is due to a request they made on your Web site. And be prepared to remind them of what the product or service is that you're offering.

Practical Tips

Just as we've tried to stay in the mainstream on design considerations, we're also limiting ourselves to the presentation of the most standard practical tips for Web site construction. These have to do with tips that will help you make your pages load faster, how to maximize your use of graphics when you use them, and some ways to use color.

Make Your Site Load Faster

It's in your interest as a Web page builder to have a fast modem and be connected to the Internet via services that are also fast. So it's easy to forget that the average Joe probably has a modem that's less than half the speed of yours and may be accessing the Internet from a service provider that adds lots of layers of processing to his connection, therefore slowing down the process even further. Hence, it's important to make your page as efficient as possible without sacrificing a professional and attractive appearance.

One of the most important considerations in building a Web site is to take into account the capability of your visitors. As we've said before, the biggest bottleneck in Internet performance from a surfer's viewpoint is the transmission speed of the page and not usually the ability to display the information once it arrives. The speed at which your page can be delivered to the visitor's computer is directly related to the size of your page and the speed of the connection.

The size of your page in bits is important because the larger your page, the more packets will be needed for transmission to your visitor. To give you an idea, we've captured a simple HTML document in an Internet browser with a heading and a couple of paragraphs of text as shown in Figure 7-4. This HTML code is 1 kilobyte (KB), which is the equivalent of 1024 bytes in size. At eight bits to a byte, that translates to 8,192 bits. At a modem speed of 36,600 bits per second (bps), even accounting for several hops, it's reasonable for this file to be delivered across the Internet in under a single second. To your visitor with a 36,600 bps (or 33.6 Kbps) modem it would seem as if the transmission were almost instantaneous.

HTML Is Easy To Learn

Welcome to the world of HTML. This is the first paragraph.

Here is yet another example of a paragraph. Instructions in HTML code are set off by tags. Tags are greater-than and less-than signs that indicate to the browser how the text in-between should be handled when the web page document is displayed. As you can see, there isn't much complexity to the basics of HTML!

FIGURE 7-4: *Shown as it would be displayed by an Internet browser, this 1 KB HTML file would be delivered and displayed in under a second to a site visitor with a 33.6 Kbps modem.*

FIGURE 7-5: *This GIF format image in color would take about fifteen seconds to load over the Internet to a visitor with a 36.6 Kbps modem (courtesy Corel Corporation).*

However, if we added a graphic image like the one in Figure 7-5, then the HTML file would still be delivered almost instantaneously, but this image would take considerably longer. In a GIF format, this image of a red flower on a black background in 256 color resolution is 48 kilobytes (KB) in the size shown above. Using the same calculations we used for the HTML file, the flower image would be 393,216 bits. At 36.6 Kbps, it would take this file nearly 11 seconds for the modem to receive, and that doesn't count the additional time spent in transit for a larger file. More realistically, it could take abut fifteen seconds or so for this file to arrive at our visitor's PC. These estimates do not take into account any of the myriad of problems that could further slow transmission, such as other visitors requesting the same file or a high volume of traffic on the end the visitor is using.

As you can see, there are obvious advantages in making your site as compact as possible. In addition, it's important to take into account the space the files take on the server hosting your site. This is because space on most servers is sold in megabytes, usually in chunks of 5 to 10 MB each. The less space you use to store your site, the less you'll pay. Linda Hammer, who runs a site to reunite people called The Seeker (http://www.theseeker.com) found storage space to be a problem because of the large number of photos she scans in and posts on her site. While she was doing all she could to optimize the photos, her ISP was charging her over $400 a month for disk space on the server, and it became obvious she needed to make her site advertiser supported in order for it to survive.

Use JPEG Instead of GIF for Photos

As we mentioned before, Internet browsers pretty much use two file formats for graphics, GIF and JPEG. Both formats offer compression, meaning the file is made smaller by squeezing it down and the browser unsqueezes it for display when it's received. However, one fact that is often lost on new Web page designers is that JPEG (which stands for Joint Photographic Experts Group) was created and optimized for use with images that have many mixed colors, like photographs. GIF was designed with images that have horizontal areas of the same color and will create a smaller image than JPEG on the same color graphics like logos, colored text stored as graphics, and cartoons.

The upshot is photographs are usually smaller in a JPEG format, while logos and other graphics with fields of a solid color are usually smaller when stored in the GIF file format. The difference can be significant—like four to five times the file size. Of course, we care about this because the smaller we can make our graphics, the faster they will load to our visitors.

Use a White Background

The default background color for a Web page, meaning the color that is displayed if you don't specifically state a color, is gray. While any HTML book or guide will tell you don't use that gray background, it's important to note that the wildly successful team of David Filo and Jerry Yang has used the default background on their well-known Yahoo search engine site for many years. The choice of this background doesn't appear to have hurt those guys. Yahoo has been designed so that anyone with any browser connected to the Internet at any speed can have a satisfying experience. It might be worthwhile to take another look at the Yahoo site with this in mind.

However, the next least obtrusive and fastest-loading color is white. (Some browers automatically switch a gray background to white for the user.) While some people get away with using other background colors, we want to warn you that most of the time the use of wild or complex backgrounds gives the site an amateurish, clumsy look. We recommend avoiding such backgrounds and sticking with white. It makes for a clean look and allows you some tricks with graphic images, which we'll explain next.

Transparent Graphics

Graphics are usually rectangles, as you can see in Figure 7-5. However, you can get that cool "transparent" look without a lot of trouble by simply changing the background color of the graphic to the background color of your Web page. If you use white, as we recommend, this works very well and often can be done without buying any graphics software. For example, we used Paint, the graphics program that comes with Windows 95, to change all the background color of the graphic shown in Figure 7-5 to white, as you can see in Figure 7-6. Since the background of our printed page is white, we get the effect of having a transparent background.

If you have a graphics program such as Adobe *Photoshop* or Corel *Photo-Paint* (which comes with *CorelDRAW*) you can make a transparent background for your image by specifying a color of your choice as the background color. When the Web browser displays

FIGURE 7-6: *A white background color against a white page creates the illusion of transparency. Compare with Figure 7-5.*

your image on the page, it will not display the background color, and so the image appears to have a transparent background. This is important on pages where you have a more complex background and want a more elegant look.

Resolution

In graphic imaging terms, resolution refers to the number of individual "picture elements" (pixels) per inch that make up an image. While pixels don't necessarily translate on a one-to-one basis to the term "dots" used in the popular measurement "dots per inch" (dpi), it works for our purposes here for you to think of it that way. Most scanners will scan images at 300 x 300 dpi, but that is much higher resolution than is necessary for reproducing an image good enough for the average viewer. For example, most newspapers use photographs scanned at 75 x 75 dpi.

Obviously, the higher the dpi, the larger the file image becomes, but the sharper the image will look. For the purpose of transmitting images on the Internet, the lower the resolution the better, since smaller images transmit faster. While high-resolution images of 1200 x 1200 dpi make for great *National Geographic*–type photos, unless the audience you're aiming at has the money to spend for a monitor that will display an image of that quality, you're simply wasting your time and money to provide that level of resolution, not to mention the time of the people waiting to see the image. But you lose resolution as the image is scanned and reproduced, so you want to start with images that are not blurred or cluttered, but are as high quality as possible.

It's also important to note that Internet browsers will display images you create about two and a half times larger than the size of the image if you were to print it. Consequently, you'll want to create images significantly smaller than the size you want your visitors to see. As anyone in the printing business will tell you, reducing an image makes it sharper. This means you can use lower-resolution images. You can also cut down transfer time by choosing the number and type of colors used to display the image, as you'll see next.

Color Tips

Another way to make graphic images smaller so they load faster is to reduce the number of colors in an image. Most programs designed for modifying graphical images allow for a choice in the number of colors the image is saved in. For example, an image saved in 16 colors will be smaller in size than the same image saved in 256 colors or 16 million colors.

Another problem with color on the Internet is getting images to display the same way on everyone's computer. Since different people are likely to have monitors capable of displaying varying colors and since browsers also have varying ways of displaying color, you can end up with a site that looks great to you, but awful to someone visiting.

The culprit is "dithering." The way a computer display gets around displaying a color that it doesn't have available is to mix the color itself. Screen displays are made of pixels, so if the computer display doesn't have the shade of green that your site uses it may try to create it by mixing a few pixels of another color into the green it does have. This process, called dithering, works okay if the pixels are small enough, but chances are if the computer display doesn't have the color available, it's a less expensive display, meaning it also has large pixels. The combination of dithering and large pixel size makes for colors that look pretty crummy. To further complicate things, Intel-based PCs and Macintosh machines dither colors differently.

The answer is to avoid dithered colors, and fortunately there are sites on the Net that will help you with this. If you use "dithered colors" or "dithering" as a keyword in the search engines, you'll find there's always someone who is discussing this topic on his or her Web site. Usually these folks are pretty credible. For example, Netscape Communications has addressed dithering on its site.

Make Changing Information Text, Not Graphics

Internet browsers have a type style they use to display all incoming text. If you want the text to look different than the "default" type style, you must make the text into a graphic, then display the graphic as you would any other picture. If you have information on your site that changes frequently, the extra step of converting text into graphics will become quite painful in a short time. One of the most common things that occurs in trying to quickly convert text to graphic images is the introduction of spelling and grammar errors that often require repetition of the process to correct the error. A smarter way to handle this is to create an attractive setting for changing content by surrounding it by interesting graphics but leaving your text as text. This way, changes to the information on your site can be accomplished rapidly.

There is much more information on the subject of Web page creation available on the Internet and from third-party sources. This information is intended to be a springboard from which you can launch into intelligent appreciation of the information you'll find out there. We would encourage you to use the search engines employing keywords like "web page design" and HTML to find the latest information on what's happening.

While you're creating your Web site, you'll want to get the paperwork started for your domain name. That information is next.

CASE STUDY

SUSAN ESHELMAN
ART VISION INTERNATIONAL
GABRIOLA ISLAND, BRITISH COLUMBIA, CANADA
HTTP://WWW.AABC.COM
VIRTUAL ART GALLERY

Susan Eshelman's interest in marketing art led eventually to the start of her on-line business, Art Vision International (AVI). Her quest began when she herself was an artist struggling to find buyers for her own art. In marketing her work, which she as a Muslim describes as "art of a spiritual nature for the ceremonial market," Susan and her husband drove around the U.S. to find galleries and dealers who would carry her art. After keeping at it for some time, Susan said she found she had a distribution network her artist friends admired and eventually began representing them as well. AVI grew out of her representation of other artists.

Susan watched the Internet become a graphical environment, and she could see that the banking industry was committed to spending millions on the Net. "We knew the medium would turn into a good marketplace," she said. So Susan and her husband went to a "techie," described what they wanted, and asked what it would cost. They were stunned to get a six-figure estimate but decided to start anyway, feeding the venture as it went along.

Susan said the development started in February 1995, the site went up by October of that year, went through a testing stage, then they officially launched the AVI site in March 1996. "During the test-marketing period, we invited a select group of people to use the site so we could test it with different browsers, measure download times, and really look at issues of speed and image quality," Susan said.

They aimed at new artists looking for exposure, but Susan said, "Selling five-hundred-dollar application fees to starving artists was 'challenging.'" To help new clients, they put together a how-to guide to explain what was required in terms of how to get art photographed and ready for placement on the Web site. Then they hopped in the car and "beat the bushes" to attract artists. Susan said sometimes they'd stop in a town, find an art gallery, and ask the owner, "Who lives here that's good?" Now they have artists coming to them, but in the beginning Susan said it was difficult because the $500 fee didn't even cover their costs.

In dealing with buyers, Susan said they discovered that the corporate market is interested in high-quality art as an investment but does not like to spend a lot of money paying agents to find art. Consequently, there's often a single individual acting as the corporate collection agent responsible for art acquisitions. Susan says she tries to help those corporate buyers find what they're looking for, even if AVI doesn't have it. "Let's say a buyer comes to us saying, 'We're looking for pieces of alabaster sculpture.' Even if we don't make a commission on that sale, if we help the agent find what he or she is looking for, we become the important point of contact for that corporate agent," Susan added. On occasion, AVI has put together a private gallery for a specific buyer on the Net and allowed them to surf it at their leisure. "Like any other retail business—good personal customer service is necessary," Susan maintains.

While Susan said the initial six-figure estimate for building the site seemed high, she now estimates she has spent well over a million dollars in time as well as money on the AVI Web page. "This puts us in between the big commercial sites and the little individual homepages. We may be spending more than other galleries, but we want to be the most prominent and best gallery on the block," she added.

Susan said the Internet allows her to live and work from her home on an island. She uses a ferry to come and go from the mainland. AVI allows her to bring to bear what she considers her best talent, which she discovered by reading the ferry bulletin board. "Someone would have an ad saying they need a refrigerator and I'd see another ad for a refrigerator for sale. Or someone put up an ad for a lost a gray cat and I'd see another ad for someone who found a gray cat. I used to call those people and put them together. Now I do that on the Internet," she quipped.

According to Susan, more businesses fail on the Net because they can't manage the flow of contact from the world outside their Web site. She says she answers over one thousand e-mails a day. Of necessity, she has automated many of her answers to standard e-mail inquiries. "We just are snowed in always by e-mail."

One of the things that Susan believes has helped AVI is that she's been able to get "super" professional people to come work for her because they want to live on the island. "People are leaving the big eastern cities, and we can get them to work for us for less. We also get pregnant women and new mothers. Many of our pages were designed by a programmer who was home nursing a child. I see people who want to build a successful business but are not willing to do deals and bargain and cut-rate fees. We couldn't afford to build this business in Montreal."

Susan said it takes a lot of skills to make a business on the Internet happen. But her advice to those starting out is to always keep your eye on the primary ball. "In our case, it's selling fine art. If you diversify too much, you forget why you're in business."

As for the future, Susan is aiming at expanding via affiliate galleries. "One of the remarkable parts of the unfolding of AVI was we came to the attention of other professional art brokers around the world. We had a couple come along who wanted to buy the business and we said, 'You can't buy the business—we're just building it.' So we sold them a franchise. We did the programming for them and they gather the artists and make the lion's share of the commission on sales." AVI now has affiliate galleries in Latin America,

Spain, Vietnam, Ireland, Singapore, and Australia and is expecting more countries to be represented in the future.

Domain Names

A domain name is an Internet address made up of letters instead of the cryptic IP address numbers that computers use to contact each other in cyberspace. A good domain name is easy to remember and has something to do with your business. For example, the domain name for Putnam, who is the publisher of this book, is *www.putnam.com* and its IP address is *192.251.67.92*. While you can use the IP address as a URL to direct your browser to Putnam's site, it's much easier to remember the domain name.

The InterNIC Registration Service physically located at Network Solutions in Herndon, Virginia, assigns IP addresses and domain names based on an application and payment of a fee. (You'll remember Network Solutions is a cooperative effort of the National Science Foundation and AT&T.) However, you can visit there on the Internet to get application forms and other information at http://www.internic.net. Currently, domain name registration is $70 for two years, then $35 a year for each year after that, due on the anniversary date that your domain name was assigned.*

Domain names follow certain conventions. For example, a domain name of a business for profit will end in the three-character extension *.com* for *commercial*. A table of common extensions for the United States follows. (There are more extensions for domain names than these, but these are the most common.)

While you and your visitors can use the URL provided by your ISP, you probably want the more professional look of your own "virtual" domain name so it looks like this: *www.yoursite.com*. You can get your own domain name by applying to the InterNIC via fax, e-mail, or regular mail (also known as "snail mail")—or your ISP can do it for

---

*Those who registered domain names on or before March 31, 1998, paid $100 for two years and must pay $50 a year starting the third year to keep their domain names. Starting April 1, 1998, the fees for new domain name registrations were reduced to $70 for the first two years and $35 a year thereafter.

EXTENSION	CONVENTIONAL USE
.com	commercial organizations
.org	nonprofit organizations
.net	Web servers and Internet maintenance sites (Your ISP may have a .net extension instead of .com)
.edu	educational institutions like universities
.gov	government sites
.us	local government sites such as county courthouses, state-run libraries, and state legislatures

you. The advantage of having your ISP do the application is that a domain name requires a unique IP address and the InterNIC is becoming increasingly reluctant to hand out these unique numbers. The number of IP addresses available in the current format is about four billion, but at the present rate of Internet growth, the InterNIC has already expressed concern it may run out of IP addresses. Your ISP probably already got a block of IP addresses just for the purpose of providing domain names to business clients, so that all that needs to be done is to request a unique domain name assignment to that IP address. Some ISPs charge extra for this and others will do it without an additional charge, so check with your ISP to see what its policy is on domain name registration.

> **TIP** *While it's advantageous to you to have your ISP register your domain name for you, we recommend you make sure you get the domain name registered in your name, rather than having it registered to your ISP. If the domain name is considered yours, then if you change ISPs, you simply submit a modified application to the Inter-NIC with the new ISP and IP information and your domain name remains unchanged. Your visitors will never know you moved.*

Find a Unique Domain Name

The InterNIC has a service that allows you to test the domain names you've chosen to see if anyone else has the name, and if so, who it is. The service is called WHOIS. This allows you to see if the domain name you have in mind is taken. However, to be on the safe side, don't publish the name you've chosen until you receive confirmation from the InterNIC. Names are given out on a first-come, first-served basis, and someone might have beaten you to the domain name you registered.

You should also be aware that while the standard format for domain names is *www.yourbusiness.com*, you don't have to use the *www*. You can have a domain name that is just *yourbusiness.com* minus the *www* part. The www part stands for World Wide Web, which in the early days of the Internet was the hot spot because it was the "graphical" portion of the Internet where visitors could see pictures. Now

> **TIP** *If you are from outside the U.S. or are registering a domain name with the .gov extension for a U.S. government agency, the InterNIC doesn't handle your request. For example, Canadian domain names are handled by CA Domain. However, the InterNIC has references to the various domain name registries worldwide for each country or situation at its homepage, so that's still the place to start.*

the entire Internet is graphical, so all that remains of the meaning of *www* is its connotation for being just a little better, and that is even slipping away. This gives you additional options for a domain name.

You can also have several domain names, but each one is billed separately and treated separately. Also, if you'd like to change your domain name, that's the same as requesting a new name as far as the InterNIC is concerned.

InterNIC Domain Name Application Tips

We've provided a sample of an InterNIC domain name registration application in the appendix. There is a separate instruction document available with the application at the InterNIC site to help you fill out the application, and most of the material the form asks for is not difficult to provide. The only areas where you need to have information available to you before you start the application are for the Primary and Secondary Name Server questions.

ISPs are expected to have two computers connected to the Internet so that one is a backup in case the other goes down. These are the primary (or active) and secondary name servers. This is where the domain name service (DNS) will point any visitors who want to view your site. Your ISP will have the domain names and IP addressses of its primary and secondary servers, so you'll need to ask for that information. In addition, the InterNIC will verify the registration with your ISP, so make sure you've checked with the ISP first before you apply for a domain name.

> **TIP**   *You may want to start your domain name application after the planning stages for your site but before you build. Registration can be accomplished in a twenty-four-hour period, but if a problem arises, it can take much longer. If you give yourself some time, you can be working on your site while the paperwork is in motion.*

Conclusion

In this chapter we've given you the basic information you need to start building your own Web site. Starting with the procedure for putting together a site, we've talked about the mechanics involved, the tools you need, design considerations, practical tips including how to make your site load faster, and information on how to register your domain name. This information is intended to be a springboard. We'd encourage you to check on the Internet for additional information and ideas for your Web page. There are resources in the appendix of magazines and material to help you do just that, and we'd encourage you to use the search engines as well to look for topics we've discussed in this chapter.

The next chapter focuses on promoting your site. While we needed a separate chapter to cover this topic, we'd encourage you to read it before you build your Web pages. As we've said, it's important to take into consideration how you intend to promote your site before you build it. You'll find information on how to promote your site in the next chapter that will also influence the mechanics of how you build it.

Chapter 8

Promoting
Your Site

Advertising is what you do when you can't
go **see** somebody. That's all it is.

—Fairfax Cone,

advertising executive quoted in
Christian Science Monitor, *March 20, 1963*

Promoting your site on the Internet is criti-
cal to its success. As Bruce Clay said from the case
study in the introduction, "Building a Web site is like
putting up a billboard in your basement—no one
sees it." To make your site a success, you have to get people to visit,
and that's what this chapter is all about.

Because of the nature of the Internet, you can do as much within
your site to promote it as you can do through channels outside your
site. We'll take a look at the main ways to promote a Web site including the use of search engines, reciprocal links, banner ads, sponsorship, advertising, and awards.

Search Engines

Search engines are the Yellow Pages of the Internet. The concept
was born out of the need to find sites in the ever-changing, con-

stantly moving world of cyberspace. Over 71 percent of frequent Web users surveyed said they use search engines first to find sites, according to a CommerceNet/Nielsen study.[1] Estimates as to the number of search engines in cyberspace run in the hundreds, but there are about a dozen popular search engines such as Yahoo, Alta Vista, Web Crawler, Excite, Infoseek, Lycos, and Deja News. We list a number of these engines in the appendix.

Search engines get listings for sites in one of two ways. Some, like Alta Vista, send out "spiders" or "robots" (also known as "bots") that scour the Internet indexing Web pages based on keywords. Others allow people to submit their site for listing themselves. Some do both. Yahoo, one of the most popular search engines, has real people looking over potential listings submitted by Web sites. In an attempt to give visitors the best shot at the site that is most likely to match what they're looking for, search engines "rank" sites, then display the sites to the visitor in the order of ranking.

From the viewpoint of someone promoting a Web site, there are two issues with search engines. One is getting the site listed and the other is improving the site's ranking. While spiders and bots will eventually find and index your site in some search engines, like Alta Vista, the proactive approach brings much better results.

While you're building your site, you should prepare to list the site with the search engines. There are several ways to do this, all of which require you to state the purpose of your site in one or two sentences. These sentences should contain keywords you believe will attract the visitors you want to come to your site. We'll discuss how to use these keywords and phrases in the following two sections: META tags and Submitting Your Site to Search Engines.

Using META Tags

To understand the advantage of using META tags, you have to know a little about how automated search programs such as spiders, crawlers, and bots work. (Since spiders, crawlers, and bots work alike, we'll just

---

[1] *Media Internet Demographics and Electronic Commerce Survey*, CommerceNet/Nielsen (Spring 1997): http://www.commerce.net.

use the term "spider.") Spiders are simply designed to use words designated by the TITLE tag and the first paragraph or so of a Web site. The spider then picks up the most important words in the first paragraph of the homepage for use as keywords for indexing the site. The first one hundred characters or so of the first paragraph of the homepage (including spaces and punctuation) are copied as description of the site and are stored together in the search engine's index along with the URL and the keywords. When a search engine visitor enters one or more keywords, the engine displays all the URLs that have those word(s) as part of their keywords along with the description copied from each site.

So let's say you're selling custom skateboards in San Diego. If you didn't have the words "custom," "skateboard," and "San Diego" in the first paragraph of your site, then no one will be able to find your site using those keywords. What's worse is if you start your site by displaying a graphic image, then the search engine may display HTML code as a description of your site.

You are not at the mercy of the spider, however. A feature of HTML, called the META tag, lets you tell the spider what keywords and descriptive words you'd like to be used in indexing your site in the search engine. So, one of the most important things you can do to promote your site is use META tags in its development. "Meta" is a prefix meaning "about," so a META tag is an indicator as to what the site is about for the purpose of indexing. Tags are commands in HTML that provide the Internet browser information such as how to display the HTML document. You'll recognize tags in HTML code as they are set apart by brackets (< >).

Besides allowing you to set the keywords and description used for your site, META tags also allow you the freedom to talk to visiting spiders without the straitjacket of having to jam all the important keywords into your first paragraph. And META tags aren't displayed to other visitors, so they don't mess up the appearance of your site.

In determining your META tags, keep the terms you use as specific and descriptive as possible. Also, avoid hype such as "best site on the Net" or "world's greatest," as it appears amateurish. This is where knowing your audience will help, because you want to use terms that will appeal to the types of people you seek to attract.

We took a look at the META tags from the Harris Company, which sells walking sticks on the Internet. Like all Web sites, this one is subject to change, but at the time we visited, Figure 8-1 shows the META tags we found. Note that META tags should be immediately after the <HTML> and <HEAD> tags, but before any other significant text.

```
<HTML>
<HEAD>
<TITLE>Walking Sticks</TITLE>
<META NAME="description" content="Harris Company is a purveyor of
fine crafted walking sticks. Our extensive line of walking sticks includes
sticks crafted in our own workshop as well as handsome sticks imported
from specialty manufacturers around the world.">
<META NAME="keywords" content="walking sticks fashion cane walking
stick cane">
```

FIGURE 8-1: *The Harris Company's META tags* (courtesy the Harris Company).

C A S E   S T U D Y

ROBERT S. HARRIS
THE HARRIS COMPANY
SWAMPSCOTT, MASSACHUSETTS
HTTP://WWW.WALKINGSTICK.COM
FASHIONABLE CANES AND WALKING STICKS

Bob Harris was a retired women's shoe designer when his wife, Penny, needed hip-replacement surgery in 1992. Depressed by the metal crutches and the constant inquiries into her condition, Bob made Penny a decorated set of crutches and a beautiful customized cane to cheer her up. Penny said unwanted sympathy turned into interest and smiles from people who saw her attractive and unusual cane. The interest turned into cash when those same people wanted to buy similar canes.

So the couple went into business. Bob made the canes, and Penny did the public relations. Together, the couple sold canes by special order, mail order, and to specialty gift shops. Then they managed to get their canes into gift shops in locations such as Disney World, the Ritz Carlton in Boston, and some Marriott Hotels.

The couple recounts what happened when they approached one of the first specialty stores to carry the canes. Bob was still making the canes by himself. The store buyer, after looking at their products, said the canes might sell, but the store could only start with a few, like about 250, and they'd like to have them in thirty days. Penny said she was speechless, but Bob agreed and in thirty days they managed to fill the order!

It was Bob's son who came up with the idea of a Web site and introduced Bob to a friend who did Web page development professionally. Bob provided the Web page designer with photos and artwork used to make the Harris Company brochure. However, Bob says the Web site is not just a copy of the brochure but a reworking of the same images in a way that works for the Internet.

Once the Web site had been developed, Penny went to work writing a one-page story about how the couple got started and sent it, along with the company's URL, to newspapers and magazines. The result has been a number of articles in papers such as the *Boston Globe,* the Fort Lauderdale, Florida, *Sun-Sentinel,* and nationally distributed *Guideposts* magazine. The response from this publicity has been nearly overwhelming, Bob said.

Bob is taking promotion of the site on the Internet one step at a time. He said that before they even pursued submitting the site to search engines, some search engines had it already listed. He and Penny still depend heavily on their Web page designer and ISP for help in answering their e-mail and confirming on-line orders. But as the pace picks up, Bob says he'll get the hang of doing it himself.

Submitting Your Web Site to Search Engines

The work you do in developing META tags can also be used in submitting your Web site to search engines who accept submissions. Some search engines will ask you to choose a category or two at their site that you think your URL best fits (where you think your URL should be listed). You can find search engines to which to submit your URL by looking in the search engines themselves. Once you find a search engine you want to submit your URL to, look for terms like "How to suggest a URL," "add URL," "add/remove URL," "add a listing," or "submit new URL." Most search engines have instructions for how to make submissions.

Don't try to come up with the description of your site on the spot. Make sure you have selected and prepared your title, keywords, and description before making your submission. Again, avoid overstatement or exaggeration, as the best search engines have actual people doing the indexing and those people hate hype. Pick what is unique or different about your site and explain that.

There are also services that will submit your URL to search engines for you and help you develop your title, keywords, and descrip-

> **TIP**   *Different search engines have different rules about how many characters can be in the description. Some allow fewer than 50 words, others allow 1,024 characters. Your best bet is to make your first 40 to 50 words pack the most punch so that the most important part of your description will make it in no matter which search engine you submit it to.*

tion. (This is still easier if you provide them with something to start from.) These Web announcement services include companies such as Submit It! and PostMaster2. Some ISPs will provide search engine submission as part of their services as well.

If you want to do submission yourself, Submit It! offers help including a list of search engines and advice. There are also software programs that perform a similar function and allow you to use your Internet access to make the submissions. Most software programs for Web announcement are priced between $100 and $200. The least expensive way to go is to do it yourself, and the most expensive way is to go with a service. What you decide to do has a lot to do with how much time and money you have to spend on promoting your site.

One way to draw visitors to your site is to create separate pages for various subtopics within the site. Some search engines will then index these pages individually, which allows for several references to the site. To draw the most visitors, you need to put META tags at the top of each page and be sure every page has a link to your main page (or homepage).

Improve Your Site's Ranking

The next hottest topic in getting listed with search engines is site ranking. As we mentioned earlier, search engines prioritize sites based on a set of criteria, then display the sites in the ranking order. In doing a search, the majority of Web surfers look at the first twenty sites listed, which is usually the first two pages of the listings brought up by the search engine. This makes your site's ranking important in attracting visitors. Being in the top twenty is good, in the top ten is better, the top five is best, and number one is outstanding.

Search engine ranking is so important, services have sprung up that do nothing but track site rankings for customers, like Position-Agent, owned now by Submit It! There are also consultants who, among other things, help sites improve their ranking, such as Bruce Clay of @bruceclay.com and Danny Sullivan of Search Engine Watch.

The best way to understand how to improve your ranking with search engines is to get a glimpse of how search engines work. In general, search engines "weigh" characteristics of the words in Web pages in order to rank them. For example, the words in the title of a page will be weighted heavier than other words found on a page. Words in the headline and in the first few paragraphs tend to be weighted heavier than other words. Significant words that are repeated throughout the page are weighted heavier than other words.

But the various search engines place importance on a variety of other factors, which is what makes each search engine different. For example, Web Crawler weighs pages with a large number of links more heavily than other pages. Some search engines will index individual pages at a site, while other engines will not. If a search engine also writes reviews of sites, a reviewed site may get a higher ranking than a site that hasn't been reviewed. HotBot and Infoseek do place more weight on pages with keywords in their META tags. However, Excite ignores META tags.

Due to such differences in Web sites, there is no magic formula for improving your ranking with every search engine. However, there are several things you can do to help your position. One we already mentioned is to use META tags. The other is to make sure your site has your keywords in the title and the opening few paragraphs.

Search engines that have people looking at the sites to rank them also look at the quality of the content, the appearance of the site, the cleverness of the site, and pretty much the same stuff you would if you were ranking sites by hand. But the automated portion of search engine ranking is important as your site may not be seen by the people doing ranking if it isn't found correctly by spiders and bots. So you need to take the automated factors of site ranking into consideration when developing your site.

Unethical Practices

While we make it a practice to avoid talking about unethical tactics in business or other areas, there are some tactics used in an attempt to boost search engine ratings that you should know about. We're telling you about them for two reasons. One, these practices will help you understand how search engines work. Two, it doesn't take much thinking to come up with some of these practices, and it's possible that some of you reading this book would inadvertently put yourself in a painful position by forgetting that you're dealing with people and not just machines. The next few paragraphs outline the most common unethical practices.

Placing terms in META tags that have nothing to do with the site is considered unethical behavior. Some people do this in the hope that someone looking for those search terms will surf by and love the site even though it wasn't what they were looking for. Some sites have gone as far as to put a competitor's name in their META tag so their site will be listed whenever anyone does a search using the competitor's name as a keyword. (This practice can get you into a courtroom.)

"Spoofing" is also considered unethical. Spoofing is the practice of repeating a keyword over and over again on a site without its having any meaning. Sometimes the text containing the repeating word is the same color as the background of the page so the site visitor cannot see all these repeating words when the page is displayed, but spiders visiting the page will pick up the words. (You can see the words if you view the HTML code that makes up the page.) One of the giveaways to this practice is to find pages on a site that appear to have large portions of blank space. Search engines are wise to this tactic, and the better engines program their spiders to ignore long strings of the same word over and over.

Some sites, in the hope of gaining additional listings, spam the search engines. As we've mentioned before, spamming in any form is considered unethical behavior. The term "spamming the index" refers to the practice of submitting a large number of pages over and over in hopes of obtaining more listings in the search engine's index.

A couple of important things concerning these practices are worth noting. First, there are no secrets on the Internet. Those who participate in unethical activity have a trail of records following them as surely as if they had written their actions down on paper and sent copies by registered mail to all the parties involved. Second, while Web site developers may see a search engine as a promotional tool, those who run the search engines do not. From the point of view of the people running search engines, practices such as entering false keywords, spoofing, and spamming the index reduce the value of their search engine to the public. Search engine developers have said that if the public starts to view their search engines as no more than promotional tools for unethical businesses, the public will stop using them and the value of the search engine will be lost.

Like any other Web site, search engines can choose who and what will be allowed in the index. Increasingly, search engines have said they have limited the listings or even removed URLs to sites that persist in violating standards for conduct in competing for rank in the index. In addition, visitor complaints are encouraged and acted upon, so "tricking" visitors can work against getting a favorable listing as well. Since it's in the interest of every site to be listed in every search engine, maintaining the cooperation of each search engine is an important consideration.

Scott Banister struck out twice before he found a business he could make work. As a freshman in computer science at the University of Illinois in 1995, he wanted to start a lifetime e-mail address service for the Internet as well as an Internet public-relations firm. Both businesses eventually failed.

But another project Scott was doing on the side blossomed. He wrote a piece of software designed to automate submission of his two other business sites to search engines on the Internet. The software would record where the sites had already been submitted, uncover other search engines and directories where his sites should be listed, and make the submission appear as though it was done by hand. Scott called the software Submit It! and created a site on the university server where other people could use the service without charge. Submit It! did something anyone could do themselves using a pen and paper, but Scott said he was short on time and there was nothing else like it available.

Submit It! became popular in a hurry. "I moved it off the university server before they got a chance to get annoyed," Scott said wryly, explaining why he transitioned Submit It! to an advertiser-supported service.

While Submit It! was self-supporting through sponsors, Scott began receiving requests from users who wanted a commercial service to provide them with the technical support to get their sites placed on search engines and a fuller set of features. The demand became a little overwhelming, and Scott knew he needed help. "I had nerve-racking floods of e-mail coming at me. I went commercial as fast as I could before this thing exploded in my face." He found his answer in a company called Webpost, run by Bill Younker in Boston, who was offering a similar service targeted at ISPs.

The marriage of Submit It! and Webpost solved both companies' problems. Webpost had resources and experienced people who understood building software products, but they needed a robust, commercial service. Scott had a brand and lots of ideas. "We made a really nice team," Scott said. He became Vice President of Technology in the new organization, which adopted the Submit It! name.

"I never finished my college degree," Scott said. Once he made the deal with Webpost, he realized he could go anywhere he wanted to, so he started looking. He chose Palo Alto, California, because it's near Stanford University where he liked the atmosphere and the people.

Scott says his goal with Submit It! is to be a "credible, real company in this space." To that end, Submit It! still provides free advice and resources to those starting out. At the site, there are sections to explain how to make submissions and a list of URLs for the most popular search engines.

Submission can turn into a war between the Webmaster and the search engine, Scott said. Part of his advice to those who want to be listed with search engines is to "think a little more narrowly by thinking of particular things someone would look for if he or she wanted to find your site, then use those keywords in your META tags."

Submit It!'s biggest advantage is the size of its knowledge base, Scott said. The service has hundreds of directories and search engines categorized, reviewed, and integrated. "The directories and search engines come to us to be included because we're so well known. Our competitors have to find these directories as they pop up."

Competition in Scott's world is fierce, but Scott is liked and respected on the Internet. "We try not to be obnoxious or engage in spamming," Scott said. He added that his competitors have sent out spiders to grab all the addresses, whereas Submit It! is linked to other sites (which number in the tens of thousands), then sends out bulk e-mail to the Webmasters of those sites trying to gain links to their own submission services. "Our linkees think those other services are underhanded. Most of our competitors have spammed the Net at one point or another."

Scott encourages those who want to start a business on the Internet. "Go ahead and jump in and do it. If you fail a few times, it's a good learning experience for the next time around."

Reciprocal Links

Linking to other sites in exchange for their linking to your site is another way to promote your site on the Internet. A link is a reference on one site to another site that can be accessed directly by clicking on colored and underlined text or a graphic. The way to set up such links is to contact the Webmaster or owner of the site you'd like to be linked to to establish reciprocity. Some sites don't care if you reciprocate with a link to their site. They simply link to sites they think will be of value to their visitors. Reciprocal linking was more effective than advertising for John Wells of Netstores, who found customers by creating reciprocal links to movie fan sites for his Movie Madness site.

However, reciprocal linking has the disadvantage of being a constant maintenance problem. To keep your site up-to-date, you always want to be sure the links you have on your site are still valid. In the constantly and instantly changing world of the Internet, links change frequently and without notice. For your visitors, dead-end links are a signal that your site is being neglected and that discourages repeat visits. To keep links up-to-date you have to either frequently test the links yourself or use a service such as NetMind (http://www.netmind.com) to check the links for you and notify you if one has changed.

Some advertiser-supported sites consider reciprocal linking, or any kind of linking, to be a disadvantage because it draws visitors away to other sites. These sites feel they do advertisers a disservice by sending visitors elsewhere, even if it might benefit the visitor to know about another site. Other advertiser-supported site owners feel visitors benefit and therefore will come back more often to a site that provides them with what they're looking for. Search engines operate on that premise, even though most of them are advertiser supported. If the advertiser has a site of its own, the advertiser may want a link to its site. If the advertiser provides links to other sites, then a potential exists for visitors to be still further drawn away from your site.

Since good content is what keeps visitors coming back, the majority of advertiser-supported sites do provide links, especially reciprocal ones. There is speculation that companies will at some point find it prudent to avoid creating sites of their own and simply advertise with other sites whose topics draw potential customers, but right now companies who advertise on the Web usually have their own sites as well. Many reciprocal links are accomplished using banner ads, which is another important way to build traffic that we will talk about next.

Banner Ads

A banner ad is advertising, usually in the form of a rectangular-shaped graphics image in the GIF file format, that forms a graphical link to another site. These ads are often displayed across the top of a Web page like a banner—hence the term *banner ad*. The graphic for the banner ad is often stored on the server of another site, either a public-relations agency or the server of the site to which the banner refers.

The idea behind a banner ad is to get the user to click on it. To this end, banner ads include text, graphics, animation, sound, and even video. Obviously, it's in the interest of the advertiser to have a simple banner ad that will load to the visitor as soon as possible. But as more people on the Internet get faster access, the larger file formats of sound and video are sure to become more commonplace features of banner ads.

Banner ads come in a number of shapes, although groups on the Internet, such as the Internet Advertising Bureau (IAB) are attempting to set standards for banners. Banner ads are measured both in pixels and in file size. Because Web pages are based on placement of elements, the size of the banner ad is an important consideration for the site builders and is usually determined by the site that will display the ad. For example, the popular banner ad exchange company LinkExchange specified that banner ads for its members should be 400 pixels long by 40 pixels wide. Lycos at one time set full-size banner ads to the IAB standard of 468 pixels long by 60 pixels wide and limited the file size of the GIF to 7.5 KB.

Targeting Banner Ads

Many sites rotate banner ads so that the same visitor loading the page twice in five minutes would see two different ads. Other sites target different banner ads to different visitors who have typed a certain search word, clicked on a certain topic, or are from a certain area of the U.S. or the world.

Targeting banner ads is also made possible via HTTP Cookies. A feature of certain browsers such as Netscape, cookies allow a site to place information into a special text file on the visitor's hard disk drive. Appropriately named COOKIE.TXT, this file allows sites to gather information about each visitor and have access to that information again each time the visitor comes back to the site. Such information could include the visitor's interests, his or her contact information, the date of the last visit, other sites the visitor has gone to, a password so that the visitor doesn't have to reenter it, and so on. The more cookies the visitor gathers from surfing sites on the Internet, the larger the cookie file on the user's hard disk drive. Some Web surfers resent the intrusion of privacy involved in the use of cookies and the use of their hard disk space. Because of this, most browsers allow the option of either notifying the user if a cookie has been sent or disallowing cookies altogether.

Free Banner Ads

There are several services on the Internet that facilitate the exchange of banner ads between sites. These cooperative services are often without charge, and the best known is LinkExchange. Supported by advertisers or sponsors, LinkExchange and services like it will place member ads for free on sites that attract suitable visitors. They tack a small logo of their own (a link) onto each banner displayed. Sites wishing to be members get one of their banner ads displayed on other sites in exchange for displaying several ads from other member sites. The service keeps the banner ads from members on its own server so it controls the display of the ads and keeps a count. Many of the sites we interviewed mentioned LinkExchange and similar banner exchange services as a great source of help in promoting early traffic to their own sites.

Paying for Banner Ads

Another way for you to promote your site is to pay for your banner ads to be displayed on other sites, preferably sites with visitors who might have an interest in coming to your site. Banner advertising is sold on a pay-per-impression, pay-per-lead, pay-per-sale, and on a click-through basis. Sites with the highest number of page views, not just hits, get the most money per page impression for displaying banner ads. Sites with lower traffic get a smaller amount overall, but more per page impression, using the justification that theirs is a more targeted audience. As we've seen from case studies earlier in the book, the argument for charging more for a more targeted audience is a valid proposition. Then there's the pay-per-sale concept, which requires the advertiser to pay only if the visitor who clicks on the ad actually buys.

The most controversial type of banner ad pricing is paying on a click-through basis. The idea here is that you only pay if someone clicks on your banner. While this is strongly to your advantage, the site owner may see it as a disadvantage because you still get exposure whether or not anyone actually clicks on your banner. Also, if you have a poorly designed banner that no one is interested in, the site owner has no control over fixing it, and therefore is helpless to gain revenue from your ad. So, the bottom line is, if you can buy banner advertising on a click-through basis, this is the way to go. However, most professionals on the Web are discouraging sites from selling click-throughs, so a site that will make such a bargain may be hard to find.

The actual arrangements for buying banner ads vary all over the board. Expect to start out paying several hundred dollars a month for targeted banner ads based on page views.

Increasing Banner Ad Effectiveness

An effective banner ad gets higher click-through rates and more visitors to your site. So what makes a banner ad effective? The industry standard for a good banner ad is if 2 to 4 percent of visitors to a site click on it. A good banner ad loads quickly, is clear, and uses bright colors, good contrast, and print that is easy to see and read quickly. It

---

QUICK TERMINOLOGY UPDATE

Click — The action a visitor takes when using the mouse to select an object on the screen. Click also connotes a visitor's selection of a banner ad.

Hits — The number of files downloaded by visitors. All files are counted including HTML pages and graphic images. The number of hits can be divided by 11 to get a rough but conservative estimate of the number of actual page views involved.

Page views (or page impressions) — refers to the number of times an entire Web page, including graphics, is served up to visitors. This term is often used to tell advertisers how many times their banner ad was seen or could be seen by visitors viewing the page.

CPM — Cost per thousand. Usually used in reference to the cost of a thousand page views.

Click rate — A comparison of the number of visitors to the number of clicks on a particular banner ad.

Click-through (or click-through rate) — The number of visitors who click on a banner ad.

Pixel — Picture element. Graphics are made up of pixels that are displayed on the computer screen or printed. In Internet advertising, specifications for banner ads include the required number of pixels an ad should be, which describes the relative size of the ad when displayed.

---

also has a call to action, such as the phrase "click here," somewhere in the banner. This may seem like an obvious point, but until the Internet is as commonplace as the telephone, visitors may not be sure that a banner ad is something they may click on. Another common technique is to create several banner ads, displaying them all until the most effective ones are identified.

Animation reportedly boosts the effectiveness of the average banner ad 14 to 44 percent, depending on the survey you read, but that still leaves only a 5 to 6 percent response rate for a good ad. However, IN2, a New York-based advertising agency, claims it is getting click-through of 10 to 30 percent for its clients.[2] The agency says it focuses on interactive polling, searching, and other direct-response activities **within** banner ads.

For example, IN2 created a drop-down banner for iVillage's Parent Soup site. The banner asked surfers to rank various Parent Soup discussion group topics, such as toddlers, teens, and pregnancy, and then linked visitors to those areas. This drop-down banner ad garnered a 10 to 30 percent click-through rate. Another interactive banner ad, which IN2 created for Barnes & Noble bookstores on-line, let users search for book titles right in the banner. It got a whopping 26 percent click-through rate. In other words, IN2 got people involved with the banner ad at the site they were viewing before asking potential visitors to change locations.

There is a certain amount of anecdotal evidence that many Web surfers don't know that several companies can be represented on a site via banner advertising. Cliff Kurtzman of Tenagra says the company regularly gets e-mail from people thanking it for the wonderful tennis racket or some other item they purchased. But Tenagra doesn't sell tennis equipment. It does run The Tennis Server site as an advertiser-supported Internet publication that includes banner ads and sponsorship from retailers who do sell tennis equipment. These companies do have their own company identities and e-mail addresses; however, visitors don't always make the distinction. The close association that visitors make between advertisers and a site is what makes sponsorship an attractive option.

Sponsorship

In order to promote your site, you can be a sponsor of other sites or of discussion lists. *Discussion list* is a term we haven't used before, so we'll define it here. A discussion list is like a group letter in which each e-mail sent is distributed to every member of the list. Lists are

---

[2]Kate Maddox, "Tech-Savvy IN2 Wins New Clients, Adds Business," *Advertising Age* (August 1997): http://www.adage.com.

oriented around a topic like advertising on the Internet or growing houseplants. Good lists have a moderator who reads each e-mail before it's sent to the entire group to make sure it's on target and appropriate for the discussion at hand. To support the moderator and the list, sponsors are usually sought and a short advertising blurb along with the Web site address of the sponsor or sponsors is included in each e-mail sent to the members of the list. Some lists are quite popular and archived for a long time, so your sponsorship can keep working after active interest in the list or the topic has died and the list discontinued. A strong benefit of sponsoring discussion lists is you can be assured that your audience is more targeted. If you're selling plants, a houseplant discussion list would be a perfect one for you to sponsor. You can be assured that everyone on the list would have a potential interest in knowing about your site.

Sponsorship, however, usually costs more than banner advertising; but it could cost you less overall. It would be less expensive to be a sponsor of a site where visitors are your targeted audience than to place a banner ad on a very busy, more general site, such as a search engine, for example. Targeting people who already have an interest in your product can be quite valuable and is therefore worth more per visitor than a banner ad.

Sponsorship requires a greater commitment to the sponsor from the site owner or the list moderator. Further, sponsorship appears to visitors or list members as an endorsement. As a sponsor, you can expect your logo and mentions of your company and Web site to be placed all around the site or in prominent places on the discussion list. Sponsorship is usually a longer-term relationship than banner advertising but offers more credibility and, it is hoped, loyalty from site visitors. In addition, the site owner or list moderator will encourage visits to your site. On the other hand, you may also have more demands placed upon you, including requests to contribute to the site content and perhaps use of your resources to maintain the sponsored site. This can also be good. For example, if you sell plants, writing a short piece on flowering houseplants with your name, Web site, and company name at the bottom could provide you with additional exposure and greater credibility.

While sponsorship is a good way to promote your site, or a good way to encourage business even if you don't have a site, there are other ways to use discussion lists and e-mail to promote your site. We'll cover these next.

Electronic Mailing Lists

E-mail is one of the most powerful tools on the Internet and a low-budget way to promote your site. There are several ways you can take advantage of e-mail, including joining discussion lists, sending e-mail to people on your site who give you their e-mail address, and the controversial practice of sending personalized e-mail to people whose addresses you gather yourself.

Join Discussion Lists and Participate in Newsgroups

As we mentioned in talking about sponsorship, discussion lists are one of the uses of e-mail on the Internet. Newsgroups (also known as forums) are another. There's not much difference between newsgroups and discussion lists in terms of functionality, although discussion lists have the advantage of using e-mail, which everyone has. Newsgroups require a news reader, a program that allows you to read the messages posted by others. Most Internet browsers come with a news reader, although shareware and commercial news readers are also available.

A low-budget way to start promoting your site is to join discussion lists and newsgroups that have anything to do with your expertise and put in your two cents. While these types of interaction groups abhor advertising except from sponsors, it is perfectly acceptable for you to contribute a worthwhile comment, question, or suggestion and sign it with your name, company name, e-mail address, and the URL for your site. This is a common tactic used by many of the people we've profiled in this book, including Su Penny of PriceCheck, Bruce Clay of @bruceclay.com, and Susan Eshelman of Art Vision International. In fact, if you have the time, you can take e-mail one step further.

Personalized, Targeted E-mail

As we discussed in chapter 1, *spam,* or unsolicited e-mail, is a dirty word on the Internet. Nothing will arouse the ire of people in cyberspace faster than spam. However, if you have a lot of time and not a lot of cash, you might consider surfing the Net yourself, looking for people who might be interested in your site in various groups and forums, then e-mailing each one a personal note inviting him or her to your site. While this is still controversial, as some people believe any e-mail they didn't ask for is spam, it works and you can still maintain a personal relationship with visitors, which is so important on the Internet. One such success story is that of Andy Rebele, owner of the City Auction site, which we profile in this chapter.

Autoresponders

You can also send e-mail to visitors to see if they're interested, then tell them to send a request for more information to your autoresponder. An autoresponder is a software program that sends out text that you specify to anyone who e-mails it. If you're a tax accountant trying to round up business, you could send an e-mail to all your clients and to people who've requested information from your site that includes an invitation to get your "10 tips to avoid an IRS audit" by simply sending an e-mail to the autoresponder. That way, you don't have to reply to every inquiry yourself and the people get the information that promotes your area of expertise.

Send E-mail to Site Visitors

One of the ways you should be promoting visits to your site is by sending e-mail to people who've already been there. You collect these e-mail addresses by asking visitors for them somewhere on your site, and telling them of your intent. Then, when you make changes to your site or offer a sale or have something new of interest, you should e-mail people to let them know. Be sure when you send your e-mail updates that this was information they requested and be sure to include a method for allowing them to get off your mailing list if they'd like to do so.

Push Technology

Push is the name for sending information to visitors on a regular basis—"pushing" information at them rather than "pulling" them to your site by having information there that they want. Mainly used for information services such as automated classified ad searches and custom clipping services from news sites, push technology has been controversial because historically it's been difficult to tell if readers are reading what's sent if they don't come to the site to get it.

However, some clever folks figured out that if they sent the push information in an HTML format, they would do more than deliver something that readers like the look of. By using HTML and only delivering the HTML code itself, not the other files for graphics or related information called for by the HTML file, the sender knows when the reader attempts to read the document. This is because the HTML file, once loaded by the browser, makes calls to the server where the HTML file originated for the other files referenced in the original HTML code.

Obviously, delivering HTML files via push technology has some limitations. For one, it requires the reader be on-line when the HTML file is read, since other files cannot be requested if the user is trying to read the HTML file off-line. One benefit is that the reader will learn quickly and be motivated to be on-line since it's a better experience visually to be able to see all the graphics, and not just the text, of the HTML file. Also, it requires that the files be read using an Internet browser instead of standard e-mail programs, so users of services that are text-based e-mail only can view the HTML files, but they'll get a much uglier product because they have to pick past all the code to read the content.

One successful site that delivers HTML files is NewsLinx, run by publisher Richard Ord (http://www.newslinx.com). NewsLinx delivers HTML files to tens of thousands of people worldwide each business day. One of the concerns about HTML push technology is that people will not come to your site. After all, why should they if they're getting everything delivered to them? But in a report in the on-line magazine *ClickZ Today*, NewsLinx reported it got more visitors by using HTML push technology, not fewer. In fact, traffic on the site quadrupled when NewsLinx started delivering HTML. Further, the format wasn't a problem since most of the readers had an Internet browser to view the files, and the advertisers remained loyal because the ad impressions were still being recorded each time a subscriber opened the HTML file.[3] In fact, NewsLinx's success spurred *ClickZ Today* to start doing the same thing.

An important point to remember here is that both *ClickZ Today* and NewsLinx are aiming at audiences who are marketing or doing business on the Internet. Most of these readers are going to make a point of spending more on technology than the average computer user with a home PC. We say this to emphasize that it's important to know your audience before you step out into new territory. It's also important to note that as the technology progresses, the bottom rung of the ladder gets higher. So, if you're catering to the average guy it's worthwhile to find out what people who cater to those on the high end are doing so that you can begin preparing for the future. In the interests of covering all the bases, next we'll talk about some low-tech ways you can promote your site.

Caution

There are individuals and groups on the Internet that make it their business to organize boycotts of companies and individuals known to participate in spamming or any variation of spam. For example, Mark Welch, an attorney based in Pleasanton, California, started a boycott against bookseller Barnes & Noble, who he claims got his e-mail address by sending a spider to his Web site, then spammed him with invitations to purchase books. Mark's campaign against the bookseller received attention worldwide. We would caution you to

---

[3]Andy Bourland, "All HTML, All the Time: Sometimes, Push CAN Pull," *ClickZ Today* (October 2, 1997): http://www.clickz.com.

proceed carefully and sensitively when using e-mail to promote your site in cyberspace.

C A S E   S T U D Y

ANDY REBELE
CITYAUCTION
SAN FRANCISCO, CALIFORNIA
HTTP://WWW.CITYAUCTION.COM
LOCAL AND NATIONAL AUCTION CLASSIFIED ADS

Andy Rebele grew up in the newspaper business. His dad was a newspaper publisher, and at age twelve Andy wrote a column. He participated in nearly every aspect of the business except delivery. "My dad tried to get me to deliver papers—my friends were doing it—but I didn't want to," Andy said.

In college, Andy got a mathematical and computational science degree from Stanford and went on to get his MBA at MIT. He worked in business development for Interactive Imaginations and was the manager for Internet business at General Magic. He also worked at Trammel Crow in Houston and was a rowing coach for high school students in Seattle.

Then Andy came up with the idea for CityAuction, a nationwide, interactive approach that combines an auction with classified ads. Funded by a VISA card, Andy set out to build from scratch a site that depends on interaction. Andy tells it best himself, so we're including his post to the On-Line Advertising Discussion List run by Tenagra Corporation.

There has been some discussion about the ethics of marketing via e-mail, with Mark Welch kicking it off with his Boycott Barnes & Noble campaign (featured in today's San Francisco Chronicle). I wanted to give my two cents and to provide some results of a campaign I conducted in what I thought was an ethical way (at the risk of incurring the wrath of another boycott!).

In the off-line world, there have been various legal challenges to telemarketing, the closest analogy I can find to e-mail marketing. In the end, it became illegal to use a machine to call people and give them a sales pitch and illegal to send junk faxes. However, it is still legal for human beings to call you at home to market to you, and it is legal to fill your mailbox with unsolicited paper mail.

Why the difference? My guess: economics. It should cost the marketer about the same amount of human time to deliver a message to you as it takes you to read it. It is abusive of your prospective customers' time to find a way to intrude with your message in a way that costs you nothing and costs them time to evaluate and discard.

The analogy to the on-line world is that if you send someone junk mail using CyberBomber or FloodGate or any other auto-spammers, you are violating not only the time of your prospective customers but probably a future law (as soon as the law catches up to the medium). However, if someone (a human not a script) reads your Web page, newsgroup posting, or other public statement, and finds from the content that you are a likely interested party, and then sends you a personalized note, that is probably okay. FloodGate is like junk faxes and automatic telemarketing machines, while a human being sending you a personalized note is more like traditional telemarketing.

E-mail marketing done the right way can have fantastic results. My Web site is called CityAuction, a person-to-person auction classified ad site. The challenge was to create awareness and reach critical mass quickly, and there was no easy way to do it. Using banners or other passive means would send a lot of people looking at an empty classified ad space—not very interesting, no matter how good the underlying technology or theory is. Therefore I decided to use a highly targeted e-mail campaign to recruit visitors and sellers.

Over several weeks I read various newsgroups and Web sites where the charter is person-to-person sales. I read every post, and put relevant posts into a database with the real name, e-mail address, and other information from the content of the post. At the end of that period, when the site was ready, I sent out about 3,500 e-mails to these people, each with a personalized note (mail merged, but prepared by a human being). It had taken me two to three weeks of full-time work to read each post and to determine which people were legitimate prospects for my site and which were not. Suffice it to say it was very time-consuming.

The results over five days (with no search engine support):

3,500 e-mails
100 listings of things to sell (2.8%)
1,000 unique visitors (29%)
35 remove requests + flames (1%)

Because we had just launched and it was our only initial technique, I can be reasonably sure that these results came directly from the e-mail campaign.

My conclusion? E-mail marketing DONE RIGHT can be a very effective technique, and one to which far more people react positively than negatively. It takes a lot of time, but for a site which needs a kick-start it may be the most cost-effective way to go.

(It's a shame so many people do it wrong. Without them I'm sure doing it right would be even more effective.)

Andy's site grew and he was invited to tell his story for *ClickZ Today*. Some *ClickZ Today* readers expressed support while others felt strongly enough against Andy's e-mail approach that they canceled subscriptions to the on-line newsletter.[4] Andy told us that once CityAuction became a viable entity, he began promoting the site using other means in addition to e-mail, such as search engine listings and discussion lists.

Advertising

What we mean by advertising is traditional methods of getting the word out that you're in business, including but not limited to printed material, radio, television, billboards, etc. Advertising your site via any means open to you is not only smart, it's necessary. You should take advantage of opportunities to get the word out.

It seems obvious that once people start Web sites, they'd print their URLs on all their marketing materials. But many people forget, so this is a reminder. Don't miss the opportunity for promoting your site by printing your URL and your e-mail address on your business cards, letterhead, envelopes, fliers, brochures, catalogs, newspaper advertising, and any other of your printed materials.

And have someone proofread your URL before it's printed. People who are unfamiliar with the format of URLs make mistakes printing their Web site addresses or don't recognize when their printer has made a mistake typesetting the URL. We've seen many business cards with URLs or e-mail addresses that were obviously incorrect.

[4]Ann Handley, "Editor's Note," *ClickZ Today* (October 13, 1997): http://www.clickz.com.

Each character is important, so it's wise to print the entire URL just as someone would type it into his or her browser to reach your site. This means don't leave off the "http://" assuming everyone already knows to type it in.

It seems that many home PC users do know how to enter URLs. For some time there has been anecdotal evidence that the number of hits to a site rose sharply immediately after the URL was displayed on television. Confirmation has come from analysts at Media Metrix, who've found that not only do home PC users tend to have their computers in the same room as their television set, a whopping 40 percent of households with both computers and televisions also use both simultaneously.[5] So, if you're advertising on television or you get media coverage, you should be sure to display your URL.

Also, don't forget to pursue standard publicity with newspapers, radio, and television. There are lots of fine books out there on how to write a press release and how to contact the media, such as *How to Make Yourself (or Anyone Else) Famous: the Secrets of a Professional Publicist,* by Gloria Michels. As we've mentioned before, your local library is a good place to start for how-to instruction and for finding news organizations interested in your site.

CASE STUDY

LINDA S. HAMMER
THE SEEKER
VENICE, FLORIDA
HTTP://WWW.THE-SEEKER.COM
A SERVICE TO REUNITE PEOPLE

Linda Hammer worked in the Florida state attorney's office as a private process server. She said one day it occurred to her that she could do this type of work for herself instead of being employed by someone else, so she became a private investigator. The only problem was, as a private investigator, people disliked what she did and she felt crummy about it. "I felt like an IRS

---

[5]Media Metrix, *HomeTech Report* (September 8, 1997): http://www.pcmeter.com.

auditor. Every time I found someone, it destroyed their life." So she decided to turn her skills to helping people find others who wanted to be found.

In 1990, she started The Seeker in a printed publication as a service to help siblings and other separated relatives find one another. Then in 1995, she decided to take The Seeker on-line. She hired a programmer to build a database and allowed people to send in photos that she scanned and put on-line. The site was met with resounding support from people all over the country. She said, "Now I have a Web site and people love me."

Linda said she'd never met an adoptee before she started this project. And she said some of the stories will break your heart. Like one woman who told the story of how she got pregnant at age seventeen, had twins, but her mother told her one of the babies was stillborn. The mother told the doctor she just couldn't handle twins, got the doctor to go along with the deception, then sold the twin to an adoptive family for $5,000. When the mother died, the woman found the papers concerning the twin and started searching for this long-lost daughter who she thought was dead.

But she added that people look for each other for all kinds of reasons you'd never think of. For example, Linda says there are 27 million living veterans from wars the U.S. has been involved in and those people are often looking for friends made in these crisis times. Insurance companies are also looking for people who are beneficiaries of life insurance policies.

Getting publicity for the site has never been a problem. Linda said her site has been featured numerous times in print, radio, and television media such as *MSNBC*, *Internet World*, and even the *New York Times*. With over a million visitors a month, her numbers were good but her ISP expenses were mounting as the gigabytes of information on the server expanded and her page views rocketed. Her problem was a lack of information on how to present her site to potential advertisers. She tried to do it herself, but between running the site and her other responsibilities, she wasn't attracting the advertisers she needed to support the site. After some research in discussion groups, Linda was able to determine that her page views were high enough to get an Internet public relations agency to handle getting advertisers for her, and she signed up Flycast, who is now marketing her site to advertisers.

As for the future, Linda is mulling over writing a book on how to find someone. She plans to include actual stories from her Web site concerning the more interesting searches people have made and how they ended.

Awards

One final way to promote your site is to win awards from other popular sites. When we say awards, we mean getting special recognition from sites and publications that already have an audience. Search engines, on-line publications, large ISPs, and other popular sites choose on a weekly, monthly, or annual basis "best" sites to feature to their audience. Being recognized as a best site can bring you an increase in traffic that will peak when you're first listed, and then continue to bring you additional new visitors for weeks or months. This is because sites that give awards often archive their choices for visitors to scan through. For example, *USA Today* on-line has its daily "Hot Site" list archive of past sites, and Yahoo allows visitors to search back several months through its "Weekly Picks." Also, sites that give awards are always looking for something new, and many of them read one another's award lists for new sites they have not considered.

Registering with the search engines is a good way to get your site considered, although some sites that give awards allow you to submit a site for consideration. We've placed a list of sites that give awards in the appendix, and we recommend you visit the sites to see what their current policy is on submitting sites for consideration.

Be prepared for lots of visitors, once you receive recognition, as you're sure to get them, especially if a popular site picks your site. Also, once you've gotten an award, often you'll be provided with an icon that you can place on your homepage. The icon is usually a link to the site that gave your site the award, which has obvious advantages to the award giver.

Conclusion

Listing your site in search engines, building reciprocal links, creating banner ads, sponsoring other sites, using e-mail, making sure your URL is displayed in any traditional advertising materials, and competing for awards are all ways you can promote your Web site on the Internet. The ideas and concepts we've presented here provide you with the basics of promoting your site and are intended to serve as a starting point. As you know, the Internet is subject to rapid change, so we would encourage you to use the resources listed in the appendix as well as search engines to find further resources for promoting your site. Discussion lists and newsgroups as well as other sites will provide you with more information on the latest trends in promoting your site, creating effective banner ads, and generally keeping up to make your site a success. One of the most important parts of any successful business site is generating income. We'll talk about how to get paid in the next chapter.

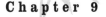

Chapter 9

Getting Paid

Be prepared, be sharp, be careful, and use the King's English well. And you can forget all the [other rules] unless you remember one more: Get paid.

—Robert N. C. Nix,

father of Pennsylvania Chief Justice Robert N. C. Nix, Jr.
(New York Times, 7 January, 1984)

 Doing business on the Internet is all about getting paid. This is an area that's received a lot of attention because it requires a new way of thinking. In the past, our banks and financial institutions were made out of granite and marble to connote strength and security. People performed transactions face-to-face. But it's now common-place to conduct transactions using a telephone, and people are be-ginning to find it's secure and convenient to perform financial transactions on the Internet as well.

Rather than talking about the obvious, like having customers mail you checks, we're going to spend our time here on the various ways to accept payment electronically—such as credit cards, demand drafts, and electronic cash. (Much of the information about accept-ing credit cards will be familar to existing businesses, but information on demand drafts, commissions, and avoiding fraud will probably be new territory for most businesspeople entering cyberspace.) We'll also talk about security precautions in conjunction with accepting payments in cyberspace. As a final note, we'll show you how commission sales can be another way to supplement your bottom line. And along the way, we'll provide ways to avoid fraud.

One thing we want to emphasize is that the cost figures are provided simply as a starting point and can change almost daily without notice. We provide these figures here so that you can get a better idea of what to expect and as a basis for discussion when you start your own investigation. So do check for yourself before making plans based on the figures we provide here.

Accepting Payment

If you're selling something, especially if you're selling something to individuals, you need to find a way to accept payment. Outside the Internet, this usually isn't a problem, but in cyberspace it can become more of a challenge. In general, accepting payment on the Internet is a lot like accepting payment through mail-order or telephone sales, which is why the term mail order/telephone order (MOTO) transaction is commonly applied to cyberspace commerce.

You can always accept payments from your on-line customers the traditional way by accepting checks or money orders by mail. This is a time-honored method though not as convenient or fast for customers. For some business operators, the mail is the only way to build credibility and establish a track record so that they can later accept other forms of payment. But in a medium as universal and fast as cyberspace, people do not usually expect to deal with barriers such as time and distance. With a focus on meeting customer expectations, we want to cover the variety of ways to accept payment on the Internet that are fast and convenient for consumers.

By far, the most widely accepted form of payment in cyberspace is the credit card, but other popular payment methods include demand drafts and digital cash. The important thing is to find a method of payment that is as convenient for your customer as possible. You may find, especially if you're a new business, that it may take some time to build up to the level of success you'll need to accept the form of payment you'd most like to offer your customers. You'll discover why as you read this section.

Credit Cards

Credit cards are one of the safest and best-understood ways for accepting payments from consumers in cyberspace. Credit card associations, such as MasterCard and Visa, have earned the trust of consumers by going to great lengths to protect them from fraud and misuse. One of the mechanisms that protects consumers is the Fair Credit Billing Act (FCBA). Under the FCBA, the consumer is allowed to dispute charges before paying them, and the consumer's liability for unauthorized charges is only $50.

Credit cards are issued by banks but run through associations such as MasterCard, Visa, American Express, and others. For determining merchant status for businesses, these associations also operate through banks. As we all know, banks tend to be very conservative, but they tend to be even more conservative when it comes to granting credit card merchant status.

How to Become a Credit Card Merchant

In order to accept credit cards, you have to be approved, usually through a bank. The approval process is the most difficult part for small and home-based businesses, especially if there is no storefront involved. Credit card associations are nervous about allowing businesses with no track record to obtain merchant status. There are businesses on the Internet that specialize in granting credit card merchant status to home-based or Internet businesses, but many of these will send a representative to your home or business to photograph your operation. They may also require a copy of your business documents, such as your business license and sales tax license from your local government authorities. The best way to get merchant status is to be able to demonstrate a track record of sales or show the bank your storefront.

What Does Accepting Credit Cards Cost?

The merchant who takes the cards is charged a "discount rate," which is really a fee for accepting the card based on the amount of the transaction and the potential risk to the bank in allowing that particular business to be an authorized merchant. Discount rates can range from 2 to 3 percent or higher. In addition to the discount rate, there's often a monthly minimum charge of between $10 and $25.

A lease agreement for the equipment you will get to process the credit card transactions is also part of the cost. This equipment is usually either a terminal that requires a phone line and allows you to enter the credit card number and other information for authorization or a software package that does the same thing and works with a modem-equipped PC or Macintosh. This equipment is leased, usually for twenty-four to forty-eight months, and you're liable for the lease payments even if your business shuts down, unless you can successfully sell the lease to another business. Lease payments are usually $35 to $50 per month automatically deducted from your business checking account, plus a balloon payment at the end of the lease of as much as 10 percent of the total lease payments. You can shorten the term of the lease, but usually at the expense of higher lease payments. If you manage to purchase credit card equipment or software from someone else, you can expect to pay a reprogramming fee of between $300 and $500.

You can also expect to pay an application fee and the first and last months' lease payments in advance. The application fee can be as much as $1,000 or more. Altogether, a new business accepting credit cards can figure on paying between $2,500 and $4,500 over a two-year period, in addition to a percentage of sales.

If you find a better deal in one cost area, it's often offset in another. For example, some banks may not require you to pay a monthly minimum but will require that all credit card payments be deposited in an account you open at that bank. This can be especially true of banks offering merchant status on the Internet since they want to have control over the deposit of credit card payments. If you have to set up a checking account out-of-state, you may face delays in accessing your funds. You may have to write out-of-state checks to pay for your business expenses or write yourself a check that you deposit

to access your funds. In addition, your bank might hold a check written on an out-of-state bank to yourself until the check clears, causing
further delays.

Credit Card Equipment

The equipment you use to accept credit cards varies from a keypad
terminal that you can swipe a credit card through to special software
for your computer. For new Internet businesses, software is recommended, because most of the time you probably will not have an actual credit card in your physical possession to swipe through a
reader.

The procedure to process a credit card sale is to enter (or write or
buy a program to enter the data into the software for you) the credit
card information including customer name, address, phone, card
number, expiration date, and the amount of the sale. Using your computer's modem and a free telephone line, the computer will call either
a local or a toll-free number at an authorization center and within a
matter of seconds receive either verification or refusal. Once the
transaction has been authorized, the money is moved into your
checking account—usually within one to three business days. You
can "batch process" sales, meaning you can enter a group of transactions for many customers and then make one call to process all the
transactions.

If you can afford the additional cost, you can have software developed that will perform this function on-line while the customer is
waiting. This can be very important for any business selling on-line
services such as access to subscription information or anything that
can be downloaded by the customer immediately. Artec International, the company that sells electronic greeting cards on-line, has
developed software and found a bank credit card system that will allow it to verify customer credit card information within a few seconds
so the customer can immediately download the product.

AVS Fraud Protection

For those starting out, we recommend you choose an option offered
by the bank who issues your merchant account called the address
verification system (AVS). Using AVS you can verify information the

customer supplies to you such as zip code and street address, which helps prevent the unauthorized use of credit cards to obtain goods. The AVS system checks the address information you supply about the customer against the information in the billing address database of the bank's computer and will tell you if there's a discrepancy. (If the customer is buying a gift and asking that it be shipped to another address, you can and should ask for both the customer's address and the shipping address.) If the information you have and the bank's address for the customer do not match up, that's one of the signs the transaction may not be legitimate.

Should the AVS detect a discrepancy in the address information, you can protect yourself by asking the customer for further verification to confirm the customer is the valid card holder. It's common to ask for a correct billing address or proof of address. If the customer claims she's moved, ask for another type of verification, such as asking for a fax of their identification with the new address shown on it. If someone is using a stolen credit card number and you ship your product or provide your service without getting a signed delivery receipt, you run the risk of getting a "charge back." This is something you want to avoid, and we'll tell you why in the next section.

> **TIP** *At the time of this writing, there was no way to get AVS verification on credit cards for international customers. Most merchants we've talked with ship to international customers using credit cards anyway because international orders tend to be more lucrative and fraud has been rare.*

Charge Backs

A hated term in the credit card industry, *charge back* is the automatic deduction from your merchant checking account of funds that were deposited there after a customer transaction. Charge backs occur because a customer successfully disputed charges you made to his credit card account. While this isn't always the case, charge backs connote that someone is fraudulently using a credit card.

Customers must dispute in writing charges they believe were incorrectly placed on their credit card accounts. You as a merchant have thirty days once contacted to show proof that the charges are valid and that the customer received the goods or services that show on their credit card account. A signed delivery slip is the most common way to answer a customer challenge.

In addition to costing you money, charge backs can also get your merchant status canceled with the bank. Too many charge backs can make the bank believe your business is not a good risk. Once your merchant status has been canceled, it is extremely difficult to reinstate. For businesses doing a brisk credit card business, a flag goes up at the bank if charge backs total more than 1 percent of total gross sales via credit card. The most common way to protect yourself from charge backs is to use AVS to get validation of each card holder's address information before you send a charge through.

Advantages and Disadvantages

The main advantage to accepting credit cards is the convenience for the customer, the fact that customers understand the use of credit cards, and credit card use is more secure than other convenient forms of payment. In addition, customers can do everything required to place orders right there on-line. They don't have to hang up their Internet connection to dial your number or find an envelope and stamp to mail you a check. The bottom line is, accepting credit cards means more business for you.

In addition, credit card processing can improve your delivery time to the customer, especially if you're waiting for orders to arrive before garnering product to ship or having another company ship the orders for you (called "drop shipping"). If you have payment guaranteed, you can order goods more quickly and deliver to your customers faster. If your business depends on recurring payments to be made by customers, such as subscriptions or installment payments, you don't have to concern yourself about customers forgetting to pay or being late sending payments. You can also skip the expense of sending monthly notices and hiring additional staff to process checks and postage costs. And you can sell to international customers without worrying about exchange rates, like Marilyn Butz of bizcardpro (profiled in the introduction).

The main disadvantage of accepting credit cards is the expense and hassle of becoming a credit card merchant, the additional work on your end to accept credit cards, and the increased cost over other methods of payment.

Demand Drafts

One way to accept payments is to simply have the customer write a check and send it to you. However, in the U.S., there is a way to accept checks without ever seeing or handling the customer's actual paper check. It's called the "demand draft." This method of payment is typically used for a fast turnaround and is perfect for Internet transactions and subscription services. Sanctioned by the U.S. Federal Reserve System, demand drafts allow businesses to serve millions of consumers with credit card–like convenience.

What Is a Demand Draft?

Demand drafts look just like checks and are printed in the location where they will be deposited. The printing is usually done by a third-party service, called a demand draft service bureau, that handles payment processing for businesses. Once a consumer provides his or her checking account number, bank number, check number, and address information to the business, that information is turned over to the service bureau.

The service bureau then generates the demand draft, which is a document that looks like one of the checks in the consumer's checkbook. These documents are imprinted with the consumer's name, address, phone number, account numbers, and the numbers necessary to route the draft through the bank's check-clearing system. The main difference is that, instead of a signature, the demand draft has either the customer's name or a statement such as "preapproved" or "signature on file" printed on it. The demand draft is then deposited and clears just like a check. The lack of a handwritten signature is not a problem in processing.

Who Uses Demand Drafts?

Millions of businesses use demand drafts for payment in lieu of credit cards from consumers who either don't have or don't want to use credit cards. Demand drafts are commonly used by *Fortune* 500 companies, insurance companies, and mortgage companies as well as airlines, car rental companies, on-line services such as AOL, and Internet businesses. Drafts can be printed on a recurring or one-time basis, and are even used by collection agencies for incremental payment of bad debits. They're most often used for recurring payments such as car payments or subscriptions.

Processing demand drafts is a lucrative business. Telephone Check Payment Systems (TCPS) of Kihei, Hawaii, a demand draft service bureau, reported to the FTC that it has over 700 business clients for whom it processes approximately 38,000 demand drafts totaling about $5 million each week. Another bureau, Baltimore, Maryland–based Accelerated Payment Systems (APS), told the FTC it processes half a billion dollars worth of demand drafts each year.[1]

What Does It Cost to Use Demand Drafts?

To accept demand drafts, you have to contract with a service bureau. Set-up costs run between $300 and $500. The service bureau will probably require you to open a checking account with its bank for deposit of demand drafts to your business, though some service bureaus will overnight to you the printed demand drafts instead of depositing them (this costs extra). Most service bureaus charge $1 per draft or 1.75 percent of the amount of the draft, whichever is more, and they automatically deduct the fee from your checking account.

Advantages and Disadvantages

The advantage of accepting demand drafts for payment is that customers can complete their orders on-line, so they don't have to hang up their Internet connection to call in the order or remember to mail

[1]Jody Bernstein, Director of the Bureau of Consumer Protection, U.S. Federal Trade Commission, from a speech entitled "Demand Draft Fraud," presented before the House Banking Committee, Washington, DC, April 15, 1996.

you a check later. You can also deliver to your customers faster. If your business depends on customers making recurring payments, you don't have to concern yourself about their forgetting to pay or being late sending payments. You also do not have the cost of salaries, paper, and mailing for processing recurring transactions. And you can sell to millions more customers because all you need is that the customer have a checking account instead of requiring a credit card.

A disadvantage of using demand drafts includes the FTC requirement that one of three methods of verifiable authorization take place: written authorization, a recording of the customer's voice authorizing the transaction, or a written confirmation notice sent to the consumer before the demand draft is submitted for payment. Penalties for failure to conform to this FTC requirement include fines of up to $10,000 per violation, nationwide injunctive relief, rescission of contracts, damages, and giving up any money obtained.[2]

Another problem is that customers may be nervous about providing their checking account information to a company on the Internet. The FTC says demand draft fraud has already cost consumers tens of millions of dollars, and demand drafts are much less secure for the consumer than credit cards.

As with accepting credit cards, you'll be faced with fees for the service bureau, but these fees are usually less than those associated with credit cards. You could face delayed access to funds, however, if the service bureau insists on depositing the drafts to a bank in another state.

Finally, demand drafts are a U.S.-only option. Unless your international customers have an account in a U.S. bank, you cannot make use of a demand draft to accept payment.

Electronic Cash

This type of service tends to be attractive to people with a lot of Internet experience, such as programmers and people who deal on the Internet on almost a daily basis. Most of the merchants who are in-

[2]Ibid.

volved in using electronic cash are those who sell software on the Internet, especially those who develop shareware.

Electronic cash is simply an account that both the merchant and the on-line customer set up with what we'll call electronic cash service bureaus. The most popular electronic cash service bureaus are First Virtual Holdings, CyberCash, and DigiCash. These companies require the customer to make previous arrangements to be assigned either an account number or special software that can be used with participating merchants for purchases on the Internet. To set up an account, customers usually call a toll-free number and give their credit card or bank account information over the phone rather than over the Internet. For people who have intimate knowledge of how the Internet works or who are concerned about Internet security, these companies are an attractive option. These bureaus say credit card and account numbers are never transmitted over the Internet or stored on a computer connected to the Internet.

For merchants, these services tend to be expensive, both in the fees paid and in cash flow. The merchant pays an application fee that can vary from $10 to $400, an annual fee that can range from $10 to $400, a percentage of sales ranging from 2 to 3 percent, and fees that can range from $1.30 to over $2.00 per transaction. Also, funds can be held by the service bureau for anywhere from four to ninety days, depending on the length of time the business has been around and the size of the transaction(s) involved.

If you're a small or new Internet business, you'll probably pay lower application and annual fees for electronic cash than other options. Also, you won't have to be concerned about special programming of your site to guarantee security to customers. But you'll face a trade-off of higher percentages and fees as well as those ninety-day hold times for funds.

So the main advantage of electronic cash is that it keeps people from having to send their bank account or credit card information over the Internet and small or new businesses can get set up easily to accept it. The disadvantage of electronic cash is that it requires more work on the part of the customer and it can stifle cash flow for the merchant, especially for smaller merchants.

What's interesting is how the concern over Internet security is giving electronic cash firms a hold in the service bureau marketplace. We'll talk about security issues in cyberspace next.

Security Issues

Anything sent over the Internet is sent through several different computers before it reaches its destination. The concern regarding Internet security is that unscrupulous hackers can capture credit card or checking account data as it's transferred or break into the computers connected to the Internet to steal the same information.

The answer is to encrypt the sensitive data into a code and send it across the Internet where it's decoded on the other end. This process of securing data is what is usually meant by the terms "e-commerce" or "e-business." With security in mind, the major vendors of Web servers and Internet browsers have implemented encryption techniques and attempted to standardize those encryption techniques across the Internet. The software handles the encryption or encoding on one end and the decoding on the other. Users are informed of the secure transaction because their Internet browser puts a special message on the screen and/or offers a visual clue. A common clue is to show an image of a broken key in the lower left-hand corner of the Web browser when regular, nonsecure transactions are taking place (see Figure 9-1) and a whole key when secure transactions are taking place (see Figure 9-2).

In order for you as the merchant to implement security functions for Internet transactions, you must use a Web server capable of those security functions. The most popular of these security codes is the Secured Sockets Layer (SSL). Other encryption schemes can be used with SSL, such as the Secure Electronic Transaction (SET) standard. Netscape and Microsoft both provide "secure Web server" software to those setting up Web servers, and the most popular Web browsers are built to accept and use these security functions. The bottom line is that you must check with your ISP about implementing security features for Internet transactions or purchase secure Web server software if you set up your own server.

One of the reasons for the popularity of electronic cash among

FIGURE 9-1: *Internet transactions that are not security encrypted are often indicated by a visual symbol such as this broken key.*

FIGURE 9-2: *Secure Internet transactions can be indicated by a visual clue such as this whole key.*

people who frequent cyberspace is that they understand what it takes to capture and illegally use sensitive information passed over the Internet. Standardizing encryption techniques can mean criminals can also learn the standard and use it to their advantage. But decoding encryption takes greater skill, so fewer criminals can do it.

Security on the Internet is much like security for your home. There's a point where the effort outweighs the advantages. As with your home, you usually stop adding security features when you feel safe. Making your customer feel safe is what's important in doing business on the Internet. If your customers tend to be very Internet savvy, then they may be willing to go to the extra effort to get an electronic cash account, and that type of security may make a lot of sense for your business. If your customers are average people accustomed to using credit cards, then more standard methods such as SSL and AVS are probably enough protection to make both you and your customers feel secure.

Knowing the needs of your customers determines the level of security you choose. In addition, if you know the needs of your customers, you may be able to provide links to helpful resources while enhancing your bottom line. We'll cover how to do that next.

Commission Sales or Pay Per Sale (PPS)

If you're selling something in cyberspace, it's often an advantage to get a smaller number of people who are interested in your product than a large number of visitors who are "looky-lou's." Visitors who don't buy cost you money since many ISPs charge more when traffic goes up or the amount of information stored to serve increased visitor traffic increases. And nonbuyers tie up computing resources, slowing things down and causing frustration for those who want to buy.

As a result, a number of retail sites have decided to share the wealth to get other sites to create links. Book retailers, florists, art dealers, electronic greeting card companies, and others are offering a cash bonus to sites who refer visitors that buy. Referral fees range from 2 to 20 percent or more of sales.

Most retailers require linking sites (often referred to as "associates") to fill out an application for approval in order to collect the referral fees, which are usually paid out quarterly. Links can be created in a number of ways from simple text to banner ads, but associate sites are provided with graphic from the retailer, usually in the form of a logo, to post as a link. Typical commissions range from 5 to 10 percent of sales. For example, bookseller Amazon.com has an associates program that allows other Web site owners to sign up to reference specific book titles for which the referring site gets as much as a 15 percent commission. Tenagra Corporation, who runs a site dedicated to the Year 2000 problem (http://www.year2000.com), said it has earned over $700 in three months by referring visitors to Amazon.com.

Commissions and the manner in which the commissions are calculated vary. Some retailers only pay a commission on certain items specifically mentioned on an associate's site. If the visitor buys the items mentioned on the referring site as well as other items, the referring site gets a commission only on the items mentioned, not on the entire order. If the visitor decides to buy other items altogether, the referring site is not paid.

Some sites offer a lower commission on referred sales but pay on any purchase made. If a specialty item is involved, such as medical book titles from a site specializing in medical texts, commissions go down even further. The argument here is that manufacturers or publishers who produce items for a narrow market don't offer discounts, so the distributor must pay a lower associate commission.

Delayed purchases present another problem. Visitors may be referred from an associate site, browse the site, and then go back hours or days later to buy. Few retailers address this problem. However, there are sites who specify that within a certain number of days, if a referred visitor buys, a commission is paid to the associate.

We would suggest if there are retail items or services that visitors to your site might want, you should look for other sites that carry those items and propose an associate deal. To find sites that already have such programs, go to your favorite search engine and use the search term *associates program*. This should bring you a number of retail sites who offer referral programs.

If you do decide that being a middleman is for you, here are three tips. First, shop around to compare commissions and reputations. Remember that the sites you refer visitors to reflect on your site. Second, compare delivery speed. You might decide that getting books or other items delivered to your visitors faster (a couple of days instead of four to six weeks) is worth more than a higher sales commission.

Third, watch how you present the items you get a commission on. We visited a site that, in an effort to come clean, said, "We list these books because we like them, not because someone pays us to. We receive a commission each time you buy one of these books." An explanation like this isn't necessary. It implies the site was just listing the books to get a commission, an idea most people wouldn't think of unless it was suggested. It is better to just list the items and the links, then let visitors make up their own minds.

DAVE BOLLINGER AND HUNTER MELVILLE
CYBERRENTALS
LUDLOW, VERMONT
HTTP://CYBERRENTALS.COM
VACATION RENTAL DIRECTORY ON THE WWW

Dave Bollinger and Hunter Melville were best friends from high school. Once they graduated, Dave worked in a bank for six years while Hunter worked in his family's bed-and-breakfast, then managed a ski resort. The two kept in touch. One day they decided to get together and start a business serving people who needed services for their rental properties, like lawn mowing and snow shoveling. According to Dave, performing services just naturally grew into handling the rental properties for the owners.

In a seemingly unrelated incident, Dave hit a deer with his Camero, and Hunter's wife started complaining about how beat-up the car looked. So Hunter started looking at photos of used cars in an auto trader publication. From that, he got the idea that he and Dave could start a similar pictorial publication for vacation rentals. So they started the *Vermont Rentals* and *Cape & Island Rentals* magazines.

In 1995, Hunter, who likes computers, got on the Internet and decided the magazines could be turned into a Web site that people could use in cyberspace to locate vacation rentals. So the pair started looking on the Internet and found an ISP in Oregon who could do their site. "We wanted something clean and user-friendly. And we wanted to avoid bells and whistles, flashy stuff, and garbage," Dave said.

The CyberRentals site now boasts rentals nationwide and in 1997 had over 2,000 advertisers and 1.3 million page impressions per month. Dave said while growth doubled in 1997, he and Hunter have taken a steady approach and are letting the results of advertising on the site speak for themselves. They've promoted the site in search engines, by purchasing banner ads on Yahoo, using strategic links with other sites, and by advertising in their own publications as well as in *Internet World* magazine.

CyberRentals takes credit cards from advertisers and has created a uniform look for the site by having people fill out a form they created. Filling out the form assures no information is forgotten and formatting of the material for the site can be uniform. Development and updates to the site are done using Adobe *Pagemaker,* which is also used for developing the print publications.

Dave said that while they allow the rental property owners and the customers to make their own arrangements, they understand the rental business, so they provide advice both to potential renters and to those new to offering vacation rentals. The advice includes information on standard confirmation and cancellation policies, check-in and -out times, how things should be cleaned, and rental agreement forms.

The Web site has grown to be a full third of the business, and Dave said international customers are starting to approach them about vacation sites. Dave and Hunter still do property management and publish the rental magazines, but they expect the Internet part of the business to continue to grow.

Page Impressions and Click-throughs

We've talked a lot already about advertising and sponsorship, but not from a monetary standpoint. As you'll recall, advertisers are looking for eyeballs and, therefore, tend to gravitate toward sites that have a high number of visitors. The standard rate of payment is on a per thousand (cpm) page impressions or page views. Sometimes advertisers insist on an "ad view" count, which is the number of times their ad was actually loaded to site visitors. Rates per thousand vary widely from $.55 to $5.00 cpm, depending on site traffic and the demographic characteristics of site visitors.

Some advertisers pay per click-through, which means the advertiser only pays when someone actually clicks on their banner ad. Click-through rates generally range from 2.5 cents to $.35 each. Click-through is considered a very good deal for the advertiser, but a poor deal for the host site because the advertiser gets exposure whether the banner ad entices people to click on it or not.

Advertising Agencies

Internet advertising agencies work to place advertisers with Web sites. Agencies typically charge Web sites 15 to 75 percent or more of the total advertising revenues. Some work on a sliding scale, paying more per cpm as site visitors reach higher levels. In addition, agencies may have a sign-up fee of $200 to $3,000. Agencies look for sites with consistently high page impression counts, starting at about 250,000 a month. They also like to control the revenue and pay slowly, often taking thirty to ninety days.

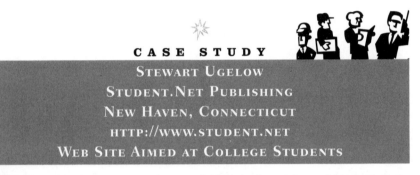

CASE STUDY
STEWART UGELOW
STUDENT.NET PUBLISHING
NEW HAVEN, CONNECTICUT
HTTP://WWW.STUDENT.NET
WEB SITE AIMED AT COLLEGE STUDENTS

Stewart Ugelow was a student studying print journalism at Yale and working summers in Raleigh, North Carolina, for the *Raleigh News & Observer* when he got the idea of setting up a Web site aimed at college students. The *Raleigh News & Observer* was one of the first newspapers to go on-line, and Stewart got to know the people in the on-line division. The paper had just launched an on-line service aimed at high-school students, and Stewart said he was hoping to start an on-line service aimed at college students.

But the *Raleigh News & Observer* was purchased by another company who changed the direction of the products and services of the paper. Stewart said he just couldn't walk away from his idea. So he got together with a group of five other students at Yale and tried to find someone to back them financially in starting a Web site aimed at college students, financed by advertising. "Companies said to us, 'It sounds like a great idea. But you're six college students with no experience, no revenue, and no site. So come back to us when you have a site.'"

So the group pooled their savings and started the Student.Net site.

Based on the business model of a magazine, Student.Net started by publishing a story per day written by college journalists around the world on topics of interest to students. The first story was a guide to brewing beer in your dorm room. While the content drew interest, the problem was that most of the early writers were volunteers. Stewart said he learned quickly that you simply cannot rely on volunteers to produce a commercial product.

Three weeks after the site was launched it was written up in the *Los Angeles Times*, *USA Today*, and then the Netscape site listed the site as a hot site. What drew attention was the site's television search and reminder service, which was the first of its kind. Site visitors can look up the times, dates, networks, and subjects of upcoming episodes of favorite TV shows. In March 1996, there was a point when the site traffic was so heavy that the Pentium PC that functioned as the site's only server was going down every four minutes.

Inside of four months, Student.Net was meeting with media companies to discuss advertiser support. At the time of our interview, Stewart said the site was selling advertising for $50 cpm or about $.05 an impression, a rate that decreased as advertisers bought volume. While the rates are higher than the industry standard, Stewart claims that Student.Net can garner higher cpm rates because of the unique nature of the site's audience.

To promote the site, Student.Net buys ads in college newspapers and on MTV. Stewart said there's also a paid staff person to handle promotion and the site has retained a college public-relations firm.

Concerning future plans for the site, Stewart recognizes it's important to stay in touch with the college crowd. "A lot of us are young and fairly close to our market. Our plan is to continue adding people recently out of college."

Techniques to Protect Yourself

Should you find yourself negotiating a deal with another party on the Internet for advertising or any other business arrangement, we encourage you to do a few quick checks to protect yourself. While it may not be possible to check everything, you can verify the most basic facts and find out a little about the company quickly and easily on the Internet. If you discover you cannot verify the address or telephone information or you cannot find out anything about this company using search engines, you should beware.

Verification Using the USPS Database

You can verify that the U.S. Postal Service has heard of a company doing business in the U.S. by doing a ZIP code look up on-line. The USPS maintains a huge database of every U.S. delivery address and the company names that go with those addresses. The database is available on-line at the USPS Web site for the purpose of helping people get the correct address and ZIP code information for sending mail, but you can use it to make sure that the company and the address you have for someone you plan to do business with are at least recognized by the USPS.

To use the ZIP code look-up feature, go to the USPS homepage at http://www.usps.gov and look for the ZIP code information look-up feature. This feature will allow you to enter the company name and address information and will check the information you enter against the USPS database. The ZIP code look-up feature will correct small errors in the address such as suite numbers, misspellings, or provide or correct a ZIP code, but if the address is bogus or the USPS doesn't recognize it, the ZIP code look-up feature will tell you that.

Verification Using the InterNIC Whois

If you remember from chapter 7, we said you could look up a domain name you're interested in by using the InterNIC's Whois on-line database to see if it is available. Well, you can also use the Whois database to get or verify information about someone who owns a domain name. Information available includes e-mail addresses, mailing addresses, telephone numbers, and the names of the people who administer the site using the domain name. If you're approached by a company you're thinking of doing business with, this is another way you can verify the information you're given. The Whois database is available under registration services at the InterNIC homepage at http://www.internic.net, and there's a tutorial to show you how to use it.

Research Using Search Engines and Usenet Newsgroups

Another technique is to look up the company's name and names of individuals involved using search engines like Yahoo or Alta Vista. If there's been something written by a third party, good or bad, you may be able to find it. Some search engines, such as Infoseek, allow you to search Usenet newsgroups for keywords as well, so you may find information there. Just be aware that all this information can be subjective and much of it is from unknown sources. Anyone can say almost anything on the Internet, but if someone is saying something about a company you're thinking of doing business with, that's information worth having, particularly if similar things are being said by a variety of people.

Conclusion

We've seen in this chapter how there is a variety of ways you can get paid on the Internet. We've talked about how to get set up to take electronic forms of payment such as credit cards, demand drafts, and electronic cash. We've also looked at the security issues involved and the types of customers attracted to each payment option. In addition, we've discussed ways to earn income via commission sales, page impressions, and click-throughs, and what to expect from advertising agencies. Finally, we covered ways you can quickly use free search and look-up tools on the Net to verify information on companies and individuals you're thinking of doing business with.

In the next chapter, we cover how to select an ISP, both from the point of view of hosting your Web site and from providing personal Internet access. We also will discuss the types of Internet connections and give you ideas for what to look for that should save you some serious headaches later on.

Chapter 10

Choosing an ISP

Being aware is more important than being smart.

—Phil Jackson,

coach of the Chicago Bulls basketball team, from
Sacred Hoops: Spiritual Lessons of a Hardwood Warrior

Now that you've determined your Web site design, decided how you're going to promote your site, and figured out how you'll get paid, you're in a position to search for an ISP to host your site on the Internet.

Basically, choosing an ISP is about speed, availability, and support. When we say speed, we mean how fast visitors can access your site. Availability means how much of the time the ISP's hardware is up and running and how long it takes to get things working again in case of a problem. And support means what the ISP will do for you in terms of technical support and giving you information about visitors to your site. If you plan to set up your own server to host your Web site, this chapter can still help you because you'll learn about the various options for connecting to the Internet and the kind of issues you need to be aware of.

To start off, we'll talk about ways to find an ISP, then work through questions you should ask potential candidates. You will probably find the answers to many of these questions on the ISP's Web site in an information section or a frequently asked questions (FAQ) section.

Then we'll discuss finding an ISP for yourself. As you've seen in some of the case studies in this book, having a Web site does not necessarily mean you have Internet access or even have a computer! Since having someone host your Web site is often not the same thing as getting Internet access for yourself, we've also included a section titled "Your Personal Internet Access" that covers tips and suggestions for getting yourself on-line.

And finally, at the end of the chapter, we have some fun with Internet terminology by offering suggestions for things you can say at parties to show your Net savvy. So first, let's talk about how to go about finding potential ISPs.

Finding an ISP

The first thing to do is to find some ISPs to evaluate. If you hire a Web site designer, the designer may know someone to handle the location of your Web site for you. In fact, some designers have a Web server in the corner of their office, connected to the Internet, where the Web sites of business clients reside. If you know someone who does Web page design, you might ask for referrals to Web servers willing to host your site.

You can also use search engines on the Internet to look up businesses who host Web sites. Your local telephone company probably offers Web site hosting, so you might check there. You might also check with sites that load quickly when you've visited to see who's hosting those sites. Geographical location doesn't have to be an issue, although if whoever hosts your site is in the same country you're in, and maybe even the same state or province, you'll have some leverage in enforcing your legal rights should things go sour.

Once you've found a few potential candidates for hosting your site, here are the questions to ask.

Questions to Ask an ISP About Hosting Your Site

Here are the questions you should ask a potential ISP that might host your Web site. We've also included some explanation of terms with each question, so that you'll understand the answer.

How Close Is the ISP to the Backbone?

This is usually question number one because the answer will tell you something about how long a visitor will have to wait to see your Web site. Sometimes the question is put this way: "How many hops are you from the NAP?" The lower the number of hops from the NAP, the better. Anything over ten is considered too many. To understand this question, we need to do some explanation of the physical structure of the Internet.

The Physical Structure of the Internet

The Internet uses the communication lines and connections put in place by telephone companies to send information. Some lines are shared, and others are dedicated. Use of this existing network is what has allowed the Internet to expand so quickly to the global network that it is today.

The function of an ISP (Internet Service Provider) is to provide access to the Internet. ISPs maintain computers with permanent connects to the Internet. These interconnected computers are in constant communication and are out of communication only if there is a hardware failure or a loss of power. There are ISPs that deal exclusively in providing connections to other ISPs, and there are ISPs that deal with business and commercial customers.

The faster and more permanent connections are called "backbones," and these form the most basic structure of the Internet. In the beginning, there was just one backbone, but in 1997 there were thirty-six backbones, run mostly by telecommunication companies such as MCI.[1] A connection to an Internet backbone is referred to as a Network Access Point (NAP, pronounced "nap").

---

[1]Jack Rickard, "ISPCon Post Mortem," *Boardwatch* (October 1997): http://www.boardwatch.com.

Another word for NAP is MAE (pronounced "may"). May stands for Metropolitan Area Ethernet and is a brand name owned by a company called MFS. The original MAE was set up in Washington, D.C., but there's another famous NAP located south of San Francisco in Silicon Valley called MAE-West. Even though technically MAE refers to the NAPs started by MFS, MAE is often used interchangeably with the term *NAP* in the same way that people sometimes use the brand name "Xerox" instead of "photocopying."

Hops

Data traveling on the Internet, whether they are Web page documents, e-mail, or any other type of information, are transferred from one router (or node) to another until they reach their destination. Each transfer is called a "hop." The fewer hops your data have to make, the better—fewer hops mean your data travel faster. It's not unusual to hear someone criticizing their ISP by saying something like "I was twelve hops from the NAP."

What Kind of Connection Does the ISP Have to the Internet?

Communication on the Internet is all about how fast files can be delivered to the computer of the person visiting your site. The bottleneck on the Internet has always been the communication speed, and not usually the speed of the computer that sends or receives the information. The type of connection to the Internet that the ISP uses will tell you the speed of the connection. In order to understand the answer to this question, we need to cover the various types of connections ISPs use to access the Internet. But first, we need to define the terms used to describe communication speed.

How Communication Speed Is Defined

In general the measure of how fast data can travel from one computer to another is measured in bits per second (bps). A bit is the smallest piece of information a computer can transmit, and eight bits make up a "byte." It takes a byte of information to describe a single character, such as the letter A.

As a shortcut, speed is sometimes referred to in kilobits per second or Kbps. This means that 57,600 bps would be 57.6 Kbps (often referred to as "fifty-seven, six"). For faster connections, the term used to describe the transfer rate is megabits per second (Mbps). A megabit is 1,024 kilobits.

Leased Lines (T-1 or T-3)

Used primarily for multiple simultaneous connections, leased lines are permanent connections to the ISP's computer and are called T-1 and T-3. The speed of a T-1 line is 1.544 megabits per second (Mbps). Each T-1 line has 24 channels capable of data transfer rates of 64 Kbps each.

A T-3 line is 45 Mbps and has 672 individual channels, each capable of a 64 Kbps data transfer rate. Internet backbone connections are T-3 lines, also sometimes referred to as DS3 lines. To give you an idea of what an ISP pays for a leased line, a 1998 *PC Magazine* column reported a T-3 leased line was about $45,000 a month.[2] Because of the expense of these types of lines, it's not unusual for an ISP to have a *fractional* T-1 line, meaning that the access and the expense of the T-1 connection is shared among several businesses.

The speed of the ISP's connection to the Internet is sometimes called its "bandwidth." The more bandwidth, or the faster the connection, the faster your Web pages will be served to those who request them.

ADSL (xDSL)

Popular in Canada and spreading in the U.S., ADSL (Asymmetric Digital Subscriber Line) is a new digital technology that works on existing copper telephone lines (also known as POTS lines). Different standards exist for this digital subscriber line, so sometimes you'll see it referenced as xDSL, with the "x" representing a term to describe the standard used. There are Asymmetric DSL (ADSL), Consumer DSL (CDSL), Rate-adaptive DSL (RDSL), High-bit-rate DSL (HDSL), ISDN-like DSL (IDSL), Single-line DSL (SDSL), and Very-high-data-rate DSL (VDSL). Each one has different speeds and require-

[2]Ben Elgin, "ISPs Work Around T-3 Rate Hikes," *ZDNet* (January 26, 1998, 1:26 PM EST): http://www.zdnet.com.

ments and is available in different areas. While speeds vary, ADSL service is about 1.5 Mbps.

Dedicated ISDN

To provide faster access, the telephone communications industry has come up with fiber-optic cable for data transmission on Integrated Services Digital Network (ISDN) lines. These are telephone connections that use digital signals instead of the old analog signals. ISDN offers a number of benefits, including security and a data transfer speed of around 128 Kbps. Dedicated ISDN is sometimes used by smaller ISPs for Internet access because it costs considerably less than leased lines.

What's the Speed of the ISP's Backbone?

Backbones can be different speeds and often use the same types of telephone company leased lines that ISPs use. The most commonly used leased lines are T-1 and T-3, although some backbones use fractional T-1 lines. Some backbones, or MAEs, are faster than others. You want to know the type of backbone the ISP is connected to because that will tell you the speed. The Business Research Group of Newton, Massachusetts, said that in 1997 half of all the ISPs in the U.S. used a backbone with a T-3 line, while another third used backbones with a T-1 connection.

How Much Space Can I Get, and What's the Cost?

The next issue is how much does disk space cost on the server. Most small businesses can get by with very little disk space to start out with. A whopping 800 pages of HTML-coded pages will fit in a mere five megabytes of disk space. However, if you get a lot of e-mail or plan to have an extensive database, you will need more disk space. Software used for tracking your hits and referral pages may also need to be stored on your portion of the IPS's hard-disk drive, which could inflate your disk space requirements. You want to find out how much more disk space costs and in what increments.

Of course, this requires that you know how much material you're putting on the ISP's hard-disk drive. So if you plan to hire a Web page designer, do that first, then find a place to house the site. The other way to handle the disk space situation is to limit yourself to the minimum space allotted by your ISP until your Web business expands enough to pay for the additional disk space.

Who Are the ISP's Other Customers?

You should talk with the other business clients that your ISP houses to find out about their experiences with the ISP. You can often send e-mail to ask these questions. While your ISP may give you a list of businesses to talk with, you can often visit an ISP's site and find businesses hosted there. In the same vein, if you find a site that loads particularly fast, you might ask the site owners who is hosting their site.

What Kinds of Additional Services Are Offered?

You'll want to ask what kind of services you can expect from your ISP. Does the ISP offer design services, site promotion, and domain name registration? (Check chapter 8 before you register your domain name.)

You might also want to ask about e-mail alias services. E-mail aliases are e-mail addresses on your site that are automatically forwarded to another e-mail address. This means you can have an e-mail address such as info@yoursite.com forwarded to your e-mail account at youraccount@aol.com. So if you have an established e-mail account or it's impractical for your ISP to offer you personal Internet e-mail, you can still have a professional look.

Also, if you can use e-mail aliases and have someone doing work on your Web site, you can automatically have certain e-mail addresses forwarded to him or her. In fact, you might be able to get the mail messages left by people who visit your site forwarded to several other e-mail addresses. But you have to ask before you can find out the answer.

Your ISP may tell you about their POP. POP, in the context of e-mail, stands for Post Office Protocol, which is the protocol used for electronic mail servers for the transmission and storage of e-mail. Sometimes you'll see POP used in conjunction with another acronym,

SMTP, which stands for Simple Mail Transfer Protocol, or IMTP, which stands for Internet Message Transfer Protocol. All that these refer to are standards for e-mail, some of which allow special features. For example, some versions of IMTP allow you to search through your e-mail messages for keywords without having to download all the mail to your own computer first. If the e-mail service has special features, you'll want to find out about those features and also find out what type of software you need to take advantage of those e-mail features.

You'll also want to ask about reports on your site activity. Does the ISP have the capability to give you referring page information, hits, page views, etc., to help you track activity on your page? This information can be gained with off-the-shelf software packages, or the ISP can write the software (and many do). Also, if there are reports available, how often can you get these reports—hourly, daily, weekly, monthly?

How Much Is the Server Available?

You want to know how much the server your Web site is on will be available. If the ISP is up all the time, they'll sometimes say "7X24" or "7 by 24," which means seven days a week, twenty-four hours a day. Servers do require maintenance, but if they tell you they're up 7X24, then the maintenance is the ISP's problem, not yours.

You also want to know about their contingency plans. Computer hardware is reliable, but problems do occur. The question is, What happens if the server goes down? How long does it take to get it running again? If only Ernie can fix it and Ernie likes to go on three-day fishing trips, then your site could be down for days if something happens to the ISP's server.

What About Technical Support?

Finally, you'll want to know what kind of support you can expect from your ISP. You want to know if the ISP caters to those starting out or are they aimed at Web professionals? What are the hours for technical support? Is there an additional charge?

Your Personal Internet Access

Most people who access the Internet from home or even from their business don't remain connected twenty-four hours a day but, instead, use "dial-up" connections. Unlike the more permanent connections, dial-up access requires that the user have software that dials a telephone number, then connects the computer to a "host" computer, which in turn is connected full-time to the Internet.

POP

ISPs call the location where you dial to gain access to their network a Point of Presence, or POP. Large ISPs have POPs in a variety of locations, so users who subscribe to the service can dial a local telephone number to get on the Internet. Most POPs allow users dial-up access, but there are POPs that allow a permanent, twenty-four-hour-a-day connection should you decide to set up your own server.

As you'll remember, POP also stands for Post Office Protocol, which is the protocol used for electronic mail servers. The only way to know which POP is being referenced is to look at the context.

Software

There are usually two pieces of software needed in order for you to "surf" the Internet using a dial-up connection. One actually dials the phone and makes the connection, so it gives your user name and password to the host computer, as well as making sure your computer and the host computer are "in sync." The other piece of software you need is an Internet browser that "talks" through the connection once it is made. Theoretically, you should be able to use any dial-up software to make the connection and any Internet browser to talk through that dial-up connection.

Sometimes the Internet browser starts the dial-up software without your help, and so you may never see the two different programs at work. But if you use other software to perform Internet tasks, such as special software to send your Web pages to your ISP, then you have to be sure the dial-up connection is working before you start the specialized software. If you have a full-time Internet connection, the software that makes the initial connection between the computers just keeps running. Usually both the dial-up software and the browser software are provided by the service who charges you for Internet access, although the dial-up software is built into Windows beginning with the Windows 95 version. You must obtain any other software yourself, although you can usually get it through the Internet using your browser.

Modems

The device that interprets the data coming into your computer is known as a modem. Modem is short for modulator/demodulator. This means the modem can translate or modulate digital data coming from your computer into an analog signal that can be transmitted and then demodulates incoming analog data into a digital format. However, the term *modem* has been expanded to include any device that performs the necessary translation of transmitted data on its way into or out of a computer. The type of connection to your computer determines the type and speed of the modem, so we'll talk about the various types of Internet connections next.

POTS

POTS is what you have if you have a telephone. We referred to it earlier as analog telephone technology. POTS stands for plain old telephone service. The top speed that data can travel over these analog phone lines is about 57.6 Kbps or 57,600 bits per second (bps). All you need to use POTS is a standard analog modem, which is built into most new PCs, and a telephone outlet near your computer.

To give you an idea of how fast (or not fast) analog phone lines are, the average floppy disk drive transfers data to your PC from a diskette at the rate of about 30,000 bps. As you know if you've ever waited for data to load from a floppy diskette, this isn't exactly lightning speed. So that means a 57,600 bps modem is capable of transferring data only twice as fast as your floppy disk drive can load data.

> **TIP**   *Sometimes you'll see modem speed referred to as the "baud rate." The baud rate is the bits per second, so a 57,600 baud modem is the same as a 57,600 bps modem.*

To get faster speed, there are more specialized connections such as ISDN, Cable, Satellite, and T-1 or T-3 leased lines. We cover those next.

ISDN

To provide faster access, the telephone communications industry has come up with fiber-optic cable for data transmission on Integrated Services Digital Network (ISDN) lines. These are telephone connections that use digital signals instead of the old analog signals. ISDN offers a number of benefits, such as two channels that can either be used separately or together and a faster data transfer speed of around 128 Kbps, or two channels of 64 Kbps each.

For our purposes here, we'll define a channel as a connection between two computers, but you can think of a channel as having the same functionality as a separate phone line. In fact, ISDN lines often offer two phone numbers, one for each channel. Use of an ISDN line requires a special modem known as an ISDN modem. You can purchase an ISDN modem that has standard modular phone line connectors so as long as the computer is on, you can use the ISDN line like a standard phone line for voice or fax and be connected to the Internet using the ISDN connection simultaneously. There is also dedicated ISDN service, which means you never dial in after the initial connection has been made but are always connected.

> **TIP**   *ISDN availability, prices, and speeds vary from area to area. Check your local telecommunications company before making a commitment of your resources to ISDN.*

Cable

Another fast connection to the Internet is via cable. Cable modems use cable television connections to provide Internet access and are aimed at residential Internet customers. The cable company provides the modem and the installation, but you need a network connection on your computer known as Ethernet. Once the Ethernet connection has been established, you never again have to "log in" to the service as you do with dial-up services. However, some cable companies also require a standard dial-up modem and telephone line for data going from your computer to the Internet, so you only receive data using the cable modem. Many cable companies also act as the ISP, so your cable modem connection fee also gives you full-time Internet access at no additional charge.

While cable modems are fast, in the 3-to-30-megabit-per-second (Mbps) range for incoming data (downloads) and 128 Kbps to 10 Mbps for uploads, a problem the cable industry is working on is security. Each neighborhood shares a single coaxial cable backbone to which every cable modem in the neighborhood is always connected, so it's not hard for someone to "pick off" signals traveling on the cable or even hack into your computer. Filters are being developed to block this potential eavesdropping, but it's something you should discuss with the cable company before signing up for this service.

Satellite

Satellite Internet connections involve installation of a card into your PC and installation of a small satellite dish. Like cable, both television programming and Internet information can be relayed using a satellite feed. Satellite technology is increasingly important to Web surfers in Europe and Asia who want access to U.S.-based Internet information. These non-U.S. Web surfers are often competing through crowded phone networks and thus face long delays in receiving U.S.-based information using POTS service. Satellite access is much faster for these subscribers.

In the U.S., satellite connections are billed as ten times faster than a cable modem with speeds up to 4 Mbps. The wrinkle here is you cannot upload, so you still need a phone line and an ISP. You also need a clear area facing south for the dish to be installed on the outside of your home or office, and professional installation of the satellite equipment is recommended.

ADSL (xDSL)

Popular in Canada and spreading in the U.S., ADSL (Asymmetric Digital Subscriber Line) is a new digital technology that works on existing copper telephone lines (also known as POTS lines). Different standards exist for this digital subscriber line, so sometimes you'll see it referenced as xDSL, with the "x" representing a term to describe the standard used. (The various types of ADSL are listed earlier in this chapter.)

ADSL modems come in pairs, one for your end and one for the telephone company or ISP. You can make a connection with an ADSL modem only to its mate on the other end, so you cannot use your ADSL modem for any other ADSL service. Also, security is an issue with ADSL. ADSL service is about 1.5 Mbps for downloads and 64 Kbps for uploads.

A Comparison of Communication Line Speeds

The table in Figure 10-1 shows the various types of lines we've talked about in this chapter as well as the type of connection, the number of channels, and the data transfer speeds for each. Pricing varies from area to area, so we advise you to check with your local telephone company.

Conclusion

We've introduced lots of terms and new ideas in this chapter with an eye to helping you decode the language when you talk to ISPs. In the way of a recap of this chapter, we thought we'd give you some of the cooler terms introduced here in sentences you can use at social gatherings to impress your friends with your knowledge of the

Internet. If you need a refresher, you can jump back into the chapter or look up these terms in the glossary.

Cool Sentences You Can Use at Social Events
to Show Your Net Knowledge

Disclaimer: Use these sentences at your own risk.

1. *I couldn't believe it when I found out my ISP was fourteen hops from the NAP.*
2. *We went with (name of ISP) because we can use their Dallas POP for local dial-up access.*
3. *Have you heard America Online bought CompuServe because of the speed of its backbone? Who would have thought they'd have such a fast MAE?*
4. *I heard the DNS database of .com names was corrupted and it slowed the whole Net to a crawl.*
5. *We thought about just publishing our IP address as our URL rather than getting a domain name because we think people will like typing all those numbers. (Not!)*
6. *I taught myself HTML and used Word Pad in Windows 95 to create my Web pages.*
7. *We got an ISDN line so our uploads to our Web site are faster. It makes surfing great, too, and it's cheaper than two regular business phone lines.*
8. *I find it hard to believe that anyone thought they could charge money for a Web browser. By the way, what browser do you use?*
9. *I downloaded a cool page off the Net yesterday. Would you like the URL?*
10. *I changed my page, but it took forever for me to upload it to my ISP. I understand the traffic on the network was unusually heavy. How is access to your ISP?*

So we've reached the end of this book, but certainly not the end of your experience in cyberspace. For you, this is just the beginning.

Description	Analog Phone Line	ISDN	Cable	Satellite*	ADSL	T-1	T-3
Type of connection	Dial-up	Dial-up	Ethernet	Proprietary	Proprietary	Leased line	Leased line
Speed in bits per second (bps)	57,600 bps max with modem	128,000 bps	2 million+ bps	4 million+ bps	Downloads 1.5 million bps, uploads 64,000 bps	1.544 million bps	45 million bps
Speed as normally referenced	57,600 bps max	128 Kbps	3 - 10 Mbps	4 Mbps	1.5 Mbps and 64 Kbps	1.544 Mbps	45 Mbps
Number of channels	1	2	1 or 2	1	2	24	672
Maximum speed per channel	57,600 bps or 57.6 Kbps	64 Kbps	4 -5 Mbps	4 Mbps	Uploads 64 Kbps, downloads 1.5 Mbps	64 Kbps	64 Kbps

FIGURE 10-1: *A comparison of the various telephone connections used to access the Internet and their speeds. *Remember: You cannot upload using a satellite connection.*

Again, here are our e-mail and Web site addresses. If we can help, we'd like to. We look forward to hearing your success story!

Paul and Sarah Edwards:
homepage: http://www.paulandsarah.com
Linda Rohrbough:
Linda@PCbios.com
homepage: http://www.PCbios.com

A p p e n d i x

Internet Resources

WEB SEARCH ENGINES

Alta Vista
http://altavista.digital.com

Deja News
http://www.dejanews.com

Dogpile
http://www.dogpile.com

Excite
http://www.excite.com

Hotbot
http://www.hotbot.com

Infoseek
http://www.infoseek.com

LookSmart
http://looksmart.com

Lycos
http://www.lycos.com

MetaCrawler
http://www.metacrawler.com

NetFerret
http://www.netferret.com

Northern Light
http://www.northernlight.com

Scrub the Web
http://www.scrubtheweb.com

Web Crawler
http://www.webcrawler.com

Yahoo
http://www.yahoo.com

INFORMATION ABOUT SEARCH ENGINES

@bruceclay
http://www.bruceclay.com

Search Engine Watch
http://searchenginewatch.com

WEB ANNOUNCEMENT SERVICES

PostMaster2
http://www.netcreations.com/
    postmaster

Register It!
http://registerit.com

Submit It!
http://www.submit-it.com

INTERNET ORGANIZATIONS

CommerceNet
http://www.commerce.net

Electronic Direct Marketing Association (EDMA)
http://www.edma.com

HTML Writers Guild
http://www.hwg.org

International Ad Hoc Committee (IAHC)
http://www.iahc.org

Internet Literacy Consultants
http://www.matisse.net

Internet Society
http://www.isoc.org

InterNIC Registration Services
http://www.internic.net

Microsoft
http://www.microsoft.com

National Association of Webmasters
http://www.naw.com

Netscape Communications
http://home.netscape.com

United States Postal Service ZIP Code Lookup
http://www.usps.gov

Whois
http://rs.internic.net/cgi-bin/whois

The World Wide Web Consortium
http://www.w3.org

INTERNET ADVERTISING AGENCIES

Double-Click
http://www.doubleclick.net

Flycast
http://www.flycast.com

IN2
http://www.in2.com

Softbank Interactive Marketing
http://www.simweb.com

ADVERTISING RATES

Standard Rate and Data Service (SRDS) On-Line
http://www.srds.com

ADVERTISING INFORMATION/DISCUSSION LISTS

Edelman Public Relations
www.edelman.com

Internet Advertising Bureau (IAB)
http://www.iab.net

MicroScope—weekly ad reviews
http://www.pscentral.com

The On-Line Advertising Discussion
  Forum List
http://www.o-a.com

BANNER EXCHANGE SERVICES

LinkExchange
http://www.linkexchange.com

ELECTRONIC CASH ORGANIZATIONS

CyberCash, Inc.
http://www.cybercash.com

Digicash
http://www.digicash.com

First Virtual Holdings, Inc.
http://www.fv.com

MAGAZINES

Advertising Age On-Line
http://www.adage.com

Boardwatch
http://www.boardwatch.com

ClickZ
http://www.clickz.com

CNET
http://www.news.com

Hits
http://www.herring.com/hits

Internet World
http://www.internet.com

NetMarketing
http://www.netb2b.com

WebDeveloper
http://www.webdeveloper.com

Web Developer's Journal
http://www.nctweb.com

Web Master Magazine
http://www.web-master.com

WebWeek
http://www.webweek.com

Wired
http://www.wired.com

PRESS RELEASE SITES

Businesswire
http://www.businesswire.com

PR Newswire
http://www.prnewswire.com

PRWeb
http://www.prweb.com

SUBSCRIPTION-BASED ELECTRONICALLY SEARCHABLE DATABASES

Knight-Ridder Information, Inc.
Dialog/DataStar
http://www.krinfo.com

Lexis-Nexis
http://www.lexis-nexis.com

OCLC
EPIC Service
http://www.oclc.org

OVID Technologies
OVID On-line
http://www.ovid.com

TRADE SHOWS

Internet World
http://www.internet.com

ISPCon
http://www.ispcon.com

Web Advertising
http://www.thunderlizard.com/tlp/
    webad.html

WEB SOFTWARE TOOLS

E-mail

Eudora
http://www.eudora.com

Web Site Development

Adobe's PageMill, PageMaker
http://www.adobe.com

Microsoft's FrontPage
http://www.microsoft.com

Sausage Software's HotDog Web Editor
http://www.sausage.com

Symantec's Visual Page
http://www.symantec.com

Web Site Statistics Software for Web Servers

ClickAudit
http://www.clickaudit.com

WebTrends
http://www.webtrends.com

WEB SITE COUNTERS

Counterstats.com
http://www.counterstats.com

Countman
http://asoftware.com/countman

i-Depth
http://www.i-depth.com

WEB SITE RANKING

@bruceclay
http://www.bruceclay.com

PositionAgent
http://www.submit-it.com

Search Engine Watch
http://www.searchenginewatch.com

AWARDS FOR WEB SITES

GIST TV magazine
Web Picks
http://www.gist.com

Lycos
Top 5% Sites
http://www.lycos.com

Tenagra Award
For Advertising Excellence
http://www.tenagra.com

Too Cool
The Too Cool Award
http://www.toocool.com

USA Today
Hot Site
http://www.usatoday.com

Yahoo
Weekly Pick
http://www.yahoo.com

Books

The Complete Guide to Self-Publishing:
Everything You Need to Know to Write, Publish, Promote, and Sell Your Own Book
by Tom and Marilyn Ross
Cincinnati, OH: Writer's Digest Books, 1985

How to Make Yourself (or Anyone Else) Famous:
The Secrets of a Professional Publicist
by Gloria Michels
New York: Cross Gates, 1988

Internet File Formats
by Tim Kientzle
Scottsdale, AZ: Coriolis Group Books, 1995

The Internet for Dummies
by John Levine, Carol Baroudi, and Margaret Levine Young
Foster City, CA: IDG Books Worldwide, 1997

PC File Formats & Conversions
by Ralf Kussmann
Grand Rapids, MI: Abacus, 1990

Publicity on the Internet
by Steve O'Keefe
New York: Wiley, 1997

The Web Server Handbook
by Pete Palmer, Adam Schneider, and Anne Chenette
Upper Saddle River, NJ: Prentice Hall, 1996

InterNIC Sample Application

(This is for information purposes only. Please visit the InterNIC site, http://www.internic.net, for a current application.)

Authorization
0a. (N)ew (M)odify (D)elete............:
0b. Auth Scheme............:
0c. Auth Info............:
1. Purpose/Description............:
2. Complete Domain Name............:

Organization Using Domain Name
3a. Organization Name (Registrant)............:
3b. Street Address............:
3c. City............:
3d. State............:
3e. Postal Code............:
3f. Country Code (2 letter)............:

Administrative Contact/Agent
4a. NIC Handle (if known)............:
4b. (I)ndividual or (R)ole?............:
4c. Name............:
4d. Organization Name............:
4e. Street Address............:
4f. City............:
4g. State............:
4h. Postal Code............:
4i. Country Code (2 letter)............:
4j. Phone Number............:
4k. Fax Number............:
4l. E-mail Address............:

Technical Contact

5a. NIC Handle (if known)............:
5b. (I)ndividual or (R)ole?............:
5c. Name.............:
5d. Organization Name............:
5e. Street Address............:
5f. City............:
5g. State............:
5h. Postal Code............:
5i. Country Code (2 letter)............:
5j. Phone Number............:
5k. Fax Number............:
5l. E-mail Address............:

Billing Contact

6a. NIC Handle (if known)............:
6b. (I)ndividual or (R)ole?............:
6c. Name............:
6d. Organization Name............:
6e. Street Address............:
6f. City............:
6g. State............:
6h. Postal Code............:
6i. Country Code (2 letter)............:
6j. Phone Number............:
6k. Fax Number............:
6l. E-mail Address............:

Primary Name Server

7a. Primary Server Hostname............:
7b. Primary Server Netaddress............:

Secondary Name Server(s)

8a. Secondary Server Hostname............:
8b. Secondary Server Netaddress............:

END OF AGREEMENT

An Alphabetical Listing of
125+
Internet Businesses

 In this section we list 125+ businesses you can start on the Internet, organized alphabetically. Virtually any business can be promoted or marketed on the Internet, but here we have sought to list businesses that enjoy a particular benefit from being started on the Web. For each entry we list the business, a description, and the chapter in which that type of business is covered. (Chapters 3, 4, and 5 cover each business type, such as Selling Goods and Services, Advertiser-Supported Sites, and Content Development.) In addition, we indicate if the business requires greater than average or lower than average financial resources to get started. Research by the U.S. Department of Commerce shows that over 60 percent of all businesses are started for under $5,000, so to be conservative, we've taken this figure as the average amount to start a business. If no financial resource is checked, then you can assume the business requires average financial resources. And since most Internet businesses can be operated from home, we've indicated those businesses that could have additional housing requirements such as rented office space or warehouse space.

The following is a key to the layout of the Internet businesses table.

Business Type	Description	1. Selling Goods and Services (chapter 3)	2. Advertiser-Supported Sites (chapter 4)	3. Content Development (chapter 5)	4. Greater Than Average Resources	5. Lower Than Average Resources	6. Outside Housing Needed

Business Type	Description	1	2	3	4	5	6
Agent / actors	Representing actors	X					
Animal breeder / pets	Breeding pure-bred or specialty pets such as dogs, cats, birds, reptiles, etc.	X					
Animator	Development of computer animation for Web sites			X			
Animator / clip art	Development of animated clip art for Web sites			X			
Antique dealer	Selling antiques	X					
Art dealer	Providing artwork for sale to the public for a commission	X				X	
Artist representative	Representing artists	X					
Artist / clip art	Development of clip art for download	X					
Auction broker	Conduct and promote on-line auctions			X			
Audio and video digitizing service	Digitizing existing analog audio and video	X					
Auto information broker	Providing information based on auto ID number of auto history from publicly available records	X					
Auto parts broker	Retail sales of hard-to-get or specialty auto parts	X					
Auto sale broker	Retail sale of automobiles	X					
Bed-and-breakfast	Providing meals and lodging	X					
Book publicist	Representing writers in public-relations efforts	X				X	
Book publisher / electronic	Publishing and promoting books in electronic form, especially those on specialized topics	X					

Business Type	Description	1	2	3	4	5	6
Book publisher / print	*Publishing and promoting printed books, especially those on specialized topics*	X					
Bulletin board service / operator	*Creating a bulletin board where people with common needs in a specialized area can communicate and gain resources*			X			
Broker / mailing lists	*Providing electronic mailing lists of e-mail addresses*	X		X			
Business coach	*Counseling business and professional people*	X					
Business stationery	*Providing businesses stationery*	X	X			X	
Calendar service	*Providing information about upcoming events for specialized audiences*	X		X			
Cartographer	*Electronic mapmaker*	X					
Clothing retailer / children	*Specialty clothing for children, such as unique baby clothing*	X					
Clothing retailer / men	*Specialty clothing for men, such as large size or short*	X					
Clothing retailer / specialty clothes	*Specialty clothing for certain activities such as hiking, skiing, working with chemicals, health care*	X					
Clothing retailer / women	*Specialty clothing for women, such as large size or petite*	X					
Collectibles dealer	*Retailing collectible items*	X					
Comics	*Comic strip development, history of comic strips*		X				
Commercial artist	*Designing art for company logos*	X	X			X	
Computer-aided design	*Designing things from clothes to traffic systems*	X					
Computer artist	*Development of art for Web sites*			X			
Computer-assisted instructional design	*Create interactive software for teaching and training in just about anything*	X			X		

Business Type	Description	1	2	3	4	5	6
Computer game reviewer	Reviewing computer games for game enthusiasts and/or offering games for sale	X	X			X	
Computer programmer	A programmer may design, write original, or modify code, compile, debug, and fix errors			X			
Consultant	Consulting services	X					
Copywriter	Writing public-relations materials for Web sites			X		X	
Corporate Web cop	Policing policies and sites			X			
Credit card service	Setting up Web sites to accept credit cards			X			
Custom wood blinds	Manufacturing and selling custom wood blinds	X					
Dance instructor	Promoting dance classes, providing instruction on videotape	X	X				
Database marketing service	Tailor mailing and direct-marketing lists to help businesses reach customers	X					
Database programmer	Programming database applications for Web sites			X			
Data recovery service	Specializing in the recovery of lost data from damaged hard-disk drives or systems working intermittently	X					
Day care	Offering live monitoring of child care	X					
Delivery service / candy	Delivering candy	X					
Delivery service / flowers	Delivering flowers	X					
Delivery service / grocery	Shopping for and delivering groceries	X			X		
Delivery service / singing	Delivering entertainment such as singing telegrams	X					
Desktop publishing service	Developing material for both internal and external communications	X					

Business Type	Description	1	2	3	4	5	6
Desktop video	*Edit and add effects to full-motion video*			X			
Dictionary developer	*Providing a reference of terms for fast look-up*		X				
Digital photography /image manipulation	*Photo retouching, image enhancement, and special-effects and editing images*	X		X			
Digital recording studio / service	*Record sound on digital media for use on computers and Web sites*			X			
Discussion list creator	*Housing and promoting a discussion list*		X				
Discussion list moderator	*Moderating an on-line discussion list*		X	X			
Electronic greeting card sales	*Developing and selling electronic greeting cards*	X					
Electronic public relations	*Helping clients get publicity in cyberspace media*			X			
Expert brokering service	*Matching highly specialized professionals and consultants with clients*	X					
Financial information service	*Providing information and/or services*	X	X				
Food production and sales	*Hard-to-find and specialty foods*	X					
Form designer	*Designing forms for use on-line (CGI)*			X			
Game developer	*Development of interactive or single-player games*	X					
Gifts / holiday, corporate	*Developing and sale of customized gift baskets, corporate gifts*	X					
Government contract information	*Organizing government contract information*	X					
Information broker	*Locating information on-line and off-line for clients*	X					

Business Type	Description	1	2	3	4	5	6
Internet consultant	Assist clients in doing business on the Internet			X			
Internet librarian	Organizing and filing information resources for easy access to Web site visitors			X		X	
Internet Service Provider / city	Providing Internet access in high-population areas			X	X		X
Internet Service Provider / rural	Providing Internet access in rural areas			X	X		
Internet trainer	Teaches people about the Internet and how to use it	X		X			
Liquidator	Sale of merchandise from defunct companies, overstock merchandise	X					
Magazine publisher	On-line magazine publisher		X				
Market mapping service	Helping companies track customer demographics and sales patterns	X		X			
Market research	Providing market research and consulting to businesses	X					
Matchmaking service	Helping people find people for special relationships	X				X	
Mortgage brokers	Home mortgage loans	X			X		
Multimedia production	Adding three-dimensional graphics, animation, sound, and motion to presentations, demonstrations, tutorials, workshops, and training sessions	X					
Music composer / sound designer	Composition of music clips for Web sites			X			
News service	Daily news reports	X	X				
Nutrition, diet, and exercise	Creating individualized plans	X					
On-line bookseller	Selling rare, specialty, and used books	X					

Business Type	Description	1	2	3	4	5	6
On-line newsletter	Highly focused specialty information published electronically	X	X				
On-line product sales	For example: • Clothing • Computer items • Customized wood blinds • Livestock • Plants	X					
Pager service	Transmitting Internet messages to pagers	X			X		
Price checker	Gathering pricing information for retailers			X			
Price locator services	Helping people find one another		X				
Printing broker	Brokering printing services, such as business cards	X				X	
Private investigator	Perform investigative services using the Internet		X				
Public relations / specialty	Unique store promotional ideas such as belt sander drag racing for hardware stores		X				
Puzzles	Development of crossword puzzles, anagrams, acronym games for on-line players		X				
Real estate agent	Selling real estate on-line	X					
Real-time image capture and display service	Virtual viewing of events such as weddings or funerals; parental viewing of day-care centers			X	X		
Referral service	Providing referrals for anything from rooms to handymen	X	X				
Reminder service	Enabling companies and professionals to remind customers of appointments, anniversaries, and service due dates	X	X				
Reporter	Reporting news events for Internet publications			X			

Business Type	Description	1	2	3	4	5	6
Résumé writing	Writing and developing résumés	X					
Scholarship service	Providing information on college scholarships and financial aid	X					
Seamstress	Custom-made specialty garments and draperies	X					
Search engine / general	Providing Internet Web site locations based on subjects or keywords		X				
Search engine / specific	Providing Internet Web site locations on a specific topic, such as cats		X				
Search engine ranking service	Services to improve a Web site's search engine ranking			X			
Search engine submission service	Submitting Web sites to search engines			X			
Sign-making service	Creating signs, posters, and fliers	X					
Software developer	Development and sale of computer software	X					
Software development / businesses	Development of software for specific business applications such as account tracking or cost estimating	X					
Software development / custom applications	Development of custom software programs for individual businesses	X					
Software location service	Finding specialized software for clients	X					
Sound effects	Creating sound effects for use in Web sites or to accompany computer applications	X	X				
Speaker's agent	Promoting public speaking and seminar clients	X					

Business Type	Description	1	2	3	4	5	6
Special-occasion and party items	Birthday decorations or surprise-party packages, birthday gifts sent automatically for customers each year	X					
Stationery designer / electronic	Design and sale of electronic greeting cards, postcards, stationery, etc.	X	X				
Syndicate	Developing on-line syndicate	X					
Teacher / instructor / tutor	On-line classes on specific topics, like computer repair, biology, or software programming languages	X					
Technical writer	Development of Web site content			X			
Therapist	Offering on-line therapy services	X				X	
Travel agent / planner	Providing travel services and information		X				
Used-computer broker	Matching buyers with sellers of used computers and related equipment	X					
Vacation rental broker	Provide information to potential vacationers concerning vacation rentals		X				
Webmaster	Maintenance of an existing Web site, answering e-mail, troubleshooting problems			X			
Web page designer	Designing Web pages			X			
Web radio and television programs	Broadcasting live programming on the Web			X			
Web security service	Tests sites for security and recommends and/or implements security measures and policies			X			
Web site content promoter	Developing contests and promotional activities on Web sites	X		X			
Web site developer / specialty	Specializing in Web site development for specific business types, like golf courses			X			

Business Type	Description	1	2	3	4	5	6
Web site reviewer	*Reviewing sites for on-line and print publications*	X					
Web site tracking service	*Notification of changes in Web sites*			X			
Web site writer	*Writing content for a Web site while conforming to stylistic conventions of the Web*			X			
Woodworker	*Custom canes, custom cabinets, furniture*	X			X		

Glossary

active name server—see **primary name server**

ad click rate—see **click-through rate**

ADSL—asymmetric digital subscriber line, a digital technology for electronic data transfer that works on existing copper telephone lines

ad views—the number of times the advertiser's banner ad is actually loaded

AOL—America Online, a non-Internet Service Provider who also provides Internet access to subscribers

ARPANET—the precursor to the Internet formed by the U.S. Department of Defense

ASCII—American standard code for information interchange, an English-language code in which each character, both upper and lower case as well as punctuation, is represented by a number

auditing—the process of verifying the number of visitors to a particular Web site or specific Web page

backbone—the main network connections that make up the Internet. These connections are T-3 leased lines.

banner—also referred to as an "ad banner" or "banner ad," it is a rectangular-shaped graphic image sized for placement at the top or bottom of a Web page and linked to another Internet Web site

baud rate—the number of bits per second, used in reference to modem speed

BBS—bulletin board service

bit—the smallest amount of information a computer can process or transfer

bot—short for robot, usually refers to an automated program designed to collect data

bps—bits per second

byte—eight bits

CDSL—consumer digital subscriber line, a variation on ADSL; see **ADSL**

channel—for the purposes of this book, a channel is a communication path between two computers

charge back—the automated deduction of funds from a credit card merchant's account because a customer disputed a credit card charge

click—the action a visitor takes when using the mouse to select an object on the screen

click rate—see **click-through rate**

click-through—a term used for when a Web site visitor clicks on a banner ad

click-through rate—the percentage of times an ad is clicked on based on the number of times it's viewed. If a banner ad is seen (via an impression) by two hundred visitors to a site and ten of them actually click on the banner ad, the banner ad has a click-through rate of 5 percent.

CLM—career limiting move

cookie—a piece of text provided by a Web server to a Web browser and stored on the visitor's computer in the COOKIES.TXT file

CPM—cost per thousand

crawler—see **bot; spider**

crossposting—posting the same article to several newsgroups. Connotes an attempt by the party posting the article to sell something or further selfish interests.

CTR—see **click-through rate**

DC3—see **T-3**

DDS—digital data service, a term used by phone companies to refer to leased telephone lines

demand draft—a "check" printed by a service bureau using account and address information provided by the customer that is processed by a bank just like a check written by the customer

dithering—a way of creating new colors by using pixels in existing colors in patterns to form the new color

DN—domain name

DNS—domain name system, a distributed database of IP addresses and corresponding domain names maintained by the InterNIC

domain name—a set of characters that are used instead of the IP address for a Web site

download—the process of sending files via telephone lines or other network connections from one computer to another

dpi—dots per inch

drop ship—the practice of selling goods, dealing with the promotion of the goods, and accepting payment, but having the goods shipped to the customer by a third party such as the manufacturer or supplier

DSU/CSU—data service unit/channel service unit, a piece of hardware equivalent to a modem and required on each end of a leased line used for on-line access. A router is also required.

EBCDIC—extended binary-coded decimal interchange code, the mainframe computer character set where each letter is represented by a unique number

e-business—see **e-commerce**

e-commerce—electronic commerce. Connotes secured business transactions on the Internet.

ECP—excessive crossposting; see **crossposting**

exposure—see **impression**

FAQ—frequently asked questions

flame—an angry or insulting comment sent via e-mail

flame bait—comments designed to incite others to respond with anger

flamers—those who send angry or insulting e-mail comments to others

flaming—the act of sending messages that are intended to be very insulting

fractional T-1—the phone company practice of leasing just part of the twenty-four channels of a T-1 line; see **T-1**

frame relay—a type of telephone service that allows a group of users to share a pool of connections for data delivery between computers and delivers from 56 to 512 Kbps bandwidth

freeware—software offered without charge

ftp—file transfer protocol

GIF—graphic image format, a compressed graphics file format designed for images with large areas of solid color

graphic—a picture

GUI—graphical user interface

HDSL—high-bit-rate digital subscriber line, a variation on ADSL; see **ADSL**

hits—the number of machine requests required to construct a page. For example, a page with eight graphics and text is equivalent to nine hits: eight for graphics, one for text.

homepage—the first page of a Web site, although sometimes the term is used to reference the entire site (e.g., Do you have a homepage?)

hop—Each time a packet of information is forwarded from one router or node to another on the Internet, it has taken a hop.

HTML—hypertext markup language, the simple language used to code Web page documents

http—hypertext transfer protocol, the code used to create Web pages

IDSL—ISDN-like digital subscriber line, a variation on ADSL; see **ADSL**

impression—see **page impression**

IMTP—Internet message transfer protocol, a standard for e-mail

in-line ad—The in-line ad is most often a vertical advertising link set off by a different color background that runs along the right or left border of a Web page.

InterNIC—the organization that supplies IP addresses and domain names

IP—Internet protocol

IP address—the numeric address of a Web site address made up of a group of numbers separated by periods like this: 192.41.3.149

IRC—Internet relay chat

ISDN—integrated services digital network, usually supporting data transfer rates of 64 Kbps

ISP—Internet service provider

Java—a programming language developed by Sun Microsystems for the Internet

Jello—Internet slang for a combination of spam and ECP

JPEG—Joint Photographic Experts Group, a compressed file format designed for photographs

Kbps—kilobits per second, or 1,000 bits per second

leased line—For the purposes of this book, a leased line is a permanent (full-time) telephone connection between two computers.

MAE—metropolitan area Ethernet, a network access point to the Internet backbone, the most famous of which is MAE-West in the western portion of the U.S.

Mbps—megabits per second, or a million bits per second

MBps—a million bytes per second, equal to eight million bits per second

MOTO—Mail Order/Telephone Order. Used to describe the methods for accepting payment when the customer is at a distance.

NAP—Network Access Point, a point where access is made to the Internet backbone

newbie—someone new to the Internet or to a particular discussion group on the Internet

newsgroup—an Internet-based forum focused on a single topic to which anyone is allowed to respond or ask questions concerning the forum topic

node—a processing location on a computer network

NSF—National Science Foundation, the government agency known for its involvement with the Internet

NSFNet backbone—the first Internet backbone

on-line—the state of being connected to a computer network, usually to the Internet

packet—a piece of a document or message that contains the destination address

packet switching—protocols for transmission of data across the Internet in which data is divided into numbered packets before being sent, so that even if each packet takes a different path to the destination, upon arrival all packets can be formed back into the original data

page impression—each time all the files necessary to create a single Web page are downloaded to a Web site visitor

page requests—see **page views**

page transfers—see **page views**

page views—Refers to the number of times an entire Web page, including graphics, is served up to visitors. This term is often used to tell advertisers how many times their banner ad was seen or could be seen by visitors viewing the page.

pixel—picture element

POP—point of presence, an ISP's connection to the Internet; or post office protocol, used for e-mail

POTS—plain old telephone service

primary name server—ISPs are expected to have two computers connected to the Internet so that one is a backup in case the other goes down, and these are the primary (or active) and secondary name servers. This is where the DNS will point any visitors who want to view your site. Your ISP will have the domain names and IP addressses of its primary and secondary servers, so you'll need to ask for that information.

protocol—a set of rules that two computers use to communicate

RDSL—rate-adaptive digital subscriber line, a variation on ADSL; see **ADSL**

resolution—In graphic imaging terms, this is the number of pixels per inch used to make up the image.

router—a computer used to connect and pass information between two computer networks

SDSL—single-line digital subscriber line, a variation on ADSL; see **ADSL**

secondary name server—see **primary name server**

server—a computer that "serves" up files or data to other computers

shareware—software offered on a try-before-you-buy basis

SMTP—simple mail transfer protocol, used for e-mail

snail mail—regular U.S. mail using paper, envelopes, and stamps

spam—Internet slang for unsolicited bulk electronic mail, sometimes also used to describe the repetition of words on a page to get the page ranked higher in search engines

spammers—those who make a living sending unsolicited e-mail

spamming—Internet slang for the act of sending spam; see **spam**

spider—an automated program that goes from page to page and link to link on the Internet for the purpose of cataloging information for use in search engines

spoofing—the practice of attempting to trick a search engine into improving the ranking of a page by repeating keywords over and over, often hiding the keywords from the user

SSL—secured sockets layer, an Internet security protocol for encrypting and decrypting sensitive information for transmission

switched 56—a type of leased telephone connection to the Internet that allows access at 56 Kbps

T-1—a telephone connection for data transmission at a speed of 1.544 Mbits, consisting of 24 channels of 64 Kbps each

T-3—a telephone connection for the purpose of data transmission at a speed of 45 Mbits, consisting of 672 individual channels of 64 Kbps each

TCP/IP—transmission control protocol/Internet protocol, an Internet protocol for communication between computers

trolling for newbies—the act of posting inflammatory messages in the hopes of exciting angry responses from new people

upload—sending a file electronically to another computer

URL—universal resource locator

VDSL—very high data-rate digital subscriber line, a variation on ADSL; see **ADSL**

Velveeta—Internet slang for ECP

Web page—a page of HTML code

Web site—a number of related Web pages linked together

xDSL—a reference to all the varieties of digital subscriber lines; see **ADSL**

Index

Complete Your Library of the Working from Home Series by Paul and Sarah Edwards

These books are available at your local bookstore or wherever books are sold. Ordering is also easy and convenient. To order, call 1-800-788-6262, prompt #1, or send your order to:

Jeremy P. Tarcher
Mail Order Department
P.O. Box 12289
Newark, NJ 07101-5289

For Canadian orders:
P.O. Box 25000
Postal Station 'A'
Toronto, Ontario M5W 2X8

			Price
_____	The Best Home Businesses for the 90s, Revised Edition	0-87477-784-4	$13.95
_____	Finding Your Perfect Work	0-87477-795-X	$16.95
_____	Getting Business to Come to You, 2nd Revised Edition	0-87477-845-X	$18.95
_____	Home Businesses You Can Buy	0-87477-858-1	$13.95
_____	Making Money with Your Computer at Home, Expanded 2nd Edition	0-87477-898-0	$15.95
_____	Secrets of Self-Employment	0-87477-837-9	$13.95
_____	Teaming Up	0-87477-842-5	$13.95
_____	Working from Home	0-87477-764-X	$15.95
		Subtotal	_____
		Shipping and handling[*]	_____
		Sales tax (CA, NJ, NY, PA)	_____
		Total amount due	_____

Payable in U.S. funds (no cash orders accepted). $15.00 minimum for credit card orders.
[*]Shipping and handling: $3.50 for one book, $1.00 for each additional book. Not to exceed $8.50.

Payment method:

☐ Visa   ☐ MasterCard   ☐ American Express

☐ Check or money order

☐ International money order or bank draft check

Card # _____ Expiration date _____

Signature as on charge card _____

Daytime phone number _____

Name _____

Address _____

City _____ State _____ Zip _____

Please allow six weeks for delivery. Prices subject to change without notice. Source key WORK

Do You Have Questions or Feedback?

Paul and Sarah want to answer your questions. They can usually respond to you if you leave a message for them at their Web site, http://www.paulandsarah.com.

If you wish to write, you can write to Paul and Sarah in care of "House Calls," Entrepreneur's HomeOffice, 2392 Morse Avenue, Irvine, CA 92614. Your question may be selected to be answered in their column; however, they cannot respond to every letter.

Other Books by Paul and Sarah Edwards

Use the table below to locate other books that contain the information you need for your business interests.

Subject	Best Home Businesses for the 90s	Finding Your Perfect Work	Getting Business to Come to You	Home Businesses You Can Buy	Secrets of Self-Employment	Teaming Up	Working from Home
Advertising			Yes				
Business opportunities				Yes			Yes
Business planning							Yes
Children and child care							Yes
Closing sales			Yes		Yes		
Credit							Yes
Employees							Yes
Ergonomics							Yes
Failure					Yes		
Family and marriage issues						Yes	Yes
Financing your business					Yes		Yes
Franchise							Yes
Getting referrals			Yes	Yes			Yes
Handling emotional/ psychological issues					Yes		
Housecleaning							Yes
Insurance							Yes
Legal issues						Yes	Yes
Loneliness, isolation							Yes
Managing information							Yes
Marketing	Specific techniques by business		Yes Focus of book		Yes Attitude	Yes	Yes
Marketing materials			Yes				
Money					Yes	Yes	Yes
Naming your business			Yes				
Negotiating						Yes	
Networking			Yes			Yes	Yes
Office space, furniture, equipment							Yes
Outgrowing your home							Yes
Overcoming setbacks					Yes	Yes	
Partnerships	Yes					Yes	
Pricing	Yes Specific						Yes Principles
Profiles of specific businesses	Yes				Yes		
Public relations and publicity			Yes				Yes
Resource directory				Yes	Yes		
Selecting a business/ career/business opportunity	Yes	Yes Focus of book		Yes			Yes
Software							Yes
Speaking			Yes				
Start-up costs	Yes						
Subcontracting						Yes	
Success issues					Yes	Yes	
Taxes						Yes	Yes
Time management					Yes	Yes	Yes
Zoning							Yes

About the Authors

Paul and Sarah Edwards, authors of eight books that have sold over a million copies, are often described as the nation's self-employment experts. They have worked from home for over twenty years. Their weekly column is syndicated by the Los Angeles Times News Syndicate and they write monthly columns for *Enterpreneur's HomeOffice* and Price Costco's *Connection.* Since 1988, they have produced and broadcasted their hour-long show *Working from Home* on the Business News Network.

Since 1990, their mission—which they express through print, via electronic media, and as speakers—has been to help people make the transition from the job economy of lifetime employment to the faster changing but potentially more satisfying world of self-employment. They live in California.

Linda Rohrbough is an award-winning author who has twice been honored by the Computer Press Association. Her book *Mailing List Services on Your Home-Based PC* was awarded Best Nonfiction Computer Book in 1994, and in 1992 she was awarded Best On-Line Service for her work with an international on-line computer news service.

On the subject of computers, Linda has been quoted by the *Wall Street Journal, SmartMoney,* the *Los Angeles Times, CNN, Money* magazine, *Home Office Computing, Home PC,* and the book *MORE Windows 95 for Dummies.* She is a columnist and a contributing editor for several publications aimed at computer enthusiasts and PC technicians. This best-selling author's other books include *Start Your Own Computer Repair Business* and *Upgrade Your Own PC, 2nd Edition.*

Linda and her husband, Mark, live in the Dallas area with their two children, Jessica and Margaret.